Garfield SLURPS and BURPS

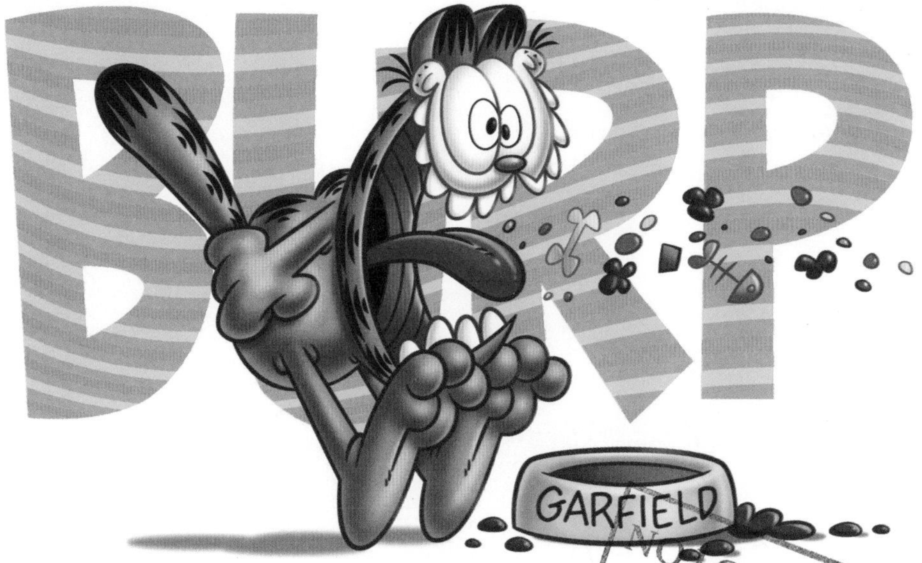
BURP
GARFIELD

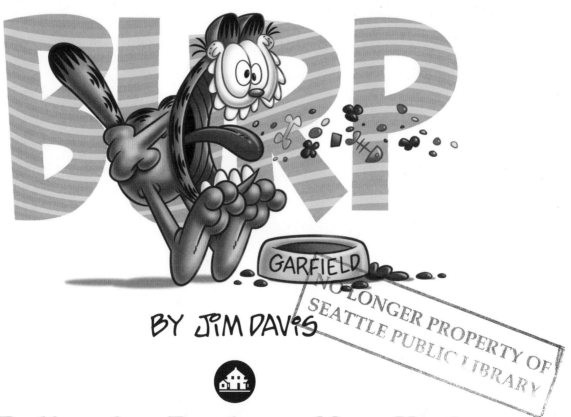

BY JIM DAVIS

Ballantine Books • New York

A Ballantine Books Trade Paperback Original

Published in the United States by Ballantine Books, an imprint of Random House,
a division of Penguin Random House LLC, New York.

BALLANTINE and the HOUSE colophon are registered trademarks of Penguin Random House LLC.

NICKELODEON is a trademark of Viacom International, Inc.

All of the comics in this work have been previously published.

ISBN 978-1-9848-1773-0
Ebook ISBN 978-1-9848-1774-7

Printed in China on acid-free paper

randomhousebooks.com

9 8 7 6 5 4 3

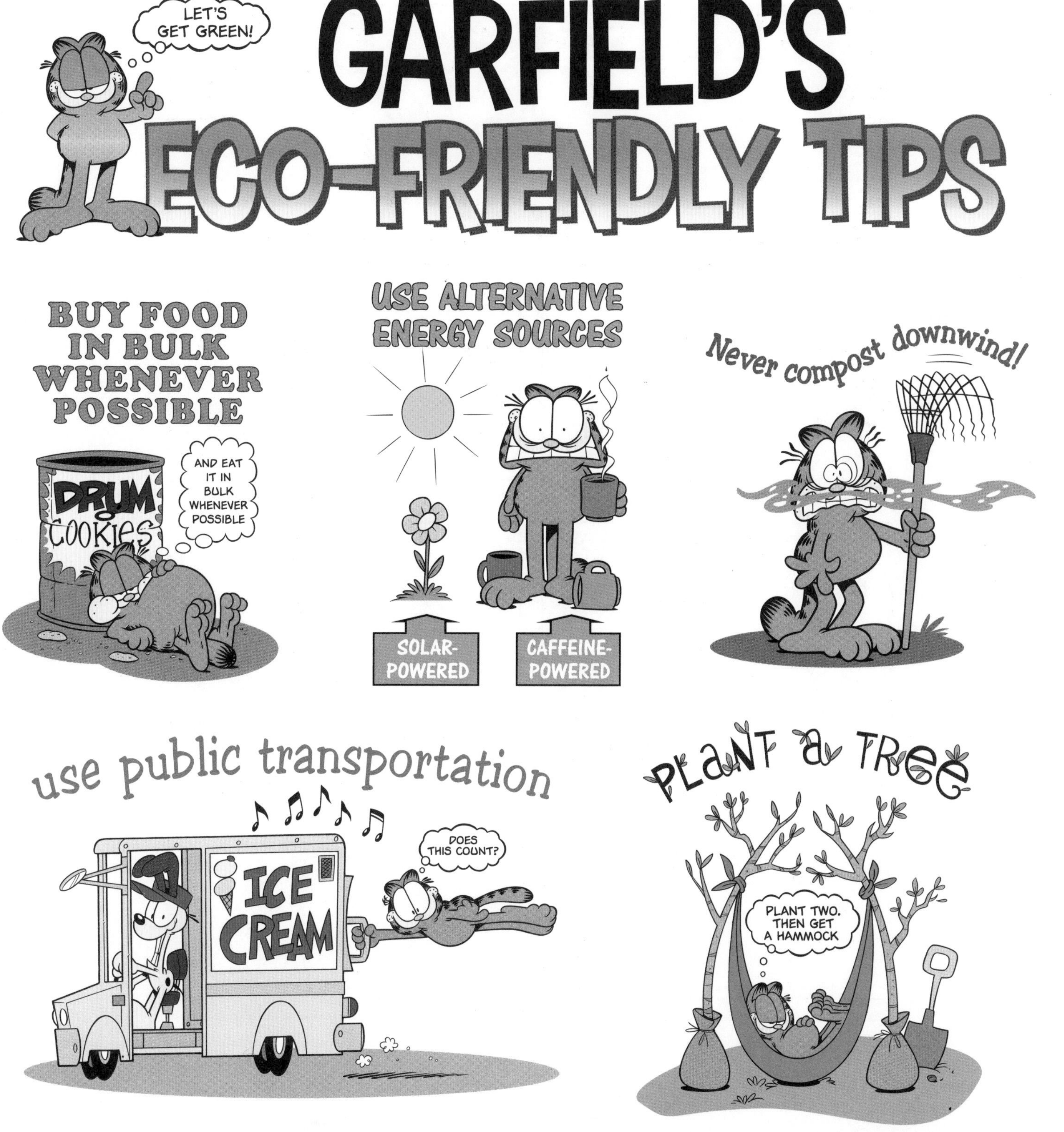
LET'S GET GREEN!
GARFIELD'S
ECO-FRIENDLY TIPS
BUY FOOD IN BULK WHENEVER POSSIBLE
DRUM COOKIES
AND EAT IT IN BULK WHENEVER POSSIBLE
USE ALTERNATIVE ENERGY SOURCES
SOLAR-POWERED
CAFFEINE-POWERED
Never compost downwind!
use public transportation
ICE CREAM
DOES THIS COUNT?
PLANT A TREE
PLANT TWO. THEN GET A HAMMOCK

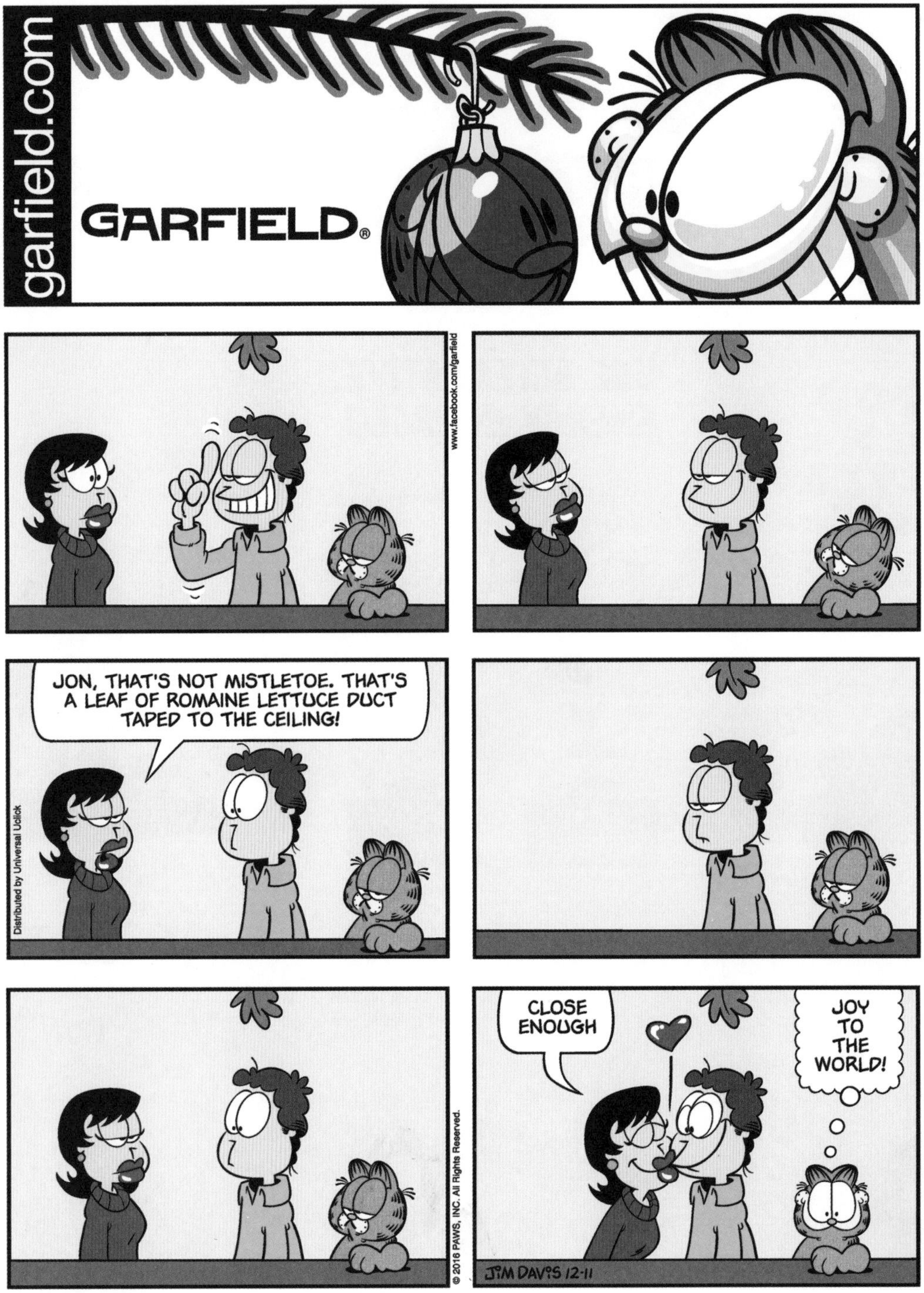
garfield.com
GARFIELD®
www.facebook.com/garfield
JON, THAT'S NOT MISTLETOE. THAT'S A LEAF OF ROMAINE LETTUCE DUCT TAPED TO THE CEILING!
Distributed by Universal Uclick
© 2016 PAWS, INC. All Rights Reserved.
CLOSE ENOUGH
JOY TO THE WORLD!
JIM DAVIS 12-11

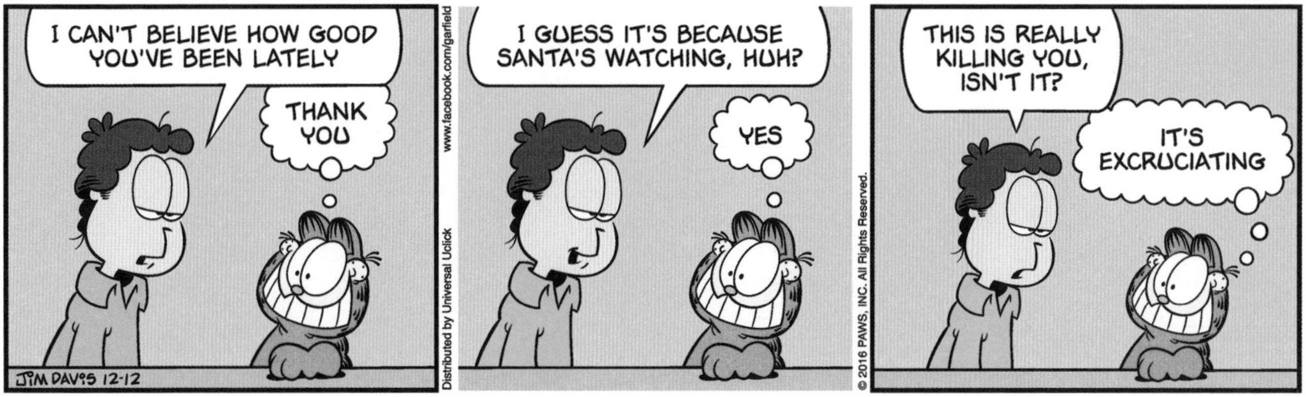
I CAN'T BELIEVE HOW GOOD YOU'VE BEEN LATELY
THANK YOU
JIM DAVIS 12-12
Distributed by Universal Uclick
www.facebook.com/garfield
I GUESS IT'S BECAUSE SANTA'S WATCHING, HUH?
YES
© 2016 PAWS, INC. All Rights Reserved.
THIS IS REALLY KILLING YOU, ISN'T IT?
IT'S EXCRUCIATING

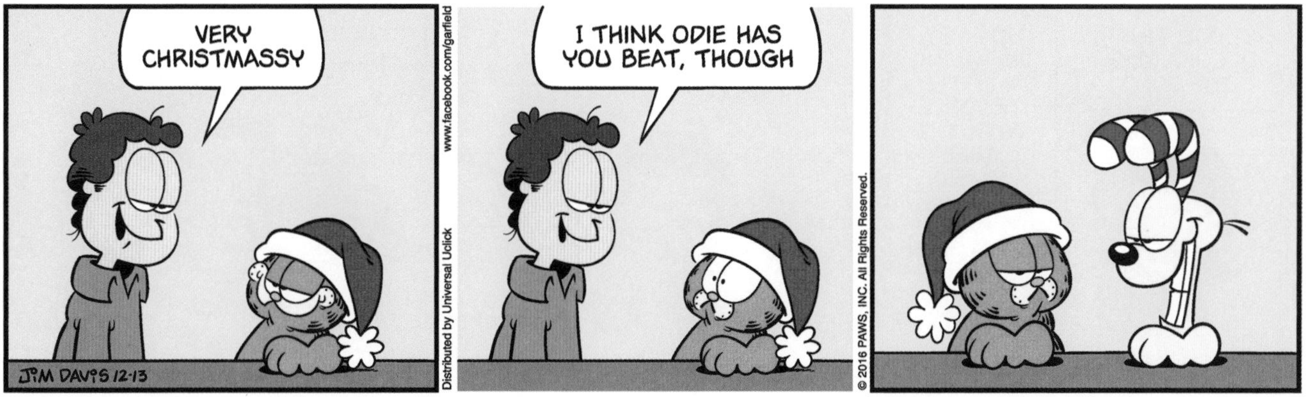
VERY CHRISTMASSY
JIM DAVIS 12-13
Distributed by Universal Uclick
www.facebook.com/garfield
I THINK ODIE HAS YOU BEAT, THOUGH
© 2016 PAWS, INC. All Rights Reserved.

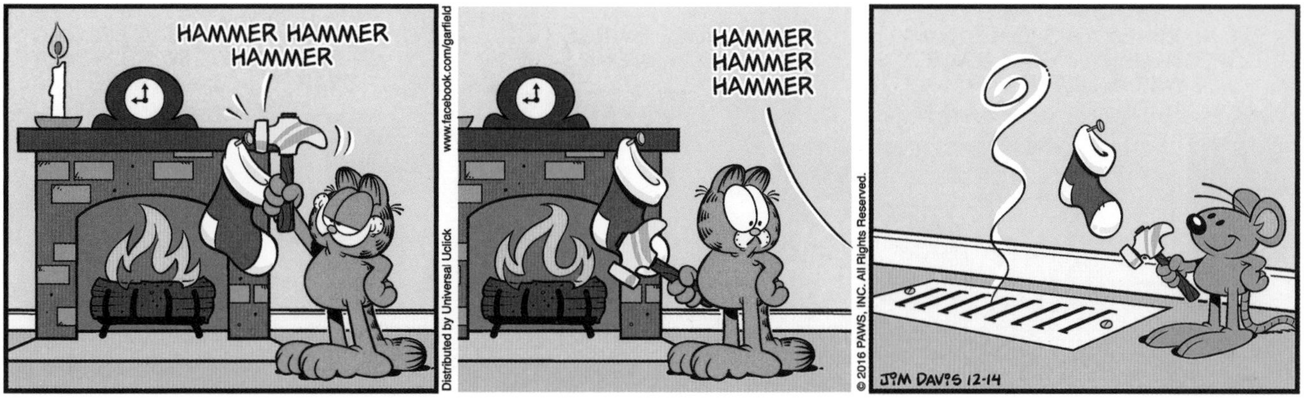
HAMMER HAMMER HAMMER
Distributed by Universal Uclick
www.facebook.com/garfield
HAMMER HAMMER HAMMER
© 2016 PAWS, INC. All Rights Reserved.
JIM DAVIS 12-14

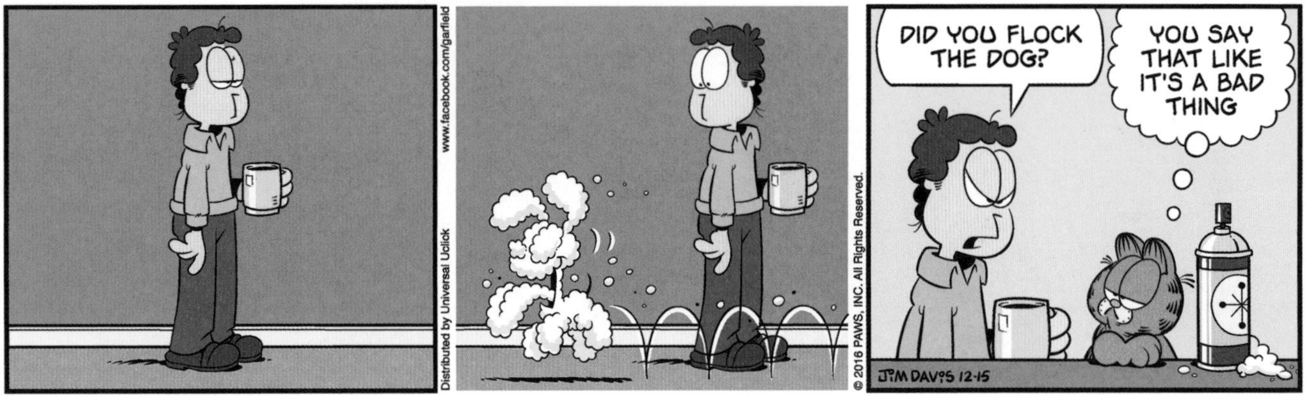
Distributed by Universal Uclick
www.facebook.com/garfield
DID YOU FLOCK THE DOG?
YOU SAY THAT LIKE IT'S A BAD THING
© 2016 PAWS, INC. All Rights Reserved.
JIM DAVIS 12-15

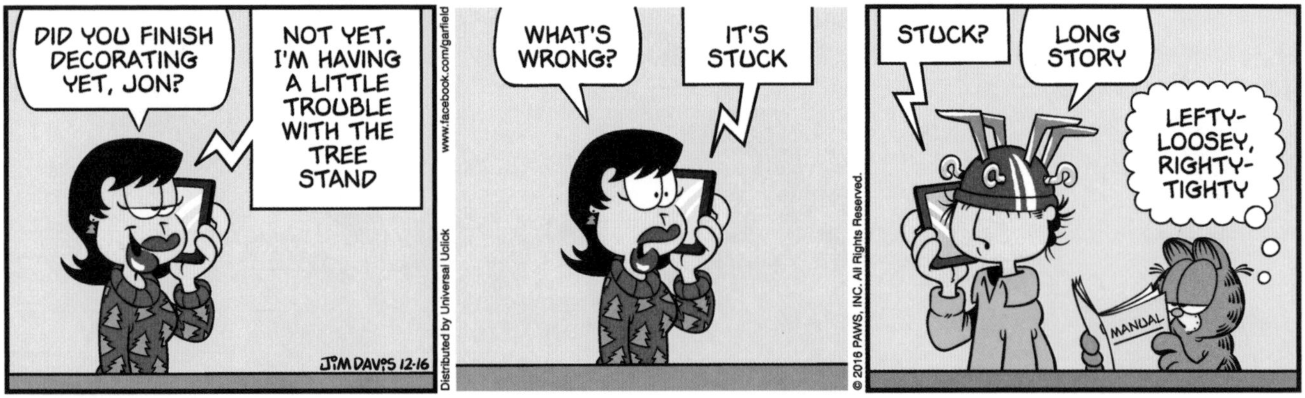
DID YOU FINISH DECORATING YET, JON?
NOT YET. I'M HAVING A LITTLE TROUBLE WITH THE TREE STAND
JIM DAVIS 12-16
Distributed by Universal Uclick
www.facebook.com/garfield
WHAT'S WRONG?
IT'S STUCK
© 2016 PAWS, INC. All Rights Reserved.
STUCK?
LONG STORY
LEFTY-LOOSEY, RIGHTY-TIGHTY
MANUAL

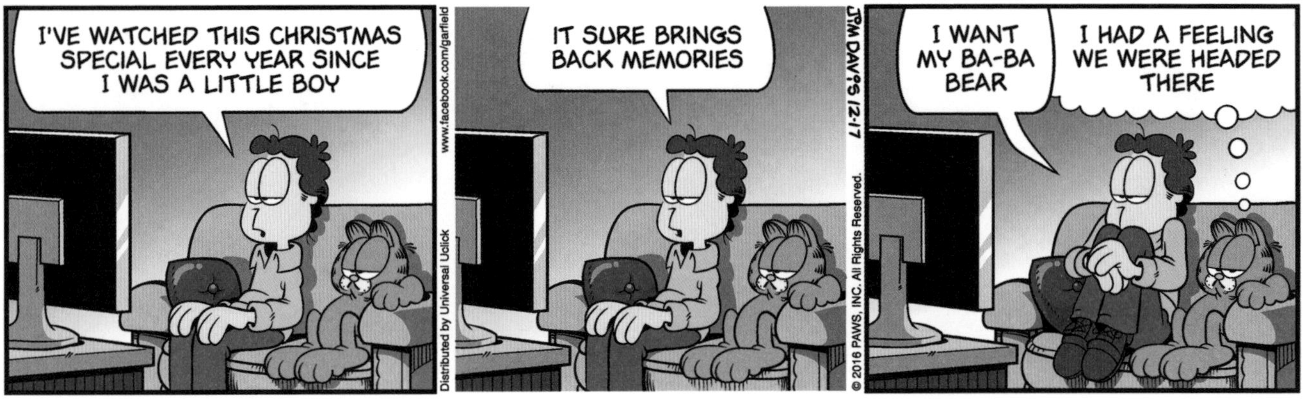
I'VE WATCHED THIS CHRISTMAS SPECIAL EVERY YEAR SINCE I WAS A LITTLE BOY
Distributed by Universal Uclick
www.facebook.com/garfield
IT SURE BRINGS BACK MEMORIES
JIM DAVIS 12-17
© 2016 PAWS, INC. All Rights Reserved.
I WANT MY BA-BA BEAR
I HAD A FEELING WE WERE HEADED THERE

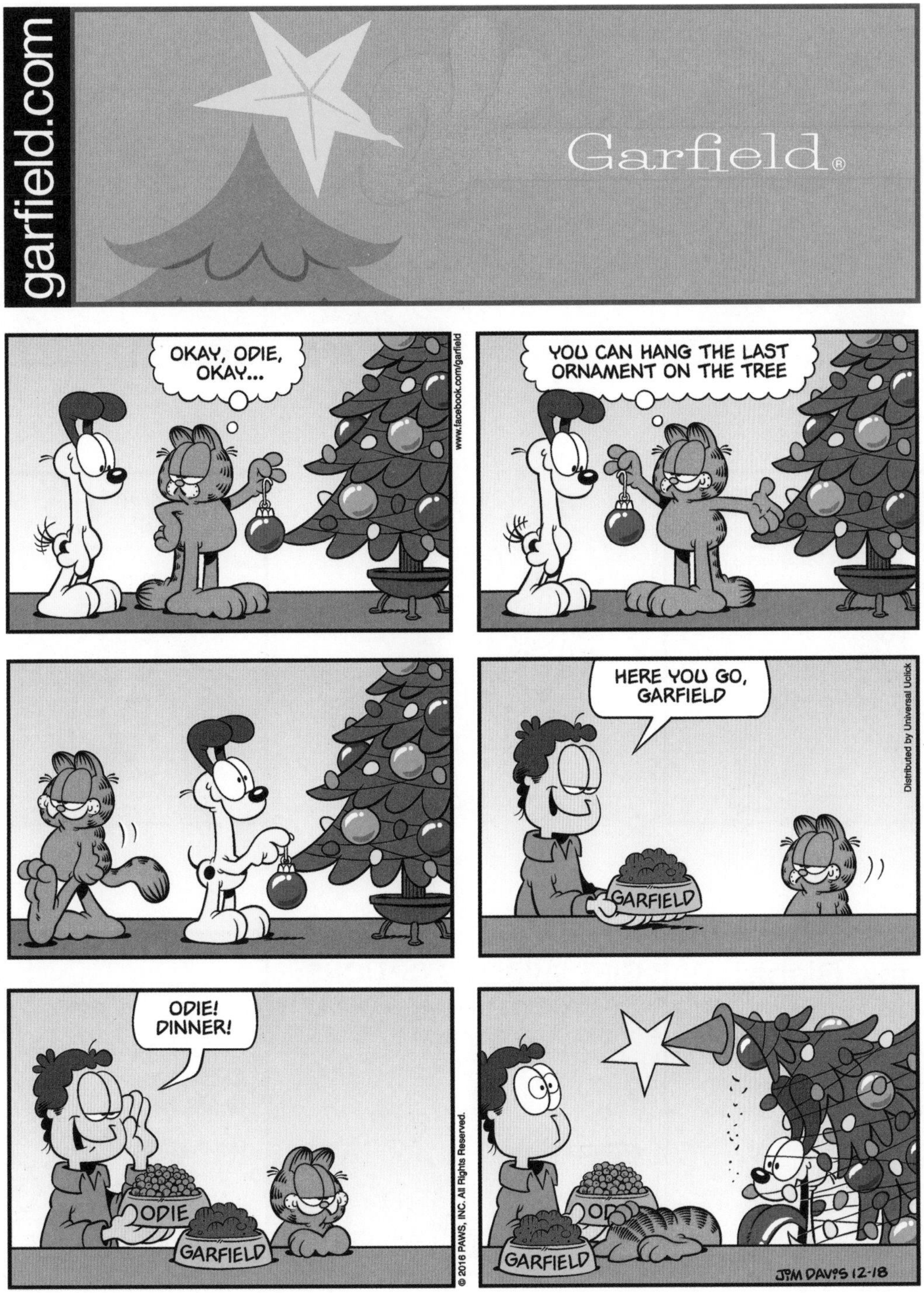
garfield.com
Garfield®
OKAY, ODIE, OKAY...
www.facebook.com/garfield
YOU CAN HANG THE LAST ORNAMENT ON THE TREE
HERE YOU GO, GARFIELD
GARFIELD
Distributed by Universal Uclick
ODIE! DINNER!
ODIE
GARFIELD
© 2016 PAWS, INC. All Rights Reserved.
GARFIELD
JIM DAVIS 12-18

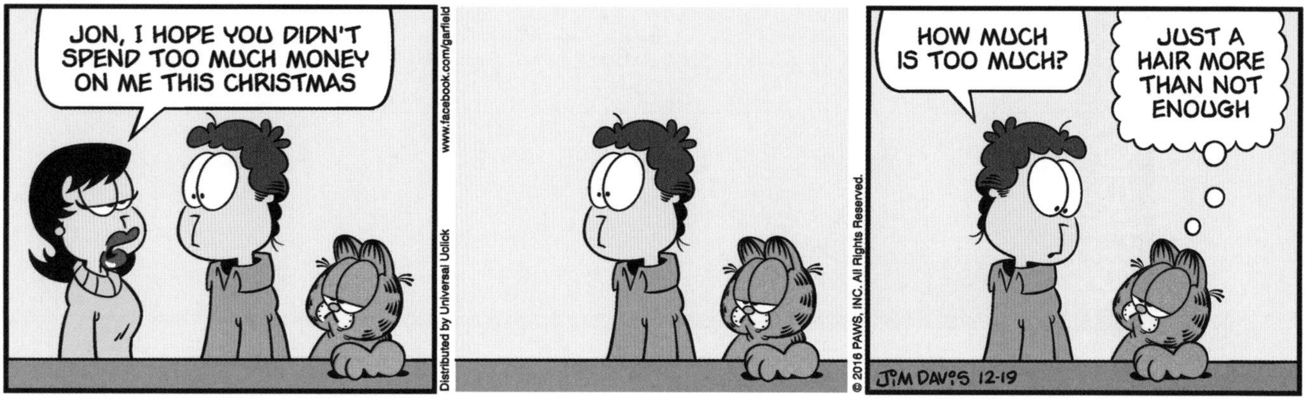
JON, I HOPE YOU DIDN'T SPEND TOO MUCH MONEY ON ME THIS CHRISTMAS
HOW MUCH IS TOO MUCH?
JUST A HAIR MORE THAN NOT ENOUGH
Distributed by Universal Uclick www.facebook.com/garfield
© 2016 PAWS, INC. All Rights Reserved.
JIM DAVIS 12-19

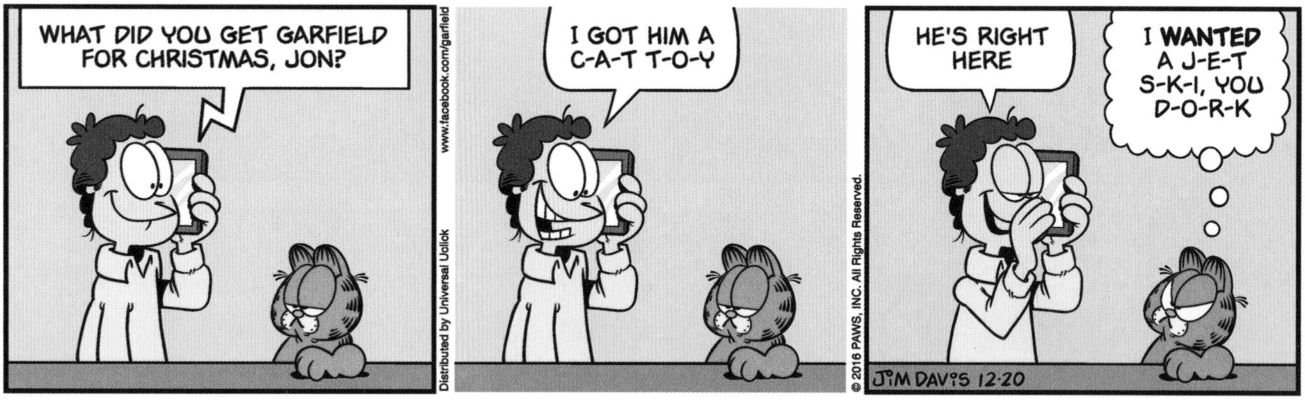
WHAT DID YOU GET GARFIELD FOR CHRISTMAS, JON?
I GOT HIM A C-A-T T-O-Y
HE'S RIGHT HERE
I WANTED A J-E-T S-K-I, YOU D-O-R-K
Distributed by Universal Uclick www.facebook.com/garfield
© 2016 PAWS, INC. All Rights Reserved.
JIM DAVIS 12-20

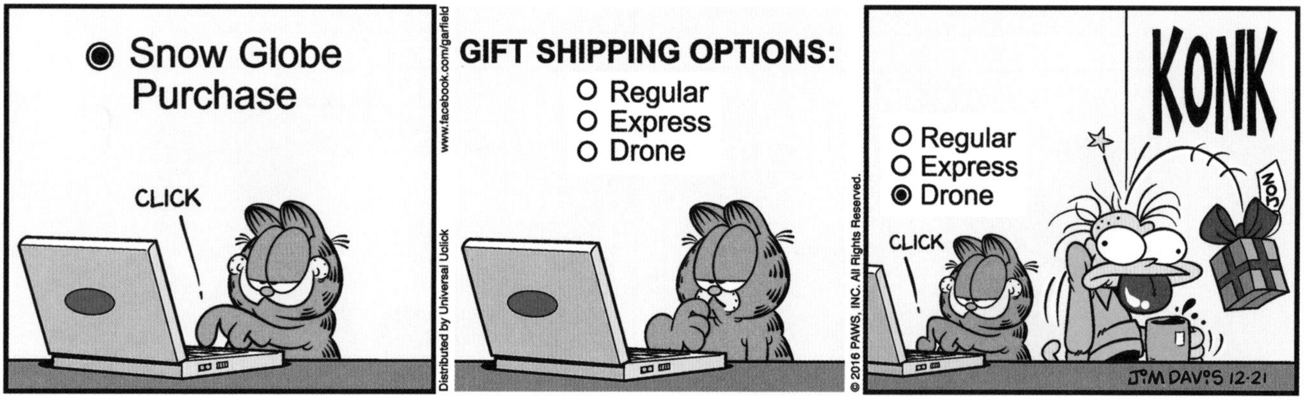
Snow Globe Purchase
CLICK
GIFT SHIPPING OPTIONS:
Regular
Express
Drone
Regular
Express
Drone
CLICK
KONK
JON
Distributed by Universal Uclick www.facebook.com/garfield
© 2016 PAWS, INC. All Rights Reserved.
JIM DAVIS 12-21

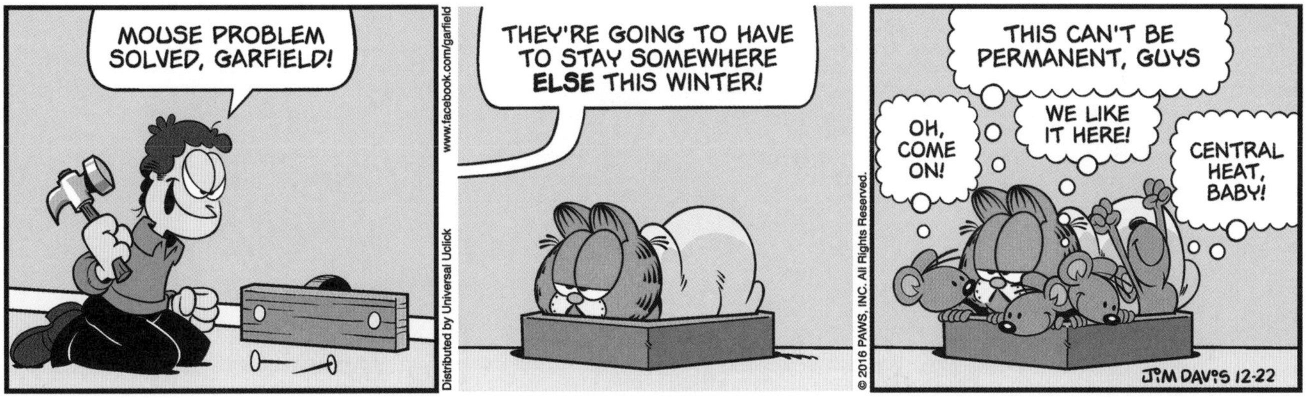
MOUSE PROBLEM SOLVED, GARFIELD!
Distributed by Universal Uclick
www.facebook.com/garfield
THEY'RE GOING TO HAVE TO STAY SOMEWHERE **ELSE** THIS WINTER!
© 2016 PAWS, INC. All Rights Reserved.
THIS CAN'T BE PERMANENT, GUYS
OH, COME ON!
WE LIKE IT HERE!
CENTRAL HEAT, BABY!
JIM DAVIS 12-22

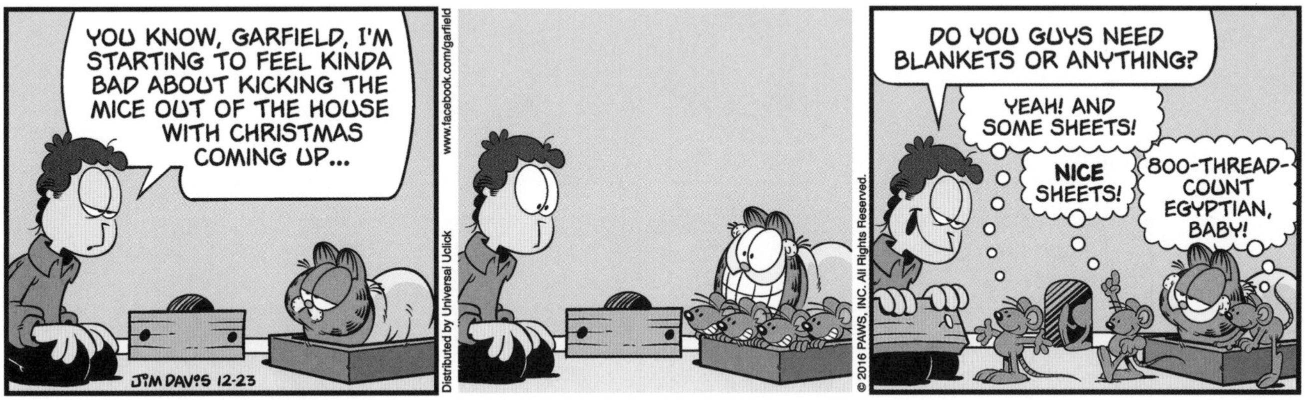
YOU KNOW, GARFIELD, I'M STARTING TO FEEL KINDA BAD ABOUT KICKING THE MICE OUT OF THE HOUSE WITH CHRISTMAS COMING UP...
JIM DAVIS 12-23
Distributed by Universal Uclick
www.facebook.com/garfield
© 2016 PAWS, INC. All Rights Reserved.
DO YOU GUYS NEED BLANKETS OR ANYTHING?
YEAH! AND SOME SHEETS!
NICE SHEETS!
800-THREAD-COUNT EGYPTIAN, BABY!

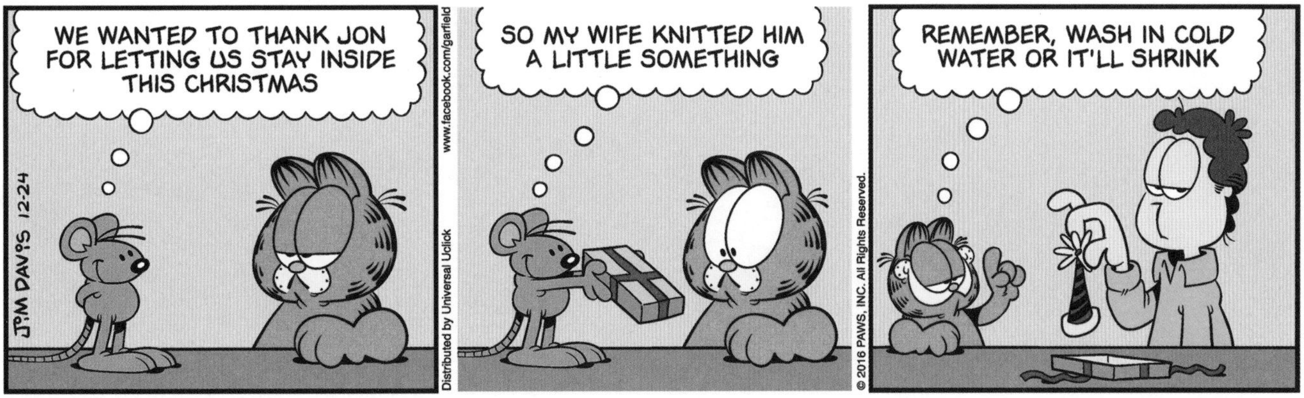
WE WANTED TO THANK JON FOR LETTING US STAY INSIDE THIS CHRISTMAS
JIM DAVIS 12-24
Distributed by Universal Uclick
www.facebook.com/garfield
SO MY WIFE KNITTED HIM A LITTLE SOMETHING
© 2016 PAWS, INC. All Rights Reserved.
REMEMBER, WASH IN COLD WATER OR IT'LL SHRINK

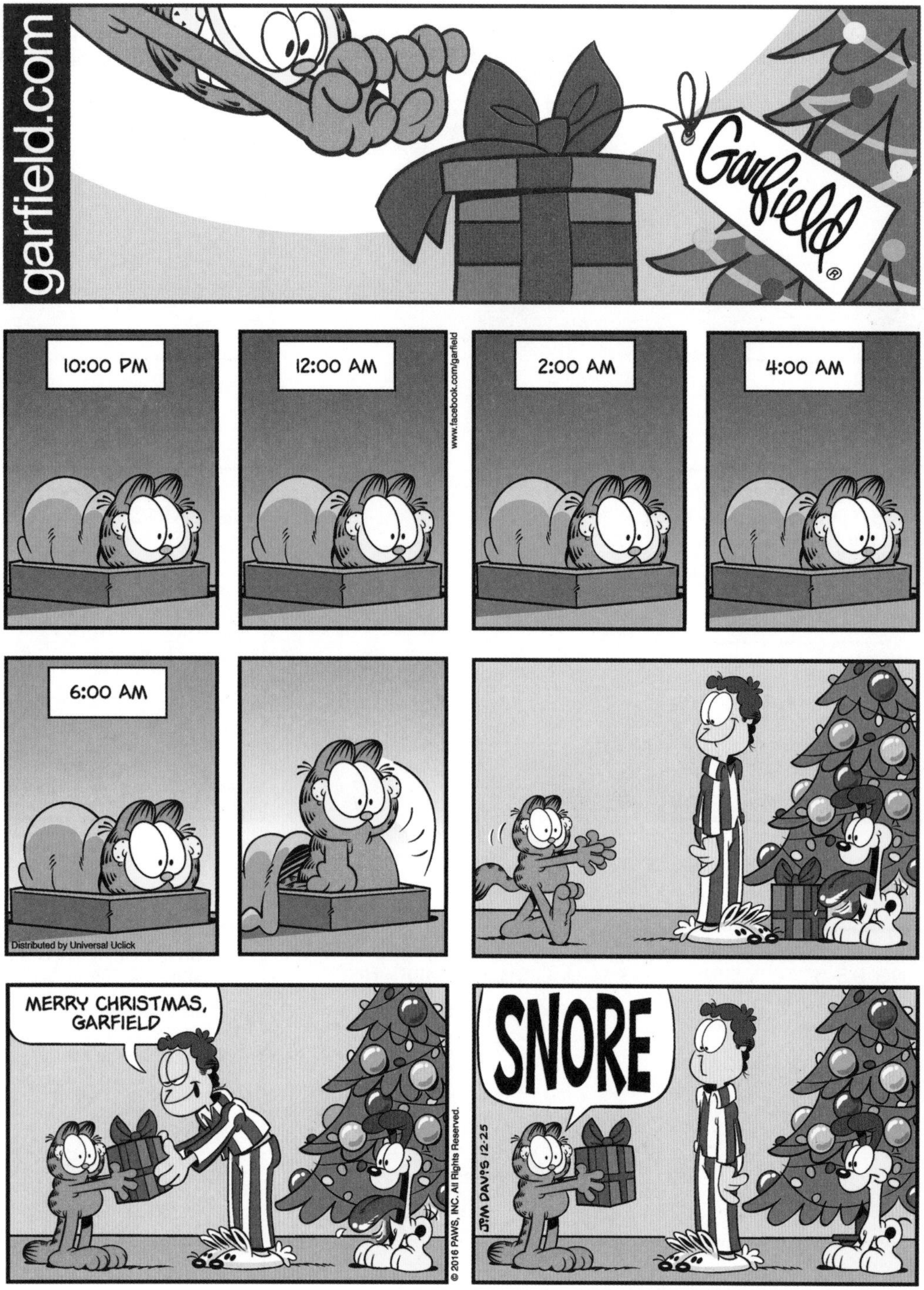
garfield.com
Garfield®
www.facebook.com/garfield
10:00 PM
12:00 AM
2:00 AM
4:00 AM
6:00 AM
Distributed by Universal Uclick
MERRY CHRISTMAS, GARFIELD
© 2016 PAWS, INC. All Rights Reserved.
JIM DAVIS 12-25
SNORE

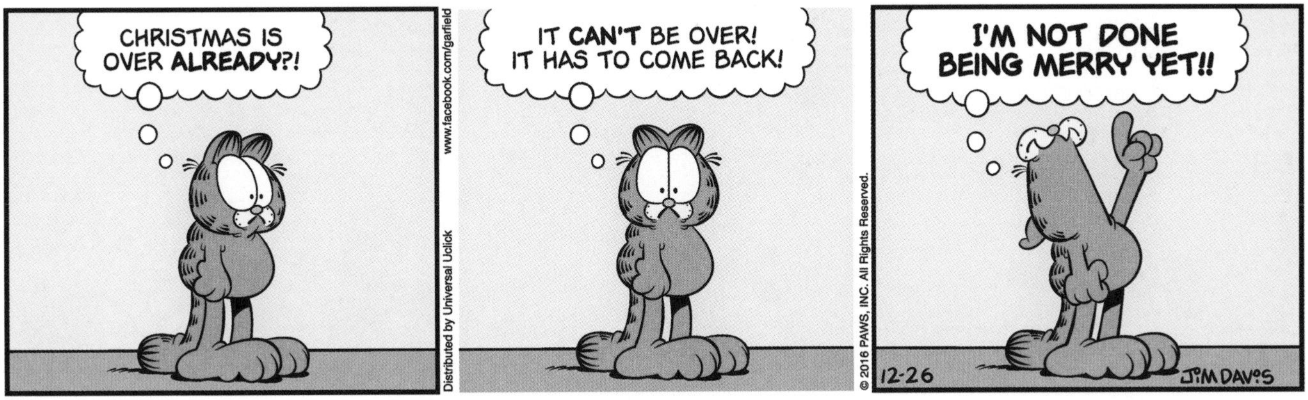
CHRISTMAS IS OVER ALREADY?!
Distributed by Universal Uclick www.facebook.com/garfield
IT CAN'T BE OVER! IT HAS TO COME BACK!
© 2016 PAWS, INC. All Rights Reserved.
I'M NOT DONE BEING MERRY YET!!
12-26
JIM DAVIS

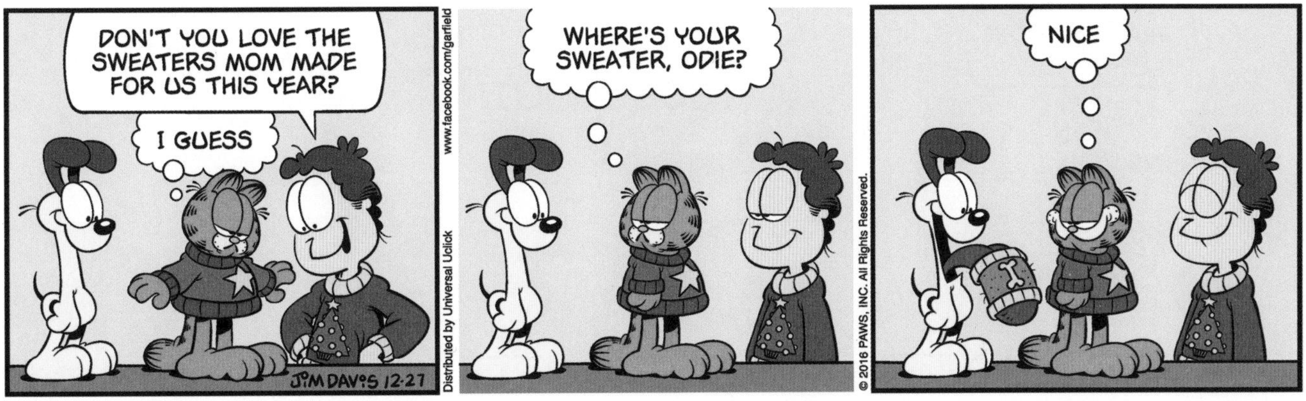
DON'T YOU LOVE THE SWEATERS MOM MADE FOR US THIS YEAR?
I GUESS
JIM DAVIS 12-27
Distributed by Universal Uclick www.facebook.com/garfield
WHERE'S YOUR SWEATER, ODIE?
© 2016 PAWS, INC. All Rights Reserved.
NICE

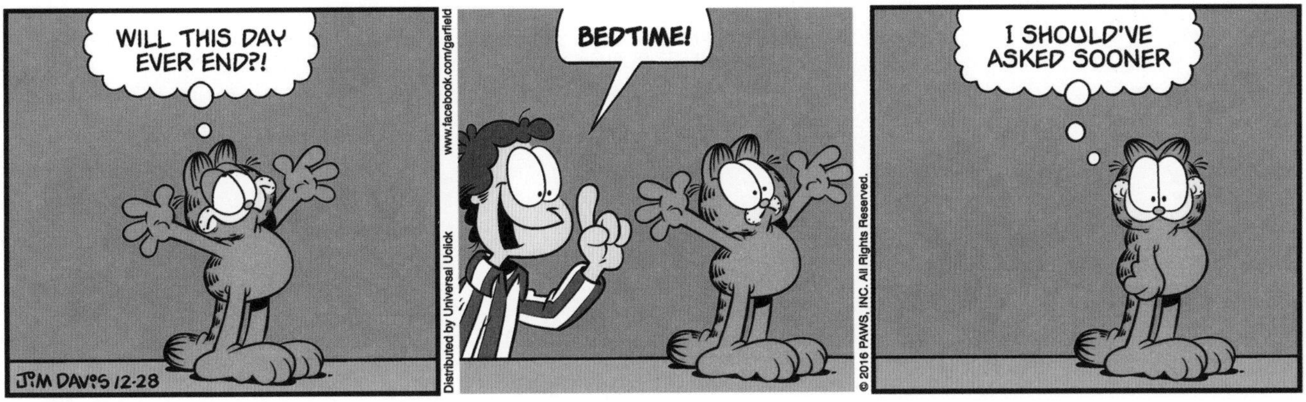
WILL THIS DAY EVER END?!
JIM DAVIS 12-28
Distributed by Universal Uclick www.facebook.com/garfield
BEDTIME!
© 2016 PAWS, INC. All Rights Reserved.
I SHOULD'VE ASKED SOONER

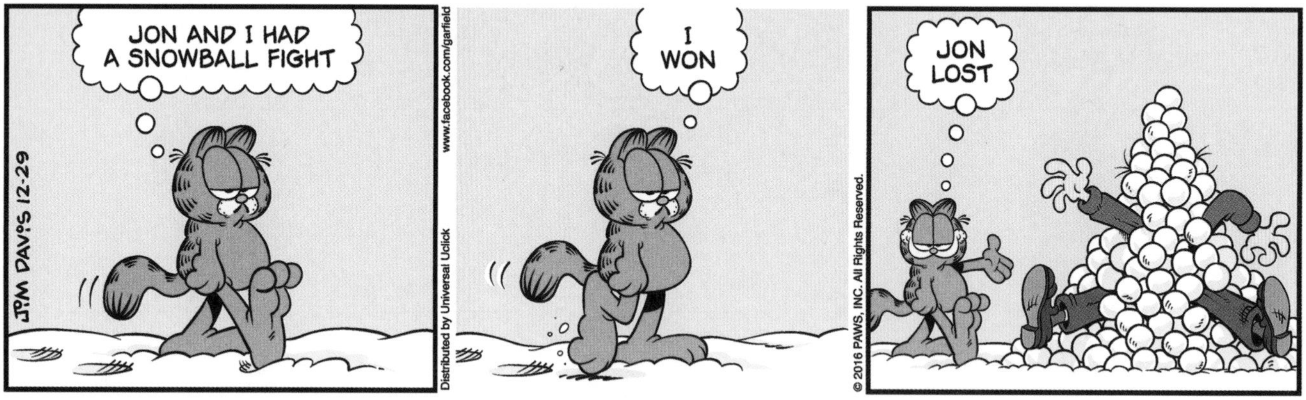
JON AND I HAD A SNOWBALL FIGHT
JIM DAVIS 12-29
Distributed by Universal Uclick www.facebook.com/garfield
I WON
© 2016 PAWS, INC. All Rights Reserved.
JON LOST

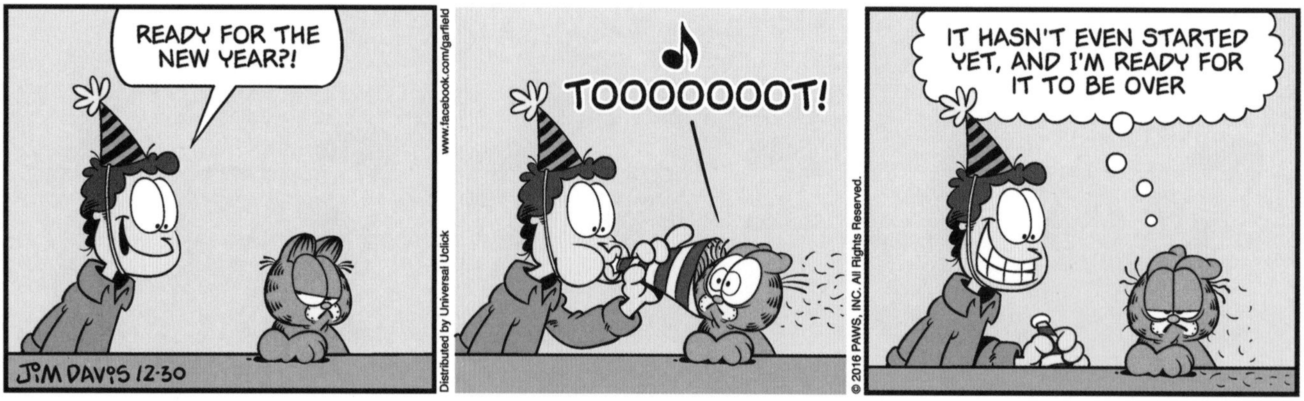
READY FOR THE NEW YEAR?!
JIM DAVIS 12-30
Distributed by Universal Uclick www.facebook.com/garfield
TOOOOOOOT!
© 2016 PAWS, INC. All Rights Reserved.
IT HASN'T EVEN STARTED YET, AND I'M READY FOR IT TO BE OVER

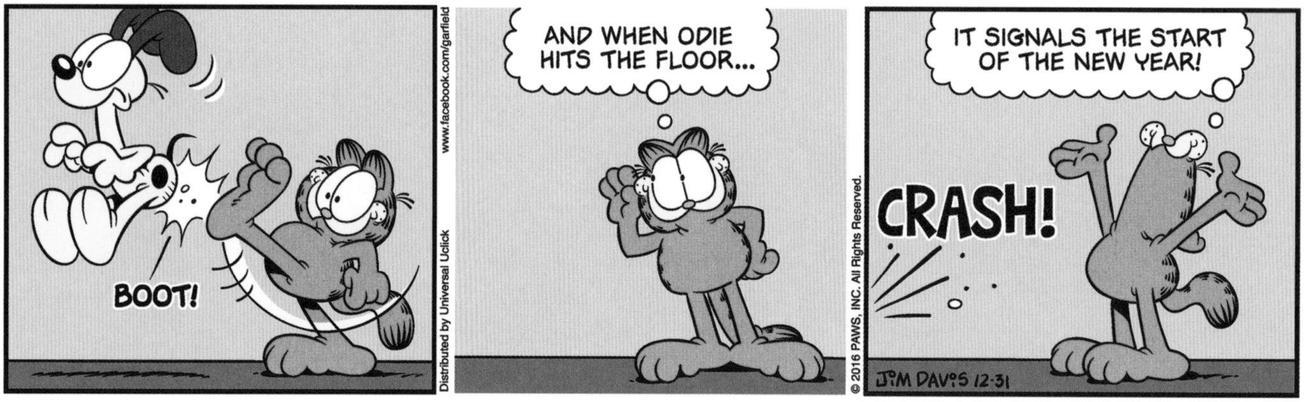
BOOT!
Distributed by Universal Uclick www.facebook.com/garfield
AND WHEN ODIE HITS THE FLOOR...
© 2016 PAWS, INC. All Rights Reserved.
CRASH!
IT SIGNALS THE START OF THE NEW YEAR!
JIM DAVIS 12-31

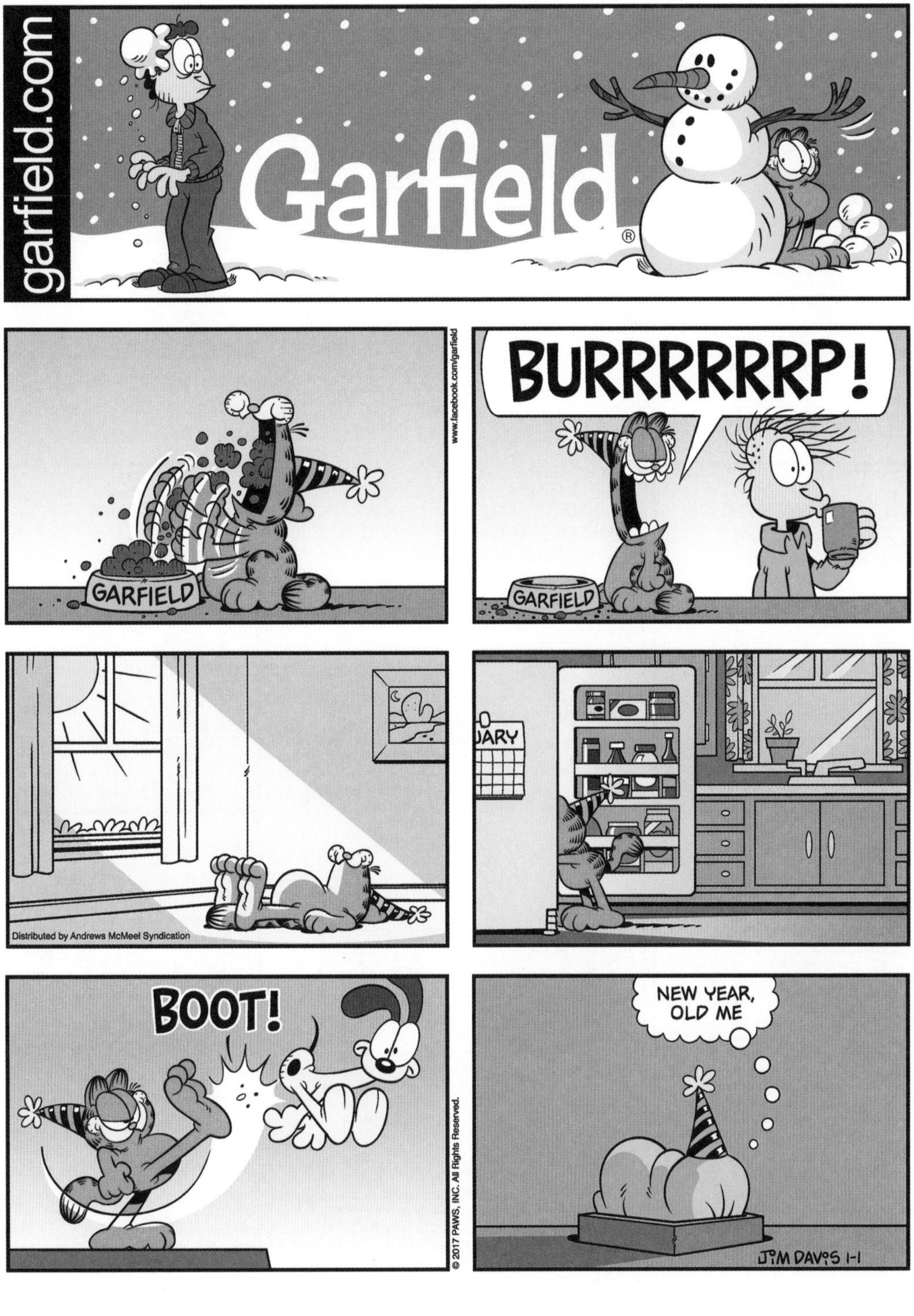
garfield.com
Garfield
GARFIELD
BURRRRRRP!
GARFIELD
www.facebook.com/garfield
JARY
Distributed by Andrews McMeel Syndication
BOOT!
© 2017 PAWS, INC. All Rights Reserved.
NEW YEAR, OLD ME
JIM DAVIS 1-1

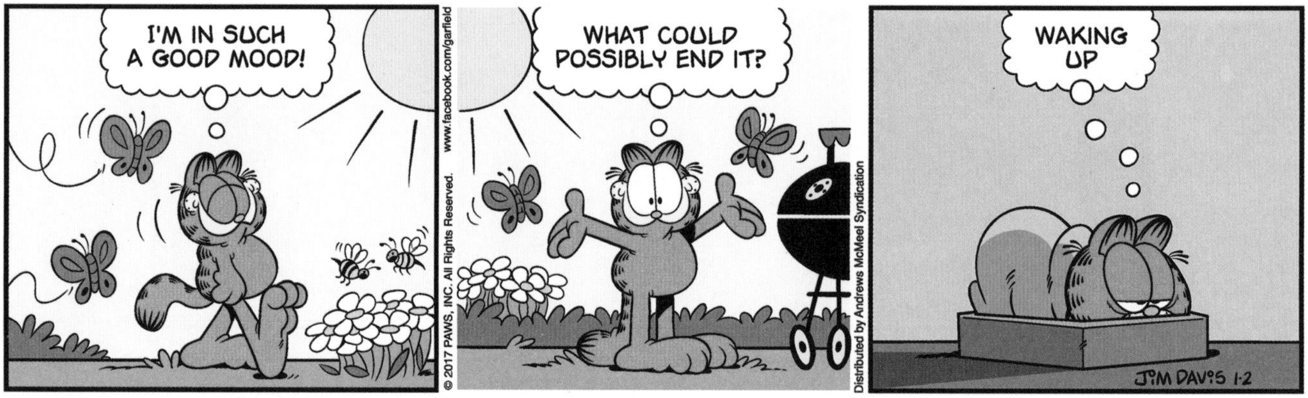
I'M IN SUCH A GOOD MOOD!
WHAT COULD POSSIBLY END IT?
WAKING UP
© 2017 PAWS, INC. All Rights Reserved. www.facebook.com/garfield
Distributed by Andrews McMeel Syndication
JIM DAVIS 1-2

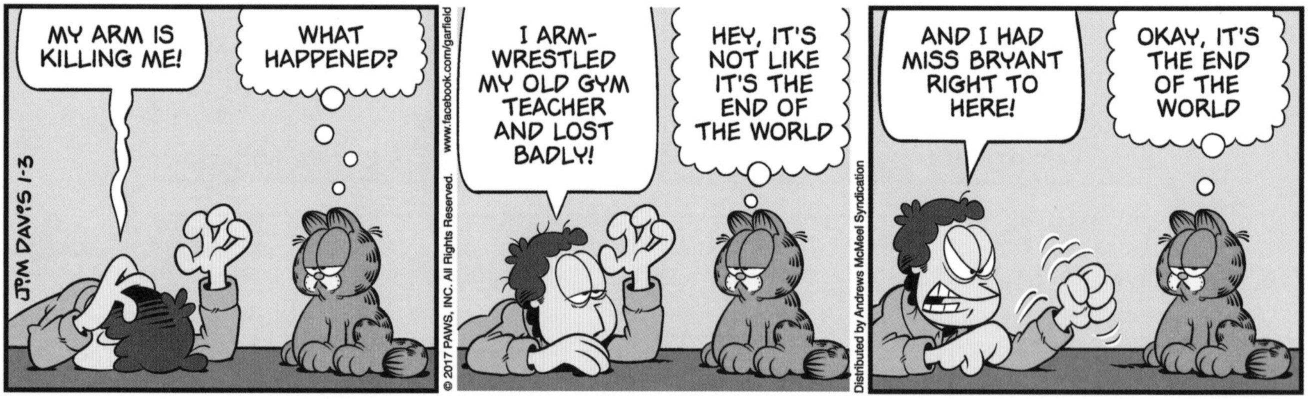
MY ARM IS KILLING ME!
WHAT HAPPENED?
I ARM-WRESTLED MY OLD GYM TEACHER AND LOST BADLY!
HEY, IT'S NOT LIKE IT'S THE END OF THE WORLD
AND I HAD MISS BRYANT RIGHT TO HERE!
OKAY, IT'S THE END OF THE WORLD
JIM DAVIS 1-3
© 2017 PAWS, INC. All Rights Reserved. www.facebook.com/garfield
Distributed by Andrews McMeel Syndication

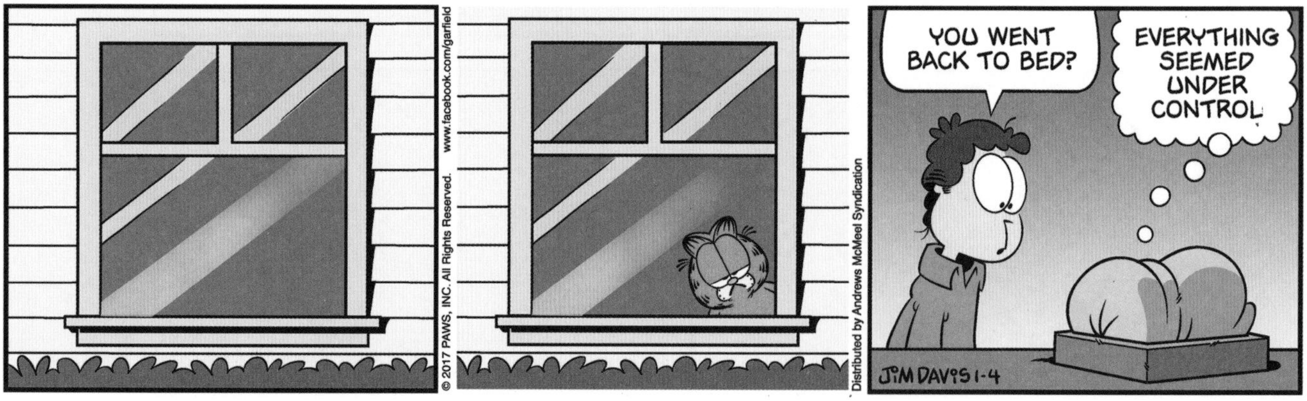
YOU WENT BACK TO BED?
EVERYTHING SEEMED UNDER CONTROL
© 2017 PAWS, INC. All Rights Reserved. www.facebook.com/garfield
Distributed by Andrews McMeel Syndication
JIM DAVIS 1-4

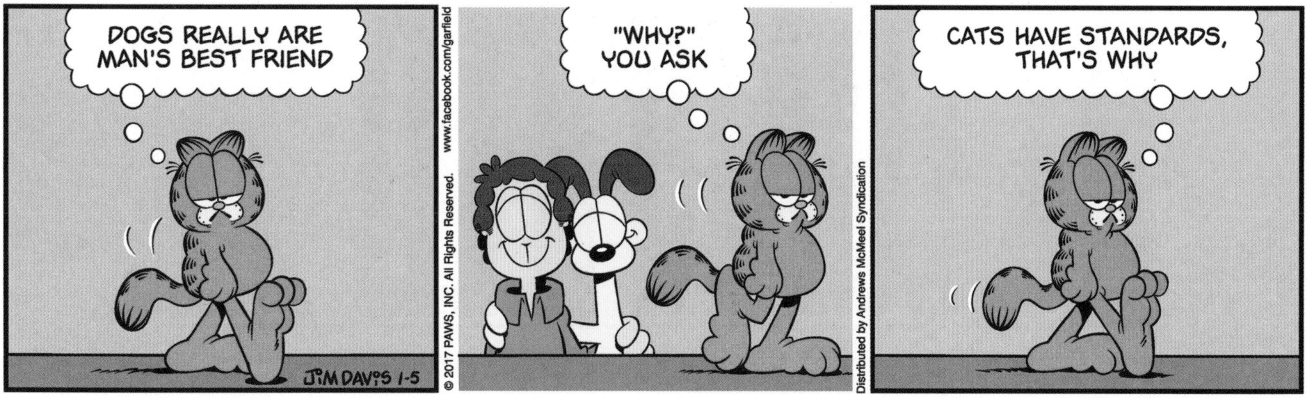
DOGS REALLY ARE MAN'S BEST FRIEND
"WHY?" YOU ASK
CATS HAVE STANDARDS, THAT'S WHY
JIM DAVIS 1-5
© 2017 PAWS, INC. All Rights Reserved. www.facebook.com/garfield
Distributed by Andrews McMeel Syndication

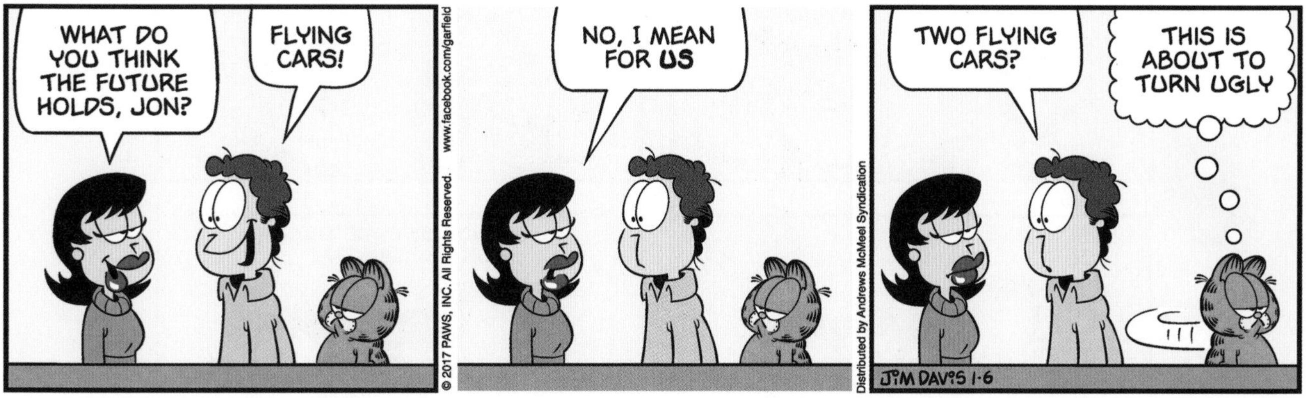
WHAT DO YOU THINK THE FUTURE HOLDS, JON?
FLYING CARS!
NO, I MEAN FOR **US**
TWO FLYING CARS?
THIS IS ABOUT TO TURN UGLY
JIM DAVIS 1-6
© 2017 PAWS, INC. All Rights Reserved. www.facebook.com/garfield
Distributed by Andrews McMeel Syndication

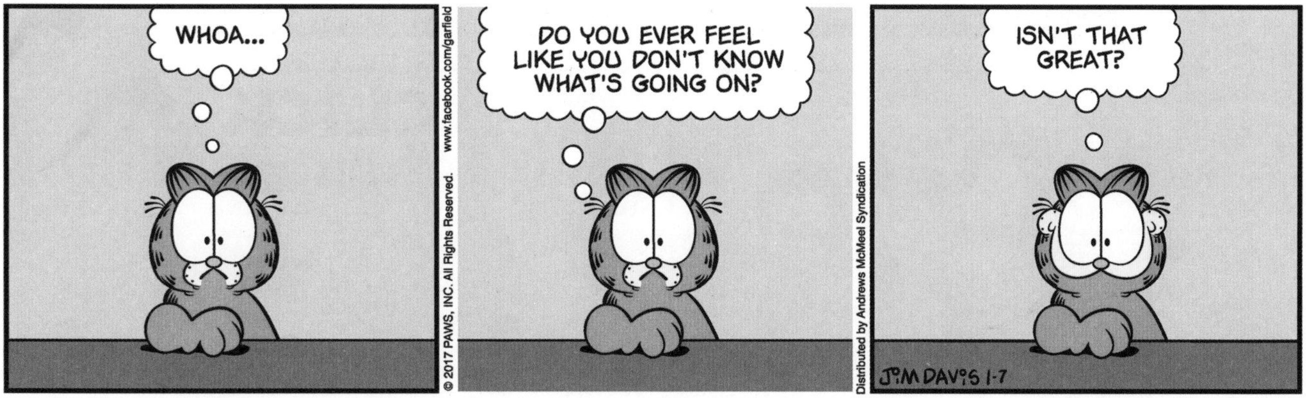
WHOA...
DO YOU EVER FEEL LIKE YOU DON'T KNOW WHAT'S GOING ON?
ISN'T THAT GREAT?
JIM DAVIS 1-7
© 2017 PAWS, INC. All Rights Reserved. www.facebook.com/garfield
Distributed by Andrews McMeel Syndication

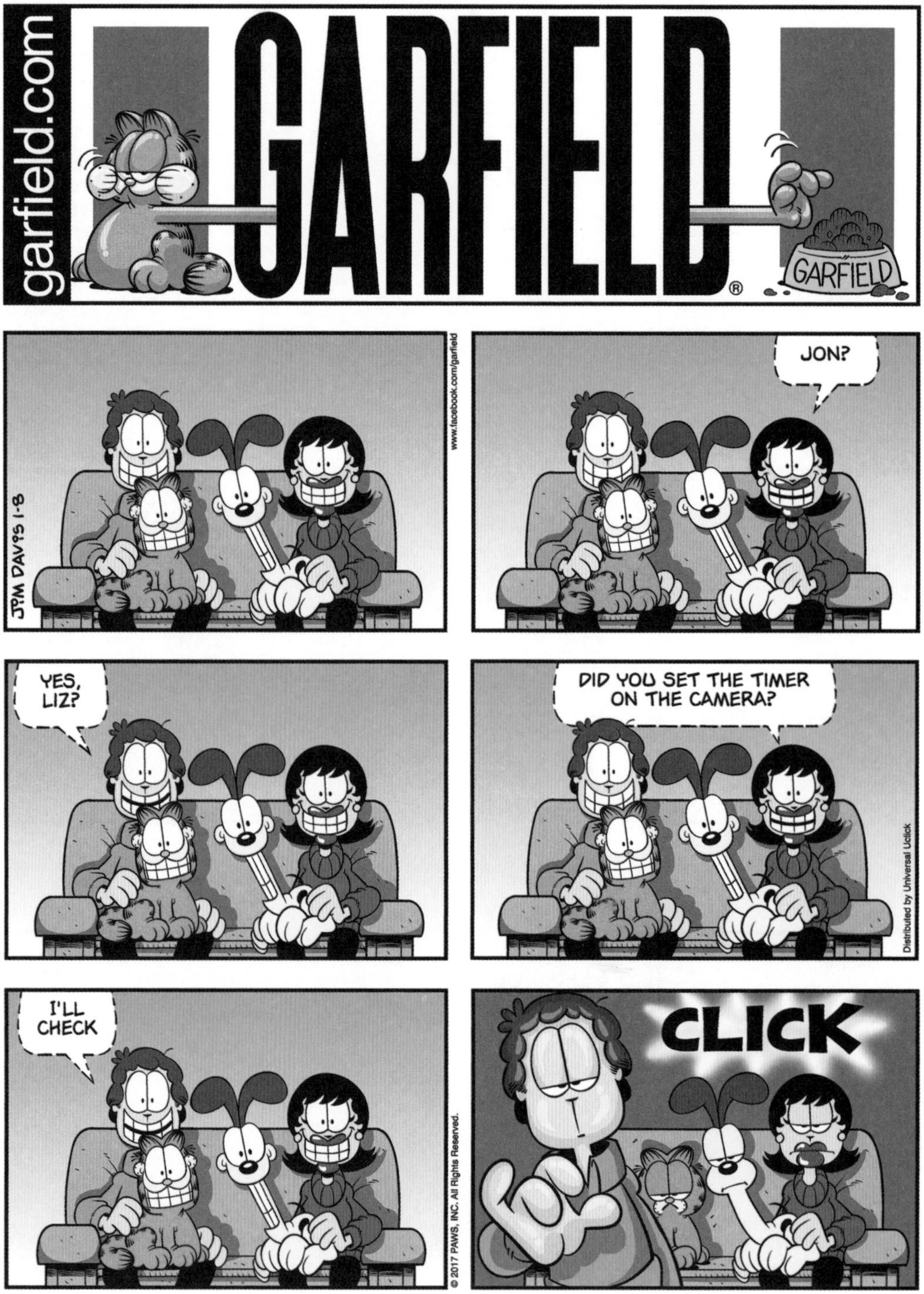
garfield.com
GARFIELD
GARFIELD
JIM DAVIS 1-8
www.facebook.com/garfield
JON?
YES, LIZ?
DID YOU SET THE TIMER ON THE CAMERA?
Distributed by Universal Uclick
I'LL CHECK
© 2017 PAWS, INC. All Rights Reserved.
CLICK

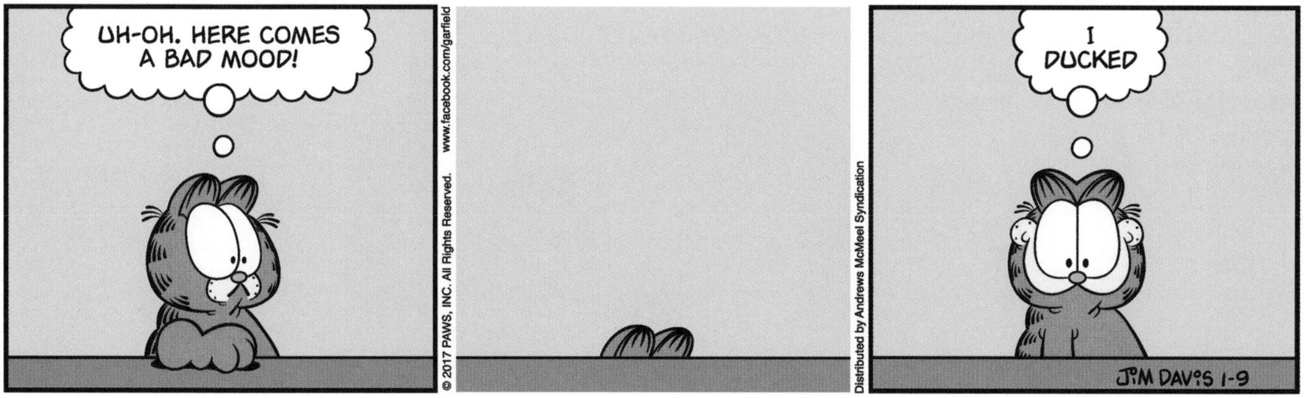
UH-OH. HERE COMES A BAD MOOD!
I DUCKED
JIM DAVIS 1-9
© 2017 PAWS, INC. All Rights Reserved. www.facebook.com/garfield
Distributed by Andrews McMeel Syndication

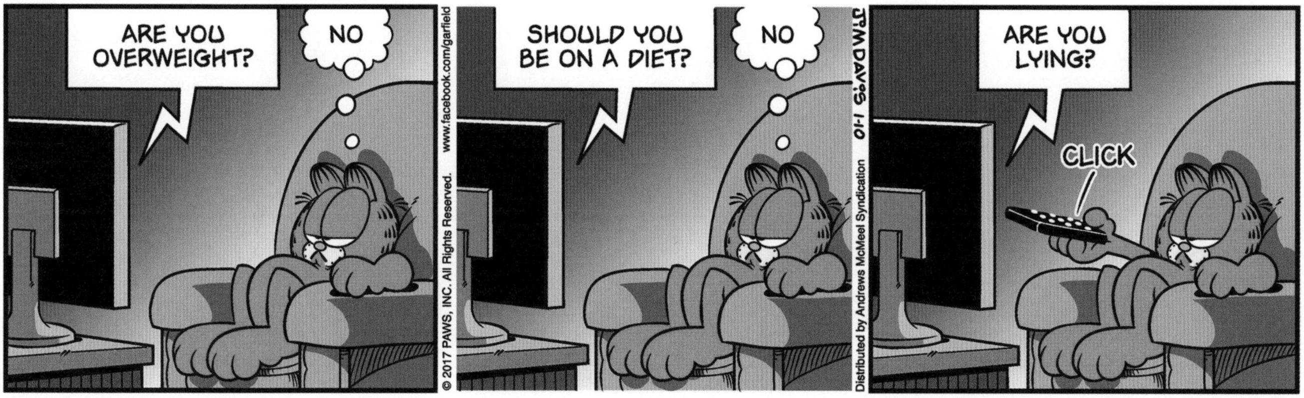
ARE YOU OVERWEIGHT?
NO
SHOULD YOU BE ON A DIET?
NO
ARE YOU LYING?
CLICK
JIM DAVIS 1-10
© 2017 PAWS, INC. All Rights Reserved. www.facebook.com/garfield
Distributed by Andrews McMeel Syndication

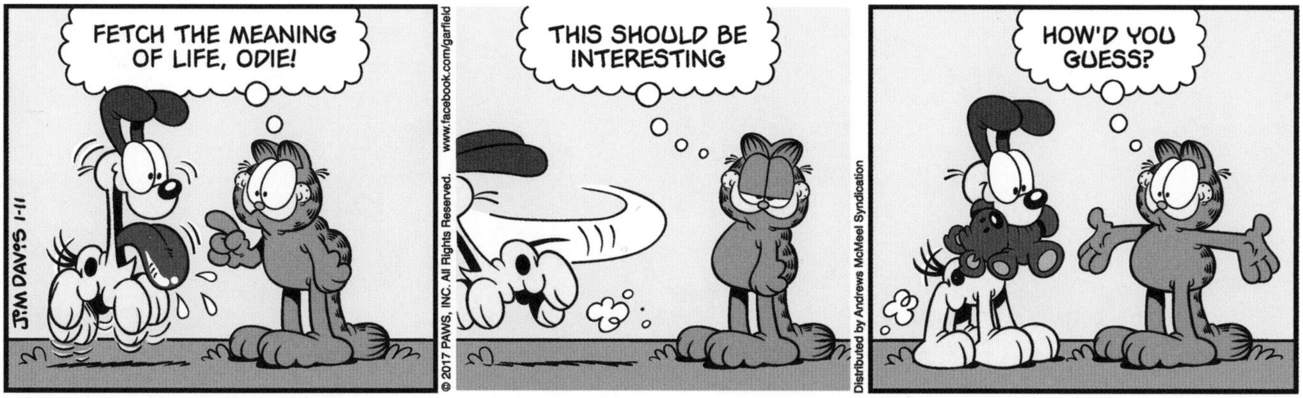
FETCH THE MEANING OF LIFE, ODIE!
THIS SHOULD BE INTERESTING
HOW'D YOU GUESS?
JIM DAVIS 1-11
© 2017 PAWS, INC. All Rights Reserved. www.facebook.com/garfield
Distributed by Andrews McMeel Syndication

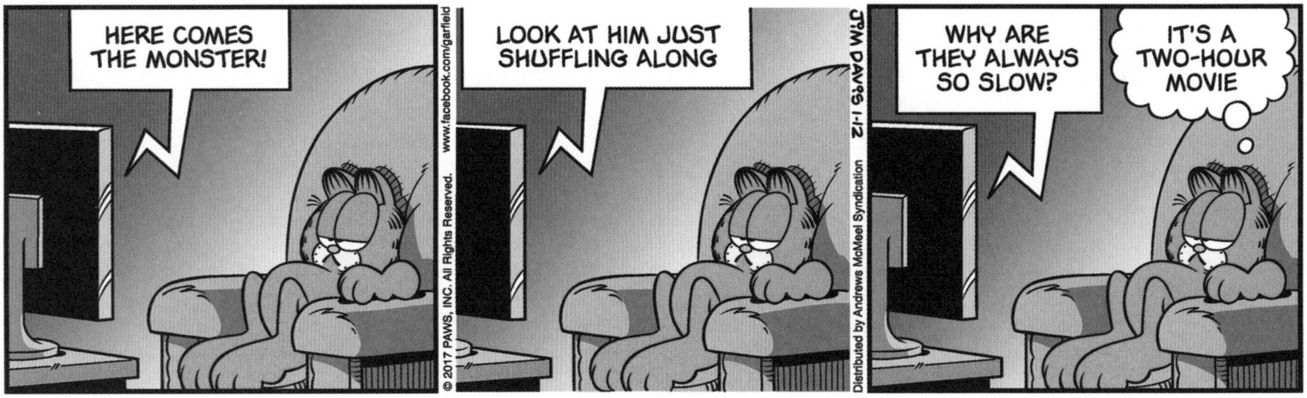
HERE COMES THE MONSTER!
LOOK AT HIM JUST SHUFFLING ALONG
WHY ARE THEY ALWAYS SO SLOW?
IT'S A TWO-HOUR MOVIE
JIM DAVIS 1-12
© 2017 PAWS, INC. All Rights Reserved. www.facebook.com/garfield
Distributed by Andrews McMeel Syndication

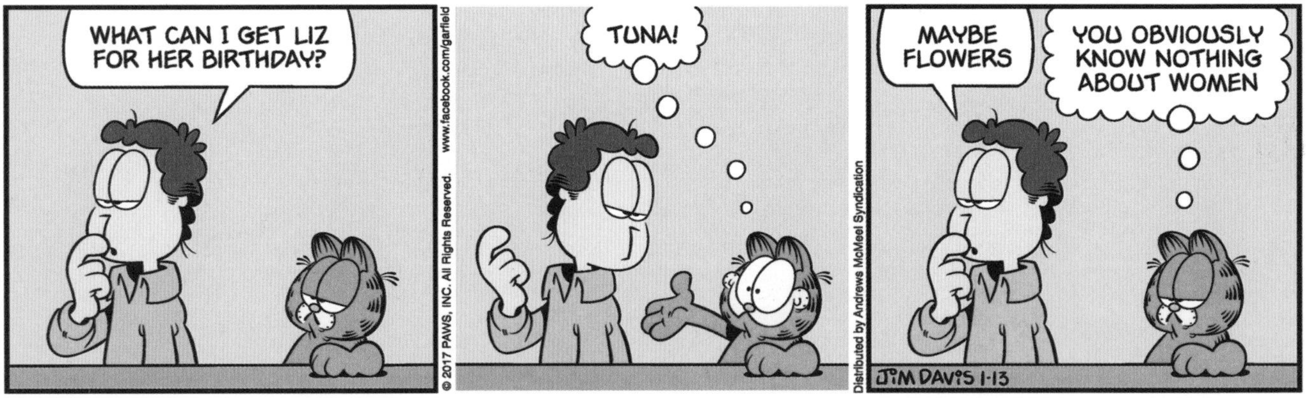
WHAT CAN I GET LIZ FOR HER BIRTHDAY?
TUNA!
MAYBE FLOWERS
YOU OBVIOUSLY KNOW NOTHING ABOUT WOMEN
JIM DAVIS 1-13
© 2017 PAWS, INC. All Rights Reserved. www.facebook.com/garfield
Distributed by Andrews McMeel Syndication

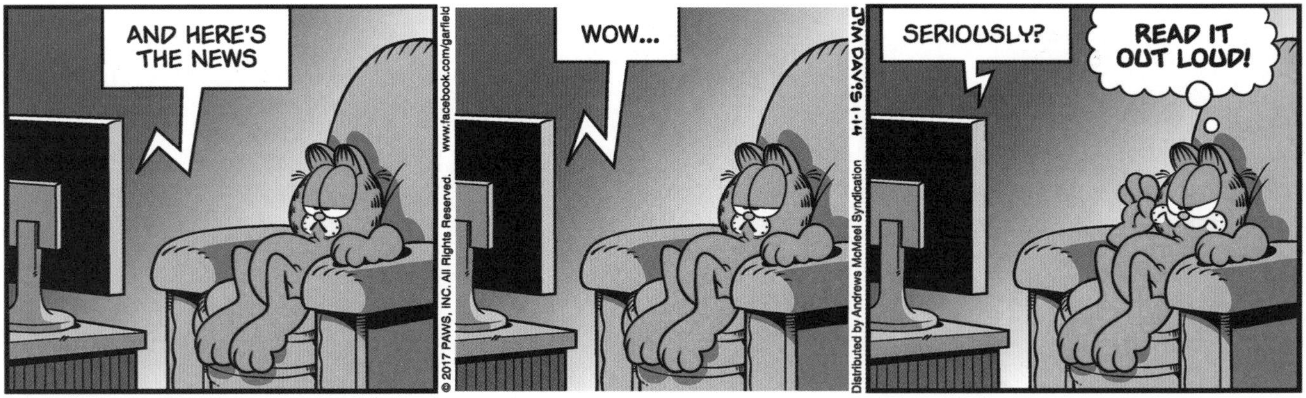
AND HERE'S THE NEWS
WOW...
SERIOUSLY?
READ IT OUT LOUD!
JIM DAVIS 1-14
© 2017 PAWS, INC. All Rights Reserved. www.facebook.com/garfield
Distributed by Andrews McMeel Syndication

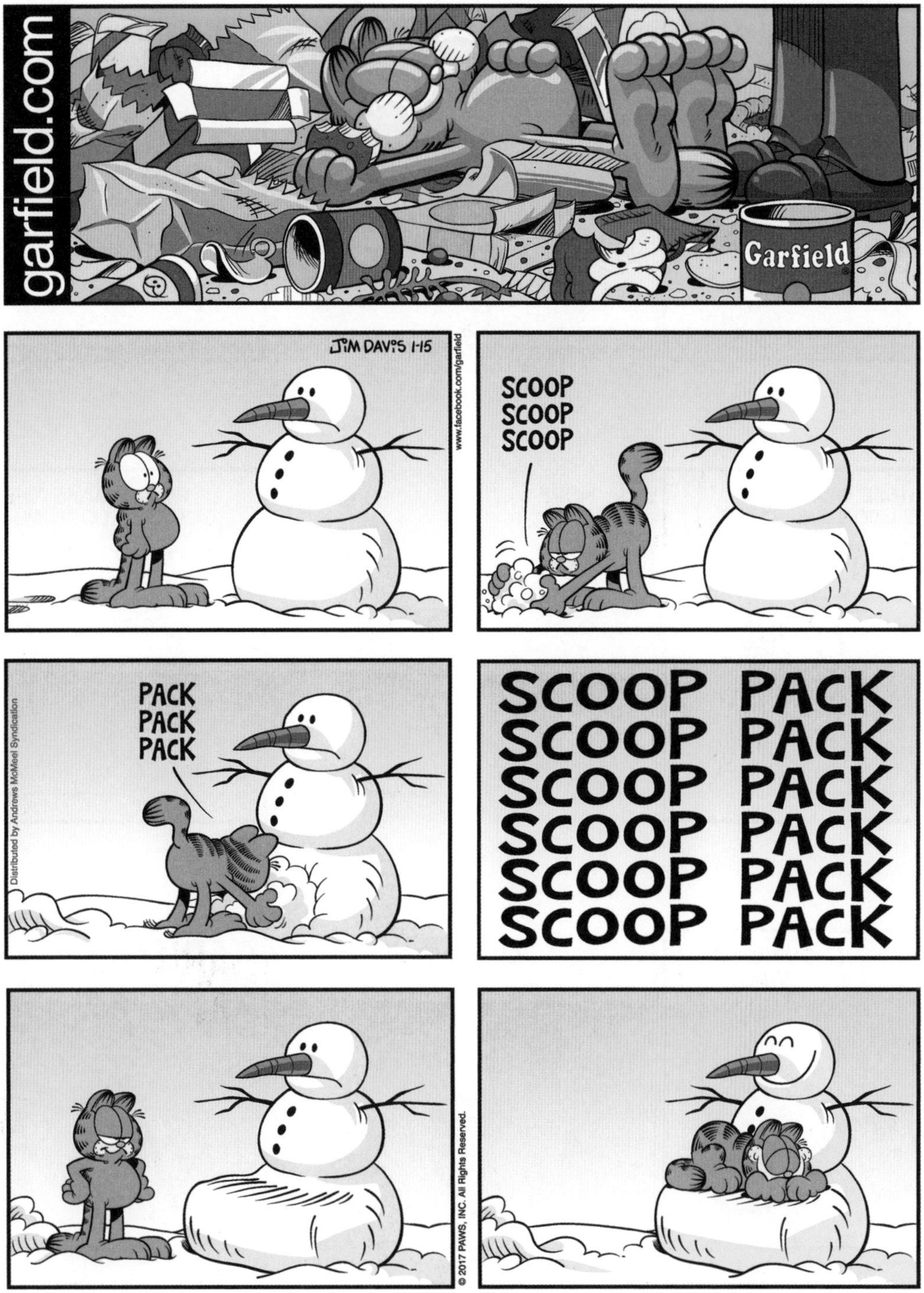
garfield.com
Garfield
JIM DAVIS 1-15
www.facebook.com/garfield
SCOOP
SCOOP
SCOOP
Distributed by Andrews McMeel Syndication
PACK
PACK
PACK
SCOOP PACK
SCOOP PACK
SCOOP PACK
SCOOP PACK
SCOOP PACK
SCOOP PACK
© 2017 PAWS, INC. All Rights Reserved.

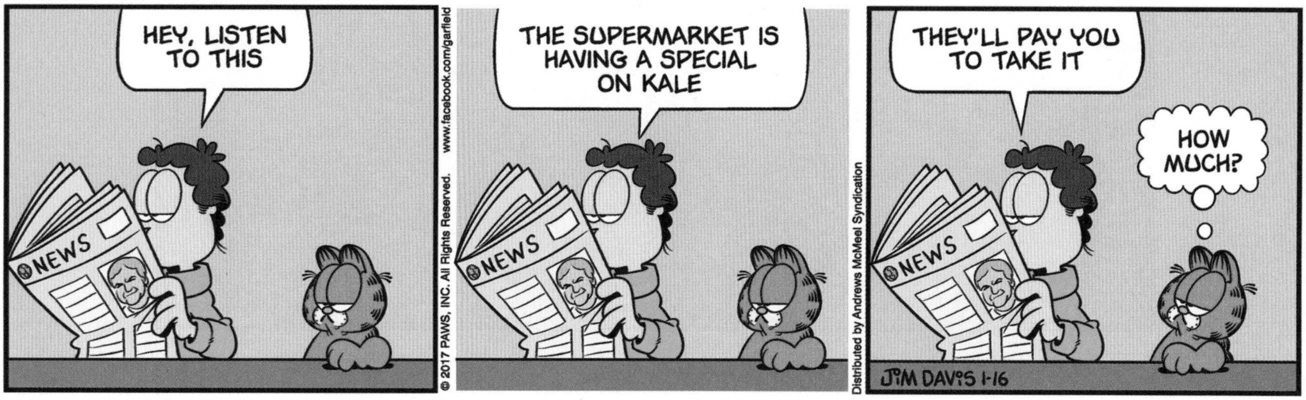
HEY, LISTEN TO THIS
THE SUPERMARKET IS HAVING A SPECIAL ON KALE
THEY'LL PAY YOU TO TAKE IT
HOW MUCH?
NEWS
© 2017 PAWS, INC. All Rights Reserved. www.facebook.com/garfield
Distributed by Andrews McMeel Syndication
JIM DAVIS 1-16

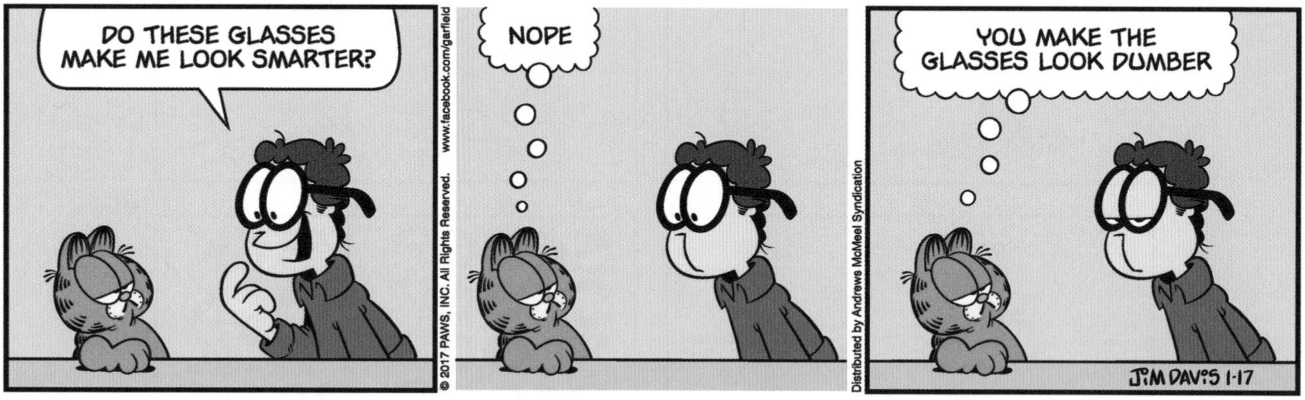
DO THESE GLASSES MAKE ME LOOK SMARTER?
NOPE
YOU MAKE THE GLASSES LOOK DUMBER
© 2017 PAWS, INC. All Rights Reserved. www.facebook.com/garfield
Distributed by Andrews McMeel Syndication
JIM DAVIS 1-17

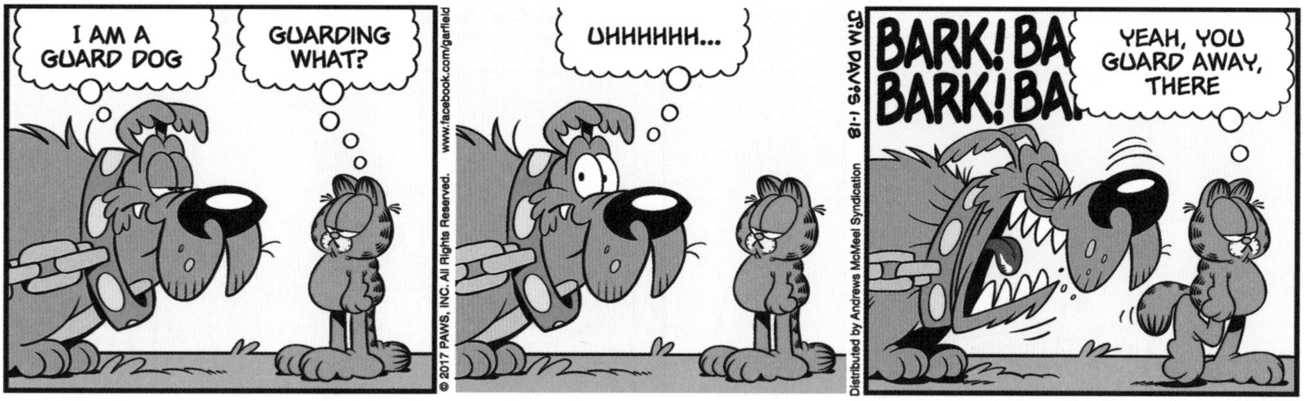
I AM A GUARD DOG
GUARDING WHAT?
UHHHHHH...
BARK! BA
BARK! BA
YEAH, YOU GUARD AWAY, THERE
© 2017 PAWS, INC. All Rights Reserved. www.facebook.com/garfield
Distributed by Andrews McMeel Syndication
JIM DAVIS 1-18

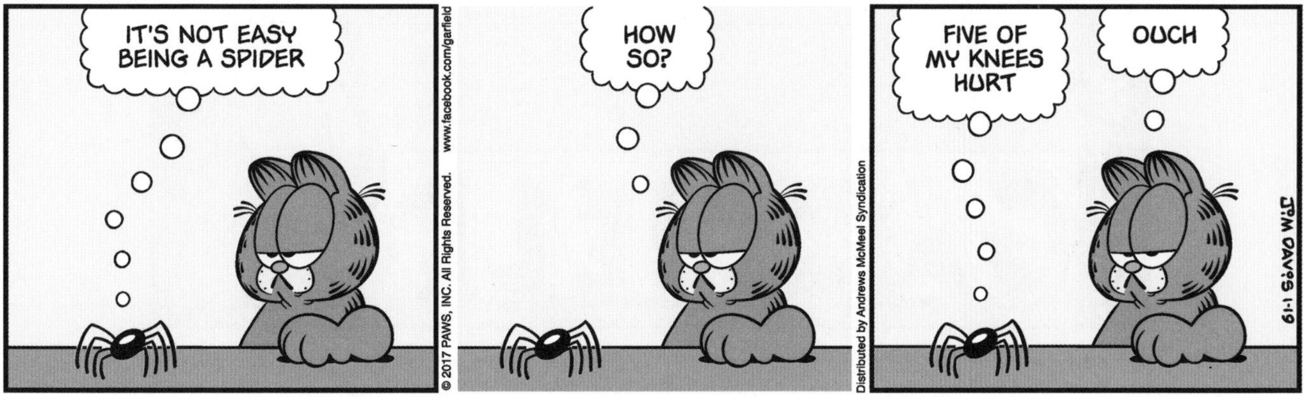
IT'S NOT EASY BEING A SPIDER
HOW SO?
FIVE OF MY KNEES HURT
OUCH
© 2017 PAWS, INC. All Rights Reserved. www.facebook.com/garfield
Distributed by Andrews McMeel Syndication
JIM DAVIS 1-19

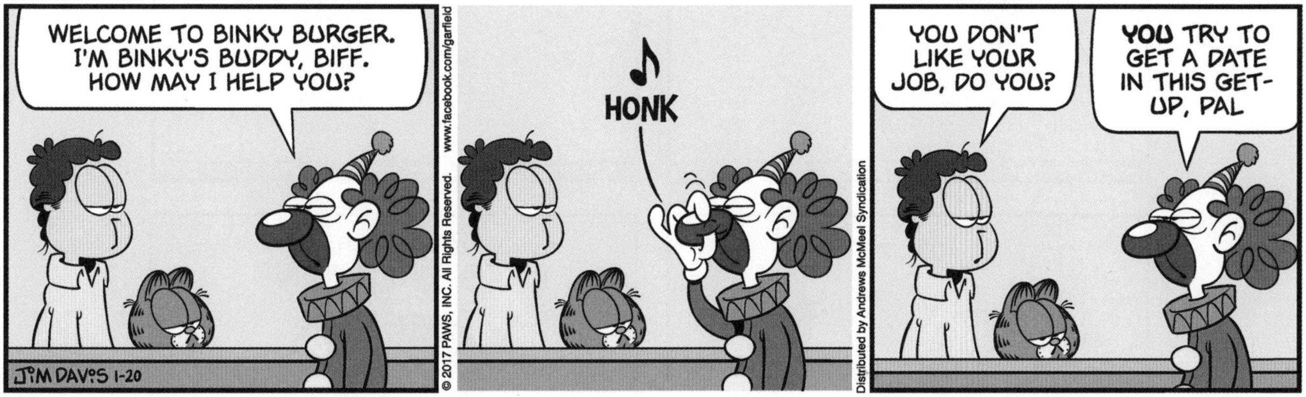
WELCOME TO BINKY BURGER. I'M BINKY'S BUDDY, BIFF. HOW MAY I HELP YOU?
♪ HONK
YOU DON'T LIKE YOUR JOB, DO YOU?
YOU TRY TO GET A DATE IN THIS GET-UP, PAL
© 2017 PAWS, INC. All Rights Reserved. www.facebook.com/garfield
Distributed by Andrews McMeel Syndication
JIM DAVIS 1-20

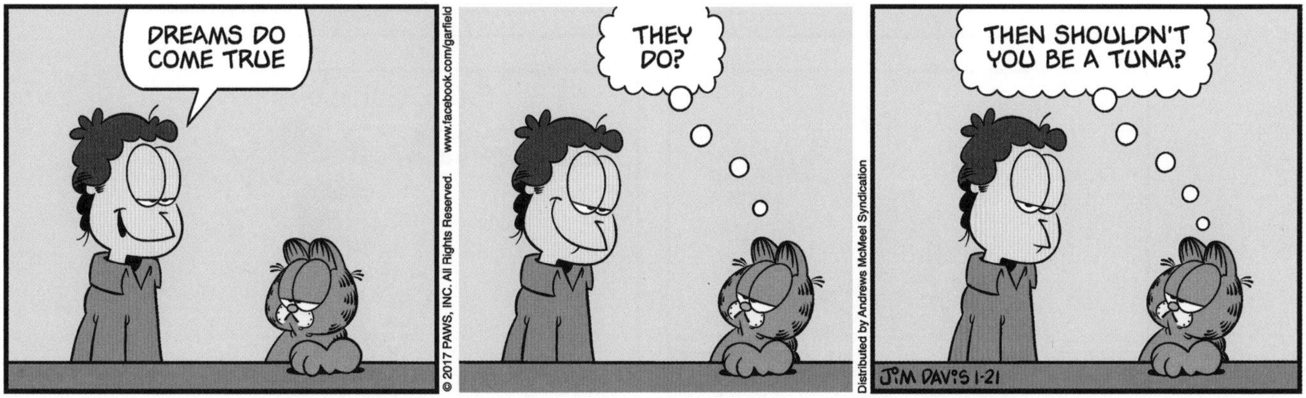
DREAMS DO COME TRUE
THEY DO?
THEN SHOULDN'T YOU BE A TUNA?
© 2017 PAWS, INC. All Rights Reserved. www.facebook.com/garfield
Distributed by Andrews McMeel Syndication
JIM DAVIS 1-21

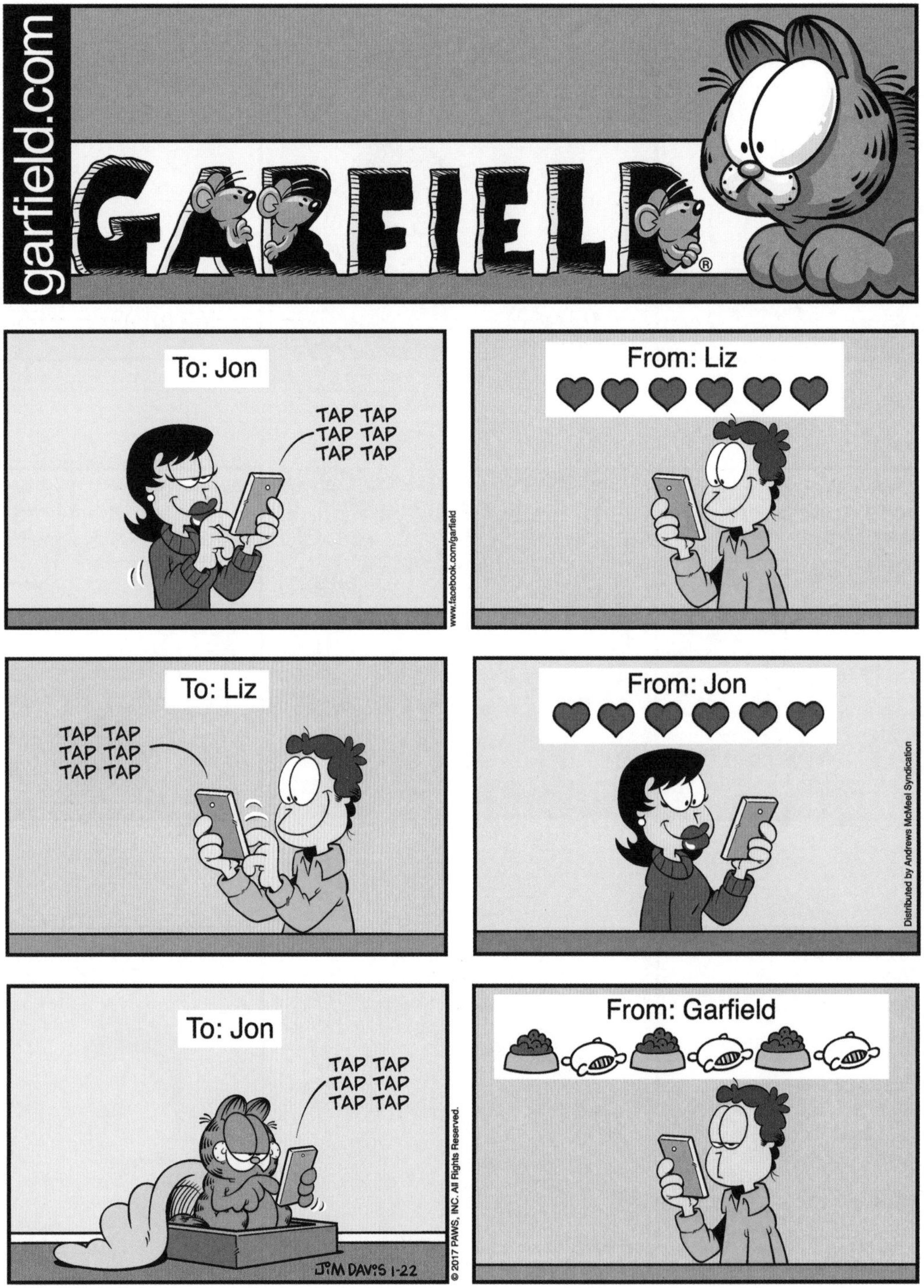
garfield.com
GARFIELD®
To: Jon
TAP TAP
TAP TAP
TAP TAP
www.facebook.com/garfield
From: Liz
To: Liz
TAP TAP
TAP TAP
TAP TAP
From: Jon
Distributed by Andrews McMeel Syndication
To: Jon
TAP TAP
TAP TAP
TAP TAP
JIM DAVIS 1-22
© 2017 PAWS, INC. All Rights Reserved.
From: Garfield

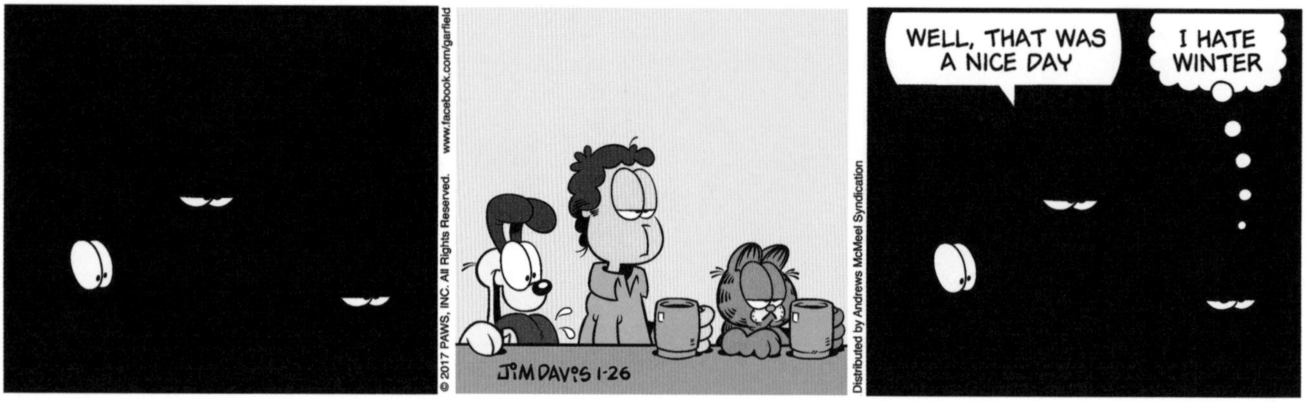
© 2017 PAWS, INC. All Rights Reserved. www.facebook.com/garfield
JIM DAVIS 1-26
Distributed by Andrews McMeel Syndication
WELL, THAT WAS A NICE DAY
I HATE WINTER

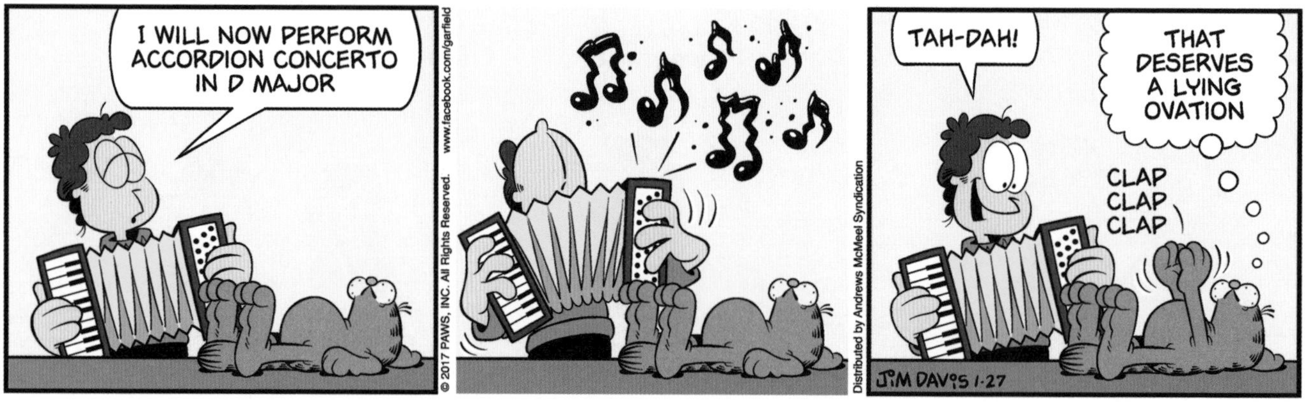
I WILL NOW PERFORM ACCORDION CONCERTO IN D MAJOR
© 2017 PAWS, INC. All Rights Reserved. www.facebook.com/garfield
Distributed by Andrews McMeel Syndication
TAH-DAH!
THAT DESERVES A LYING OVATION
CLAP CLAP CLAP
JIM DAVIS 1-27

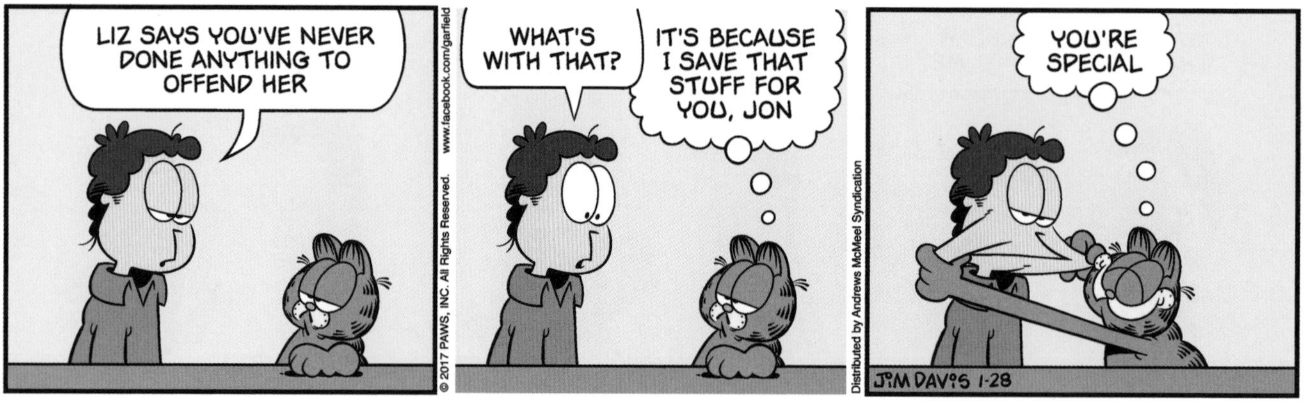
LIZ SAYS YOU'VE NEVER DONE ANYTHING TO OFFEND HER
© 2017 PAWS, INC. All Rights Reserved. www.facebook.com/garfield
WHAT'S WITH THAT?
IT'S BECAUSE I SAVE THAT STUFF FOR YOU, JON
Distributed by Andrews McMeel Syndication
YOU'RE SPECIAL
JIM DAVIS 1-28

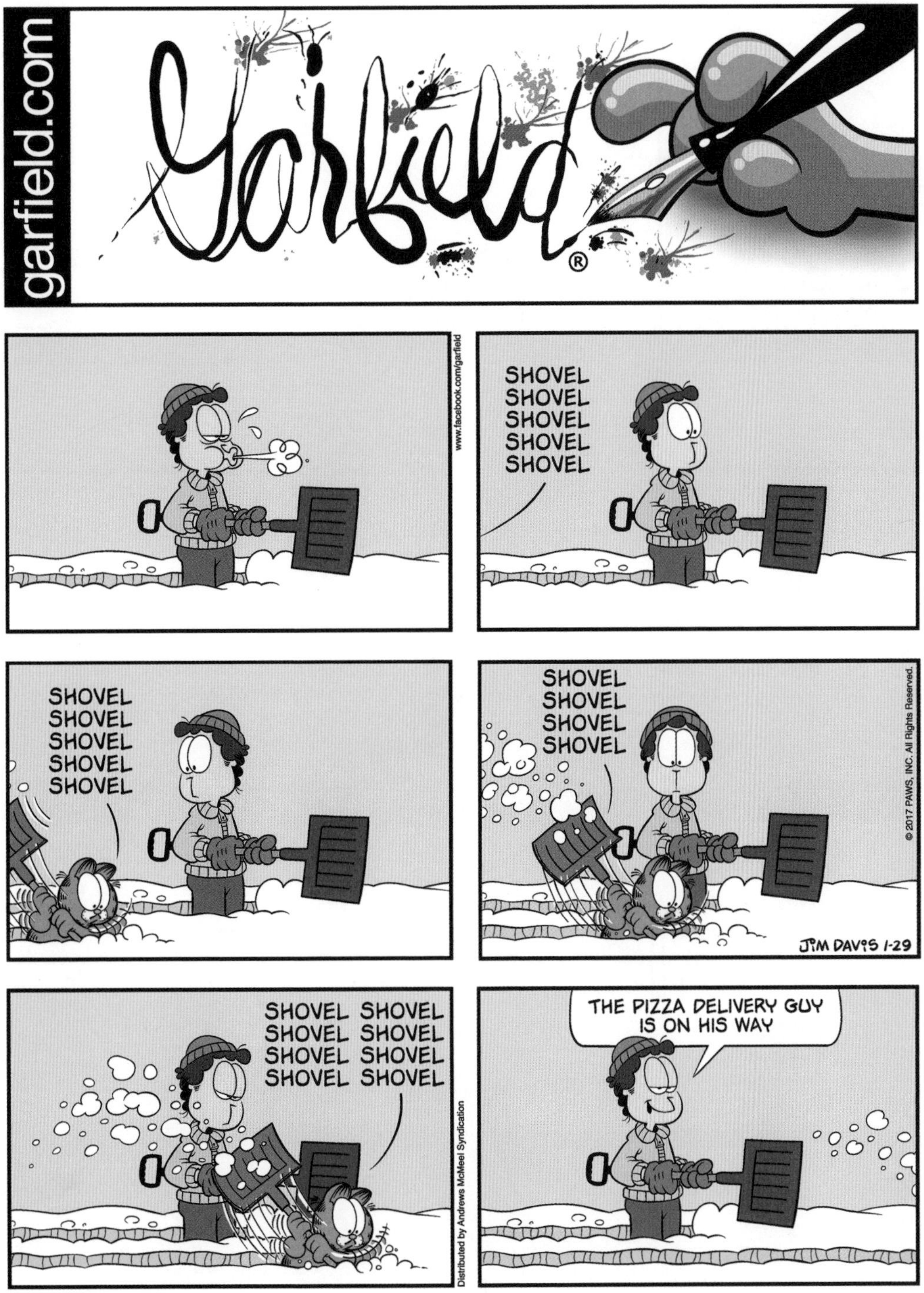
garfield.com
Garfield®
www.facebook.com/garfield
SHOVEL
SHOVEL
SHOVEL
SHOVEL
SHOVEL
SHOVEL
SHOVEL
SHOVEL
SHOVEL
SHOVEL
SHOVEL
SHOVEL
SHOVEL
SHOVEL
© 2017 PAWS, INC. All Rights Reserved.
JIM DAVIS 1-29
SHOVEL SHOVEL
SHOVEL SHOVEL
SHOVEL SHOVEL
SHOVEL SHOVEL
Distributed by Andrews McMeel Syndication
THE PIZZA DELIVERY GUY IS ON HIS WAY

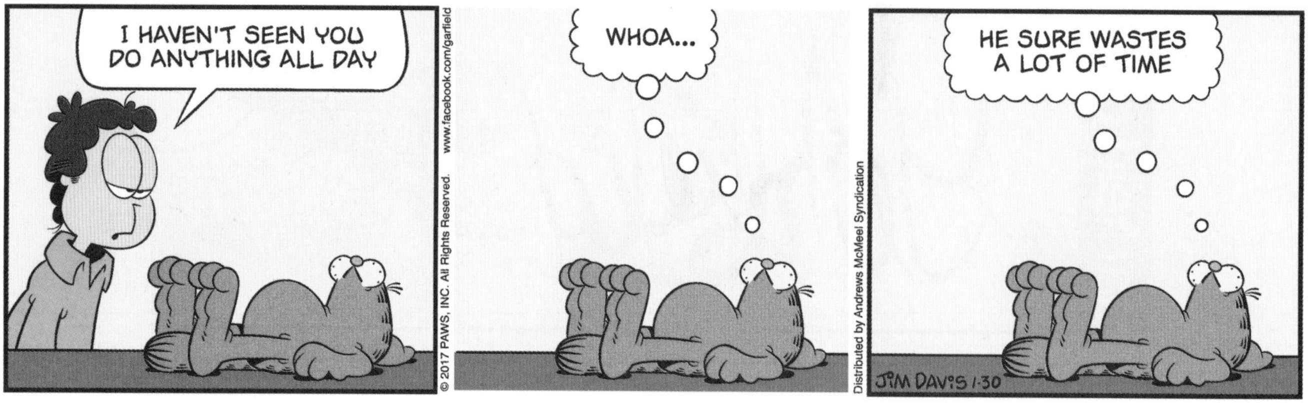
I HAVEN'T SEEN YOU DO ANYTHING ALL DAY
WHOA...
HE SURE WASTES A LOT OF TIME
© 2017 PAWS, INC. All Rights Reserved. www.facebook.com/garfield
Distributed by Andrews McMeel Syndication
JIM DAVIS 1-30

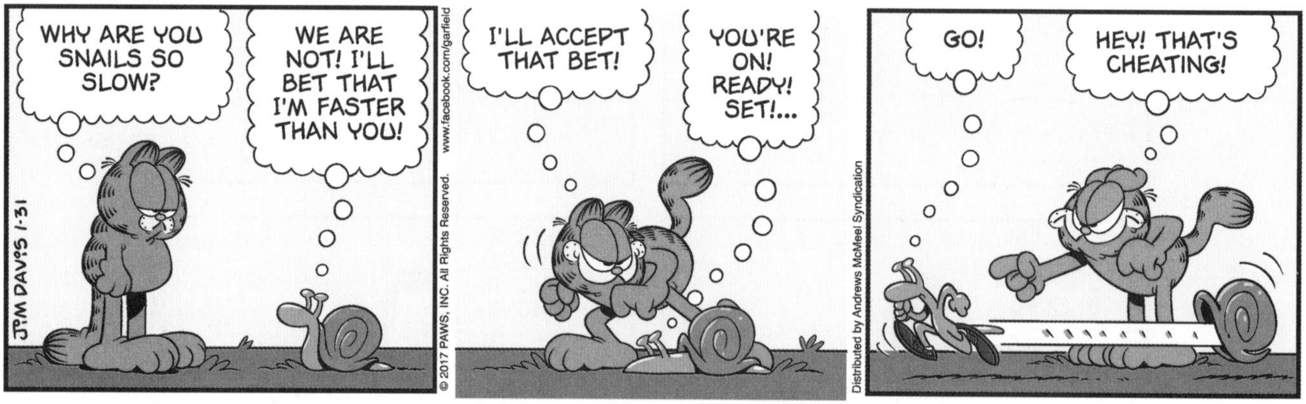
WHY ARE YOU SNAILS SO SLOW?
WE ARE NOT! I'LL BET THAT I'M FASTER THAN YOU!
I'LL ACCEPT THAT BET!
YOU'RE ON! READY! SET!...
GO!
HEY! THAT'S CHEATING!
JIM DAVIS 1-31
© 2017 PAWS, INC. All Rights Reserved. www.facebook.com/garfield
Distributed by Andrews McMeel Syndication

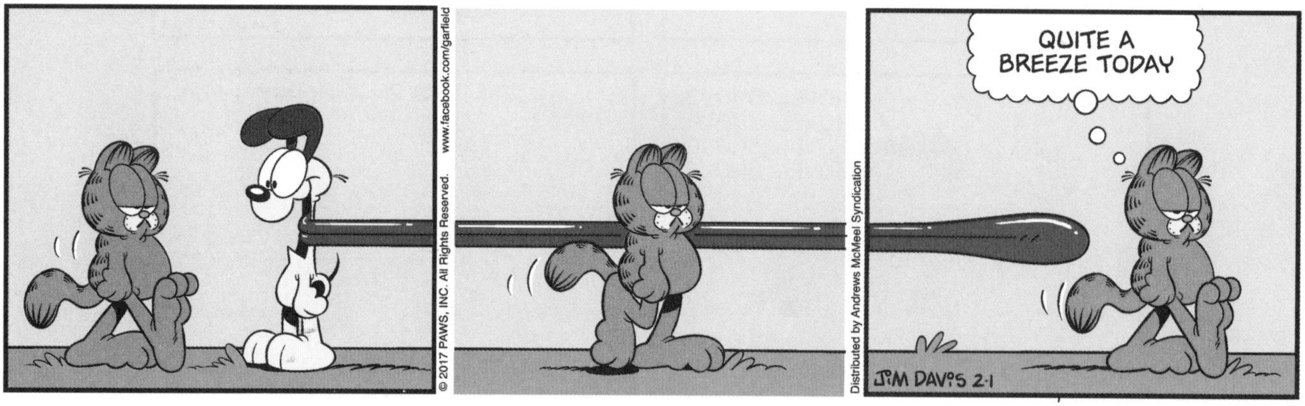
QUITE A BREEZE TODAY
© 2017 PAWS, INC. All Rights Reserved. www.facebook.com/garfield
Distributed by Andrews McMeel Syndication
JIM DAVIS 2-1

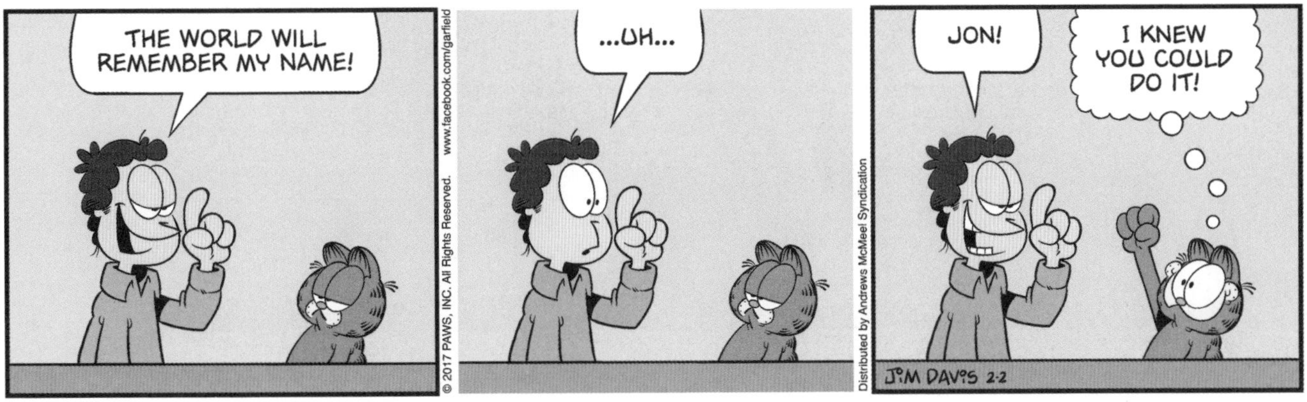
THE WORLD WILL REMEMBER MY NAME!
© 2017 PAWS, INC. All Rights Reserved. www.facebook.com/garfield
...UH...
Distributed by Andrews McMeel Syndication
JON!
I KNEW YOU COULD DO IT!
JIM DAVIS 2-2

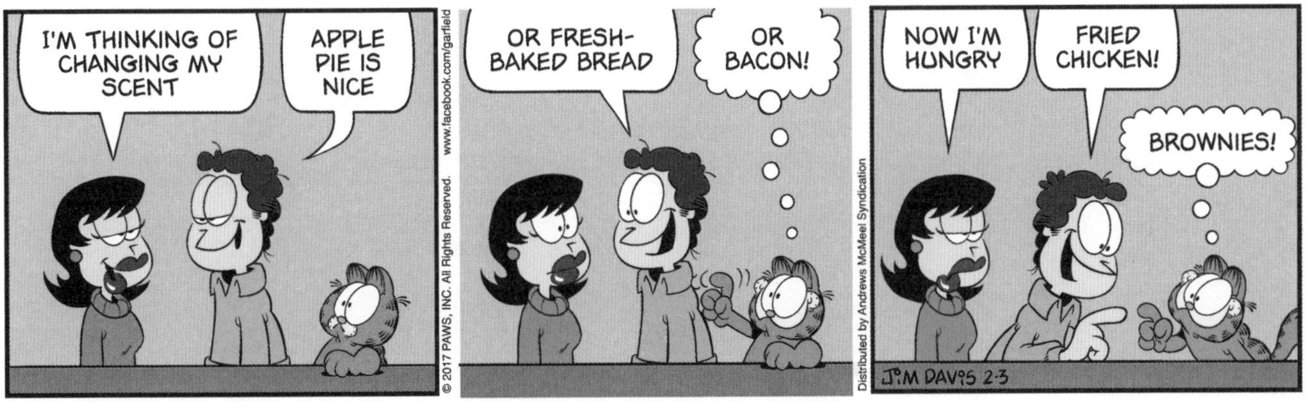
I'M THINKING OF CHANGING MY SCENT
APPLE PIE IS NICE
© 2017 PAWS, INC. All Rights Reserved. www.facebook.com/garfield
OR FRESH-BAKED BREAD
OR BACON!
Distributed by Andrews McMeel Syndication
NOW I'M HUNGRY
FRIED CHICKEN!
BROWNIES!
JIM DAVIS 2-3

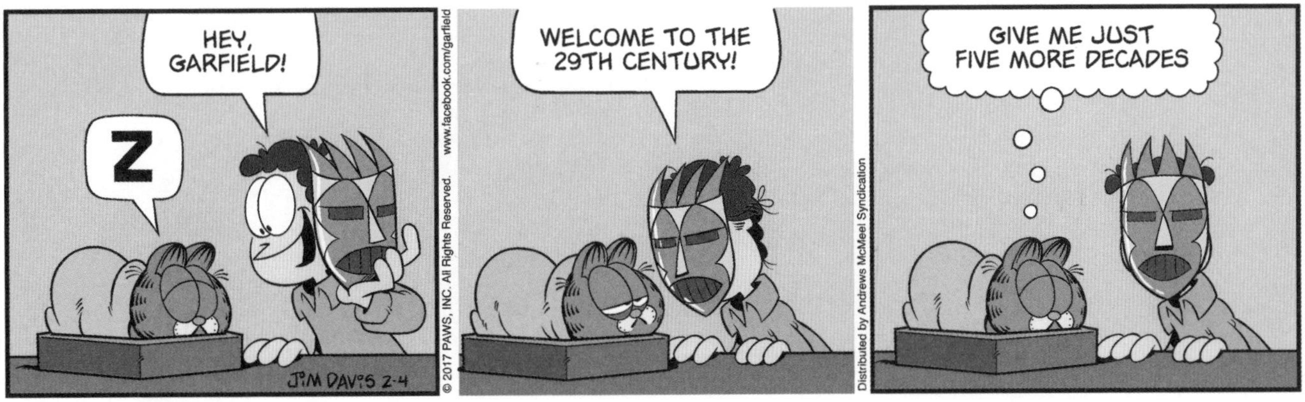
Z
HEY, GARFIELD!
JIM DAVIS 2-4
© 2017 PAWS, INC. All Rights Reserved. www.facebook.com/garfield
WELCOME TO THE 29TH CENTURY!
Distributed by Andrews McMeel Syndication
GIVE ME JUST FIVE MORE DECADES

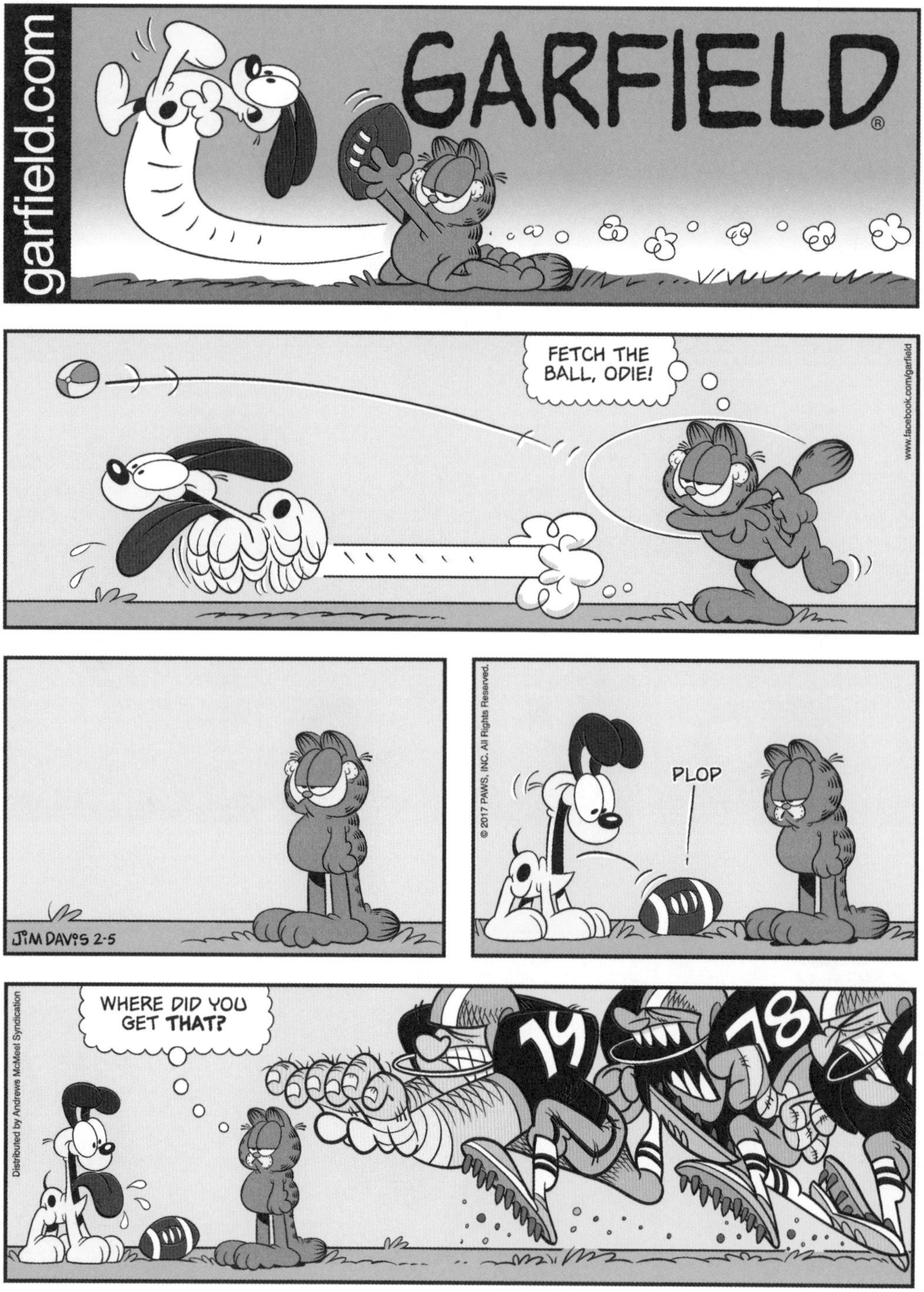
garfield.com
GARFIELD®
FETCH THE BALL, ODIE!
www.facebook.com/garfield
JIM DAVIS 2-5
© 2017 PAWS, INC. All Rights Reserved.
PLOP
Distributed by Andrews McMeel Syndication
WHERE DID YOU GET THAT?

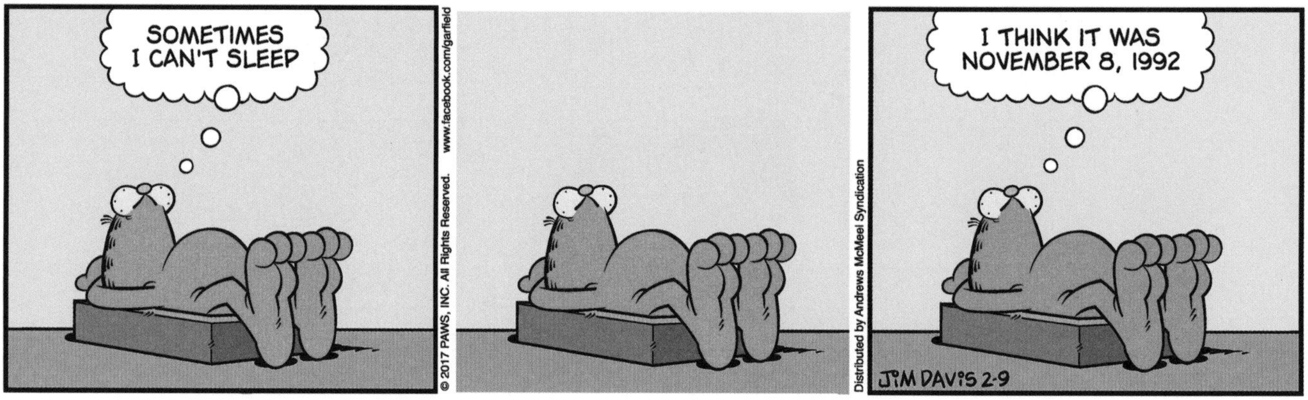
SOMETIMES I CAN'T SLEEP
© 2017 PAWS, INC. All Rights Reserved. www.facebook.com/garfield
Distributed by Andrews McMeel Syndication
I THINK IT WAS NOVEMBER 8, 1992
JIM DAVIS 2-9

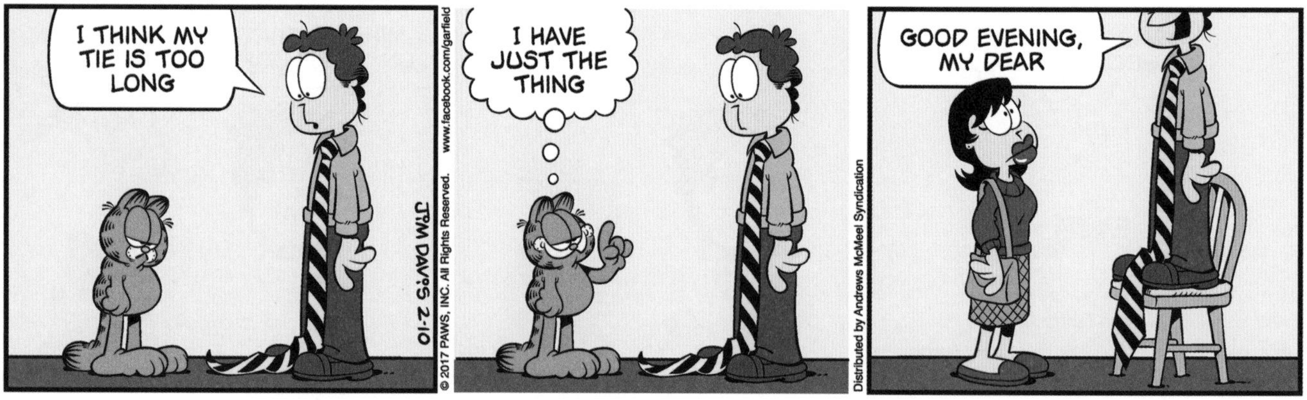
I THINK MY TIE IS TOO LONG
JIM DAVIS 2-10
© 2017 PAWS, INC. All Rights Reserved. www.facebook.com/garfield
I HAVE JUST THE THING
Distributed by Andrews McMeel Syndication
GOOD EVENING, MY DEAR

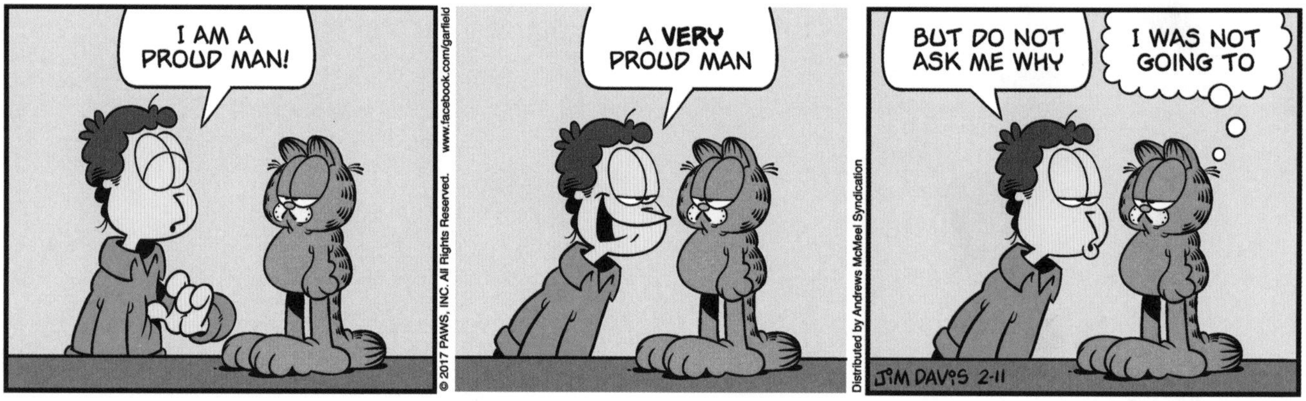
I AM A PROUD MAN!
© 2017 PAWS, INC. All Rights Reserved. www.facebook.com/garfield
A **VERY** PROUD MAN
Distributed by Andrews McMeel Syndication
BUT DO NOT ASK ME WHY
I WAS NOT GOING TO
JIM DAVIS 2-11

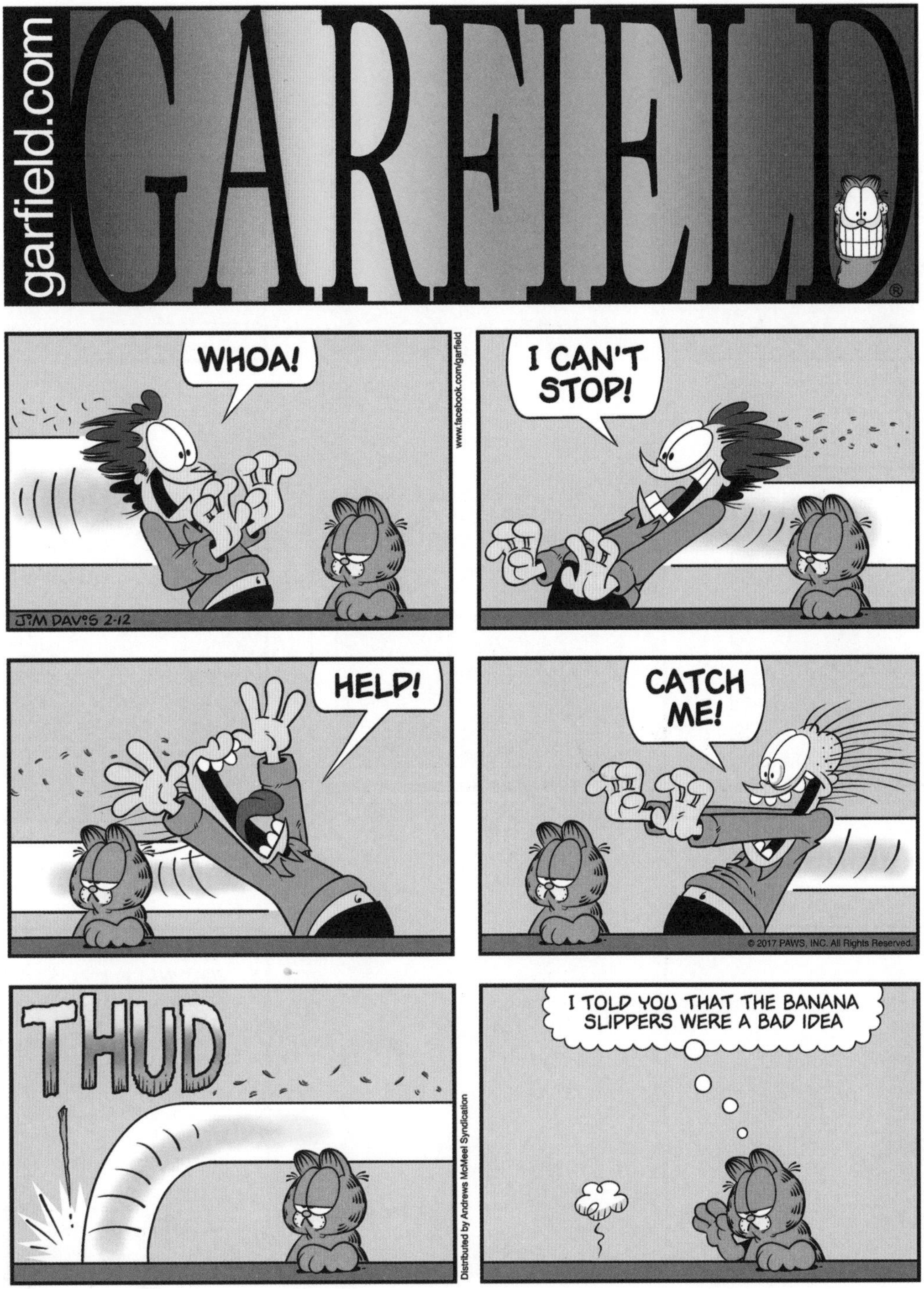

garfield.com
GARFIELD
WHOA!
JIM DAVIS 2-12
www.facebook.com/garfield
I CAN'T STOP!
HELP!
CATCH ME!
© 2017 PAWS, INC. All Rights Reserved.
THUD
Distributed by Andrews McMeel Syndication
I TOLD YOU THAT THE BANANA SLIPPERS WERE A BAD IDEA

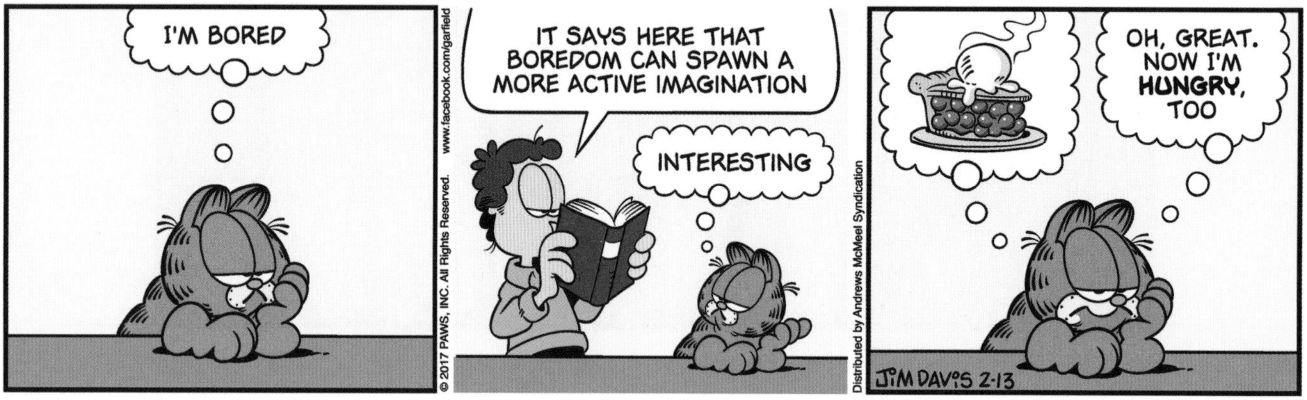
I'M BORED
© 2017 PAWS, INC. All Rights Reserved. www.facebook.com/garfield
IT SAYS HERE THAT BOREDOM CAN SPAWN A MORE ACTIVE IMAGINATION
INTERESTING
Distributed by Andrews McMeel Syndication
OH, GREAT. NOW I'M **HUNGRY**, TOO
JIM DAVIS 2-13

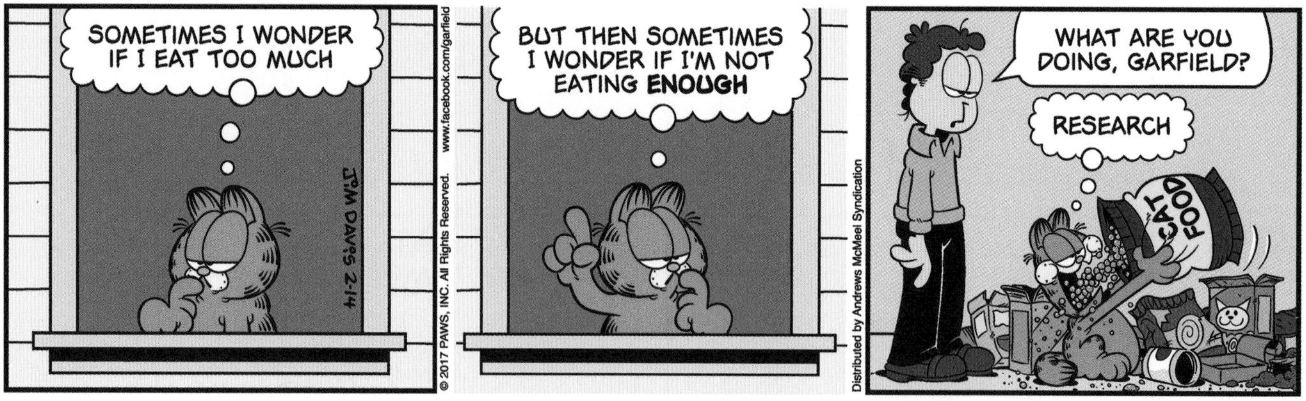
SOMETIMES I WONDER IF I EAT TOO MUCH
JIM DAVIS 2-14
© 2017 PAWS, INC. All Rights Reserved. www.facebook.com/garfield
BUT THEN SOMETIMES I WONDER IF I'M NOT EATING **ENOUGH**
Distributed by Andrews McMeel Syndication
WHAT ARE YOU DOING, GARFIELD?
RESEARCH
CAT FOOD

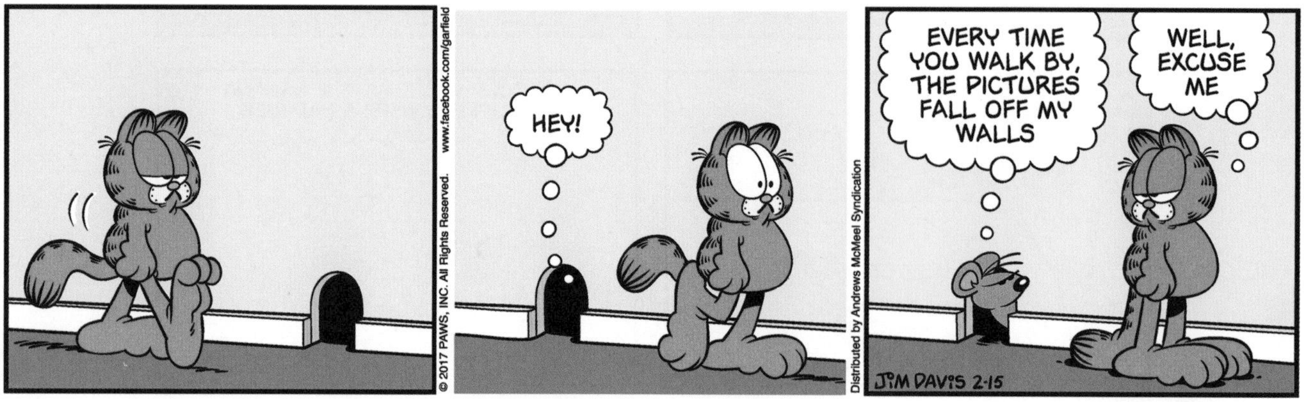
© 2017 PAWS, INC. All Rights Reserved. www.facebook.com/garfield
HEY!
Distributed by Andrews McMeel Syndication
EVERY TIME YOU WALK BY, THE PICTURES FALL OFF MY WALLS
WELL, EXCUSE ME
JIM DAVIS 2-15

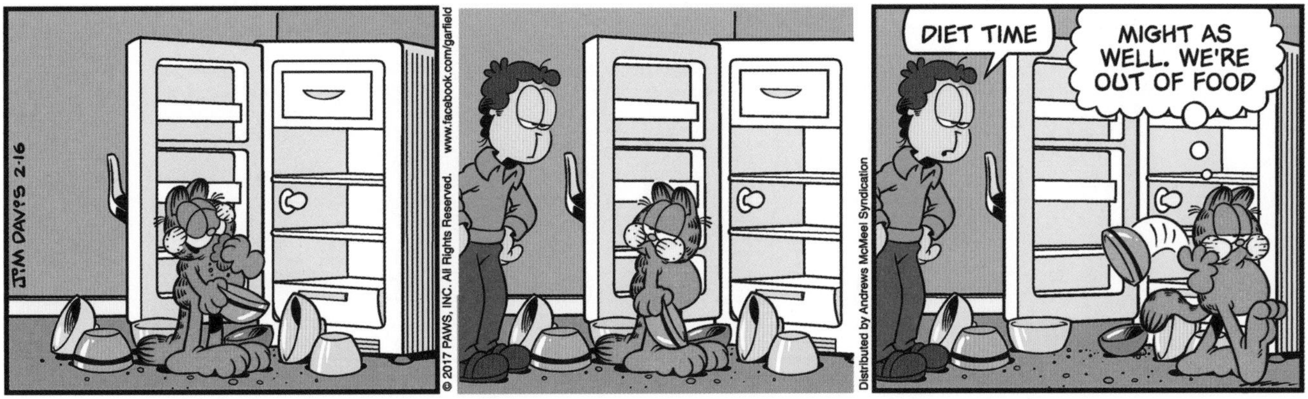
JIM DAVIS 2-16
© 2017 PAWS, INC. All Rights Reserved. www.facebook.com/garfield
DIET TIME
MIGHT AS WELL. WE'RE OUT OF FOOD
Distributed by Andrews McMeel Syndication

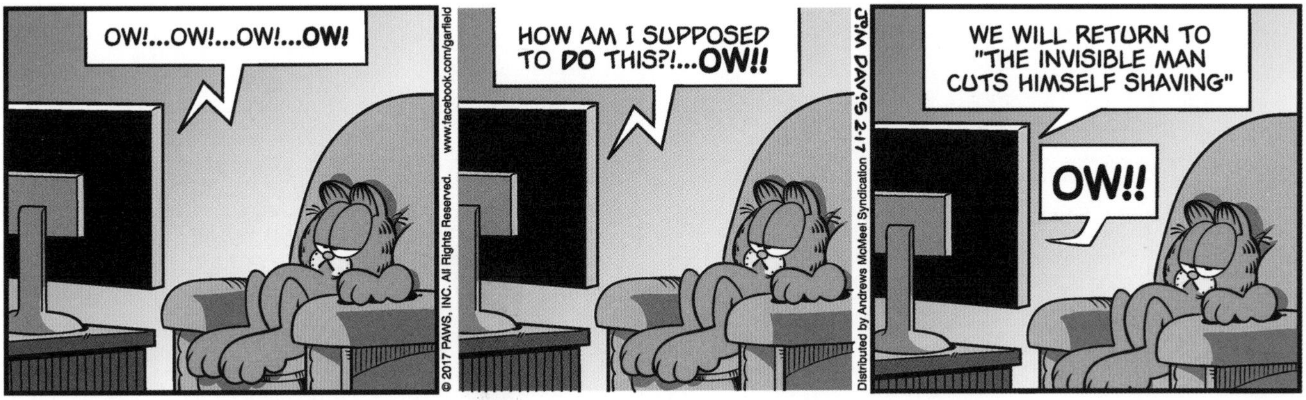
OW!...OW!...OW!...OW!
© 2017 PAWS, INC. All Rights Reserved. www.facebook.com/garfield
HOW AM I SUPPOSED TO DO THIS?!...OW!!
JIM DAVIS 2-17
Distributed by Andrews McMeel Syndication
WE WILL RETURN TO "THE INVISIBLE MAN CUTS HIMSELF SHAVING"
OW!!

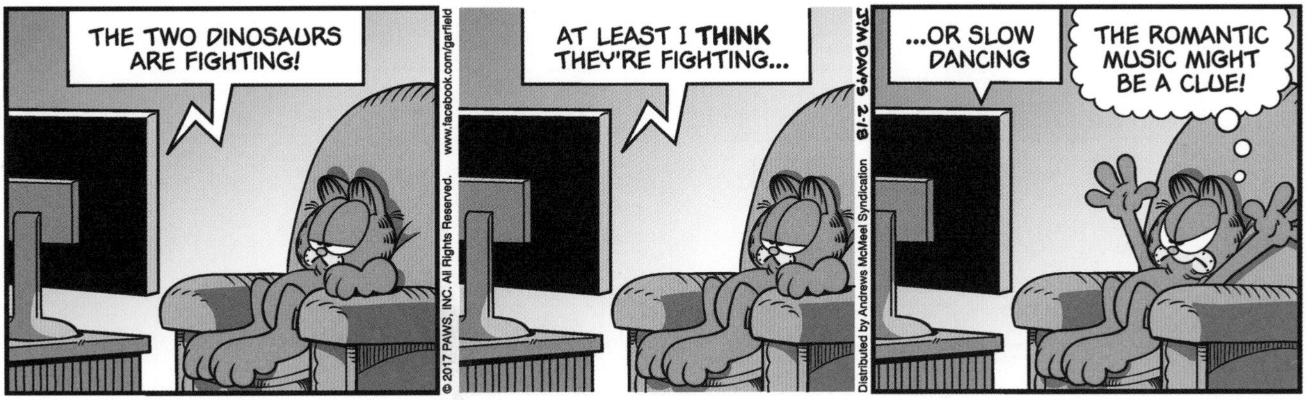
THE TWO DINOSAURS ARE FIGHTING!
© 2017 PAWS, INC. All Rights Reserved. www.facebook.com/garfield
AT LEAST I THINK THEY'RE FIGHTING...
JIM DAVIS 2-18
Distributed by Andrews McMeel Syndication
...OR SLOW DANCING
THE ROMANTIC MUSIC MIGHT BE A CLUE!

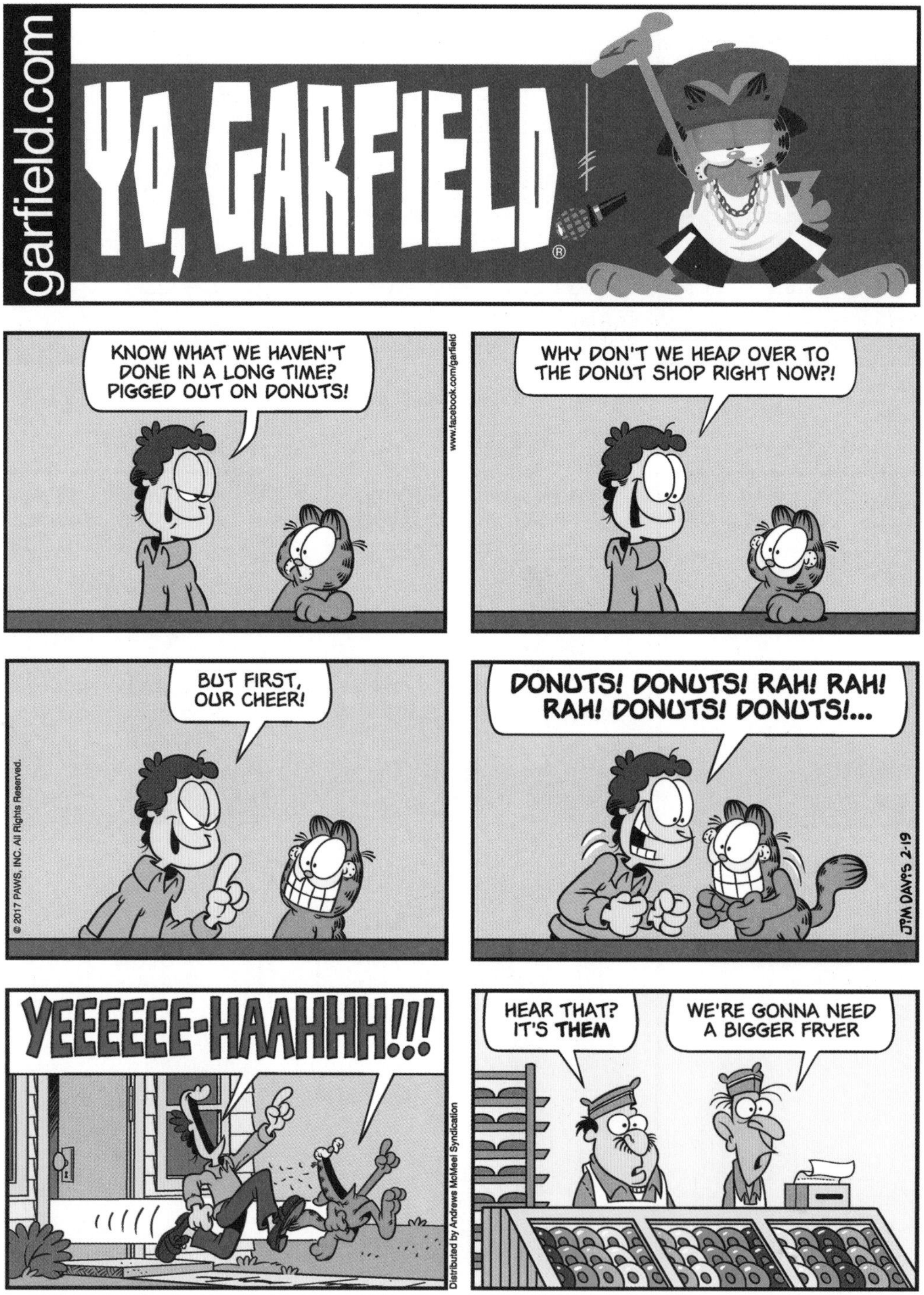

garfield.com
YO, GARFIELD®
KNOW WHAT WE HAVEN'T DONE IN A LONG TIME? PIGGED OUT ON DONUTS!
www.facebook.com/garfield
WHY DON'T WE HEAD OVER TO THE DONUT SHOP RIGHT NOW?!
BUT FIRST, OUR CHEER!
© 2017 PAWS, INC. All Rights Reserved.
DONUTS! DONUTS! RAH! RAH! RAH! DONUTS! DONUTS!...
JIM DAVIS 2-19
YEEEEEE-HAAHHH!!!
Distributed by Andrews McMeel Syndication
HEAR THAT? IT'S **THEM**
WE'RE GONNA NEED A BIGGER FRYER

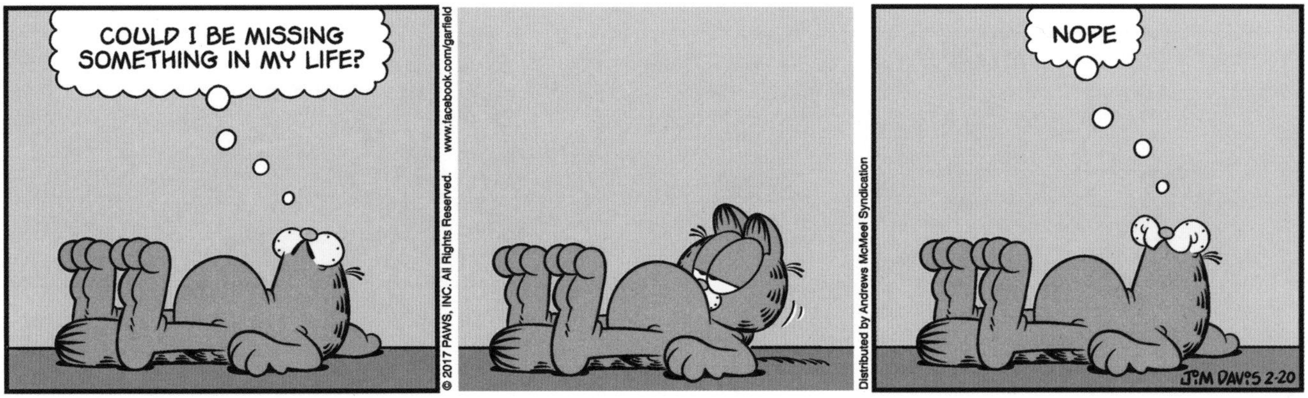
COULD I BE MISSING SOMETHING IN MY LIFE?
NOPE
© 2017 PAWS, INC. All Rights Reserved. www.facebook.com/garfield
Distributed by Andrews McMeel Syndication
JIM DAVIS 2-20

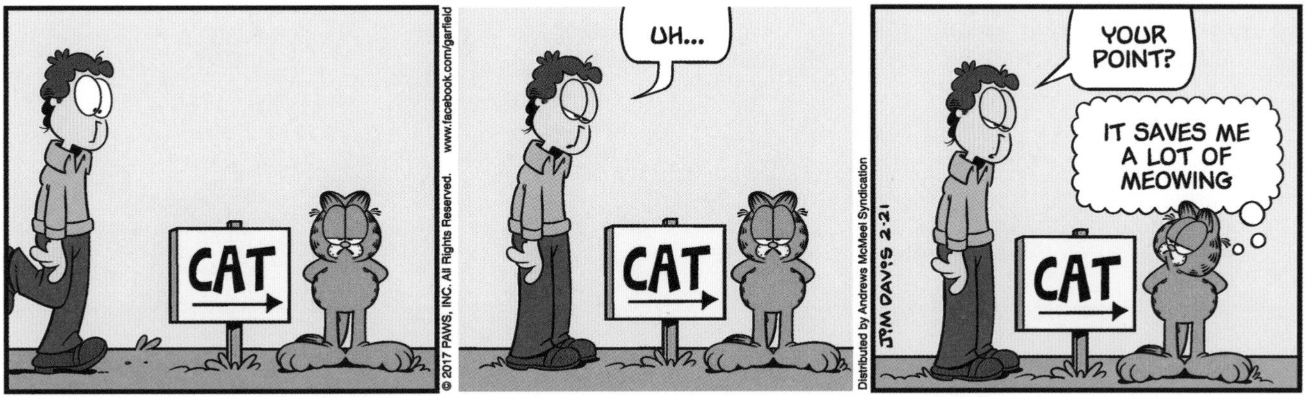
CAT
UH...
YOUR POINT?
IT SAVES ME A LOT OF MEOWING
© 2017 PAWS, INC. All Rights Reserved. www.facebook.com/garfield
Distributed by Andrews McMeel Syndication
JIM DAVIS 2-21

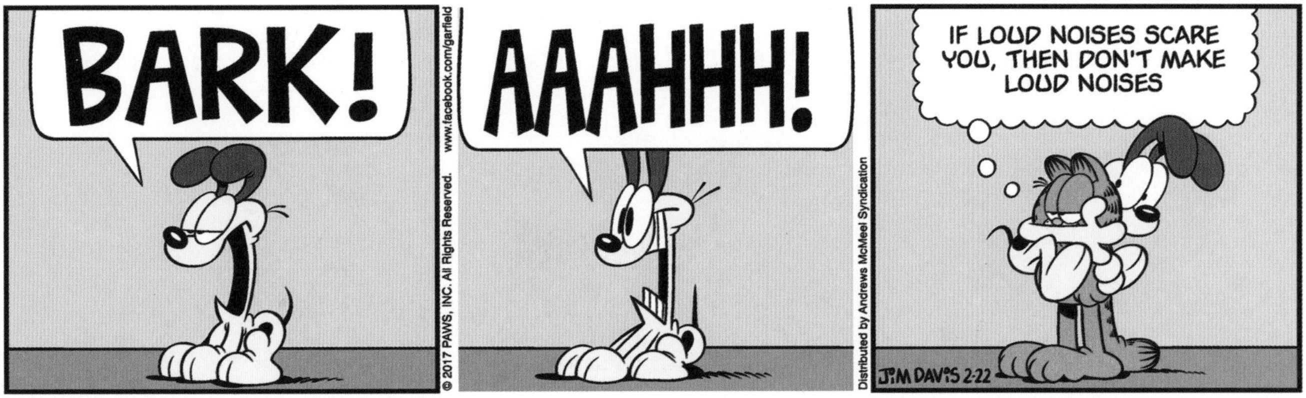
BARK!
AAAHHH!
IF LOUD NOISES SCARE YOU, THEN DON'T MAKE LOUD NOISES
© 2017 PAWS, INC. All Rights Reserved. www.facebook.com/garfield
Distributed by Andrews McMeel Syndication
JIM DAVIS 2-22

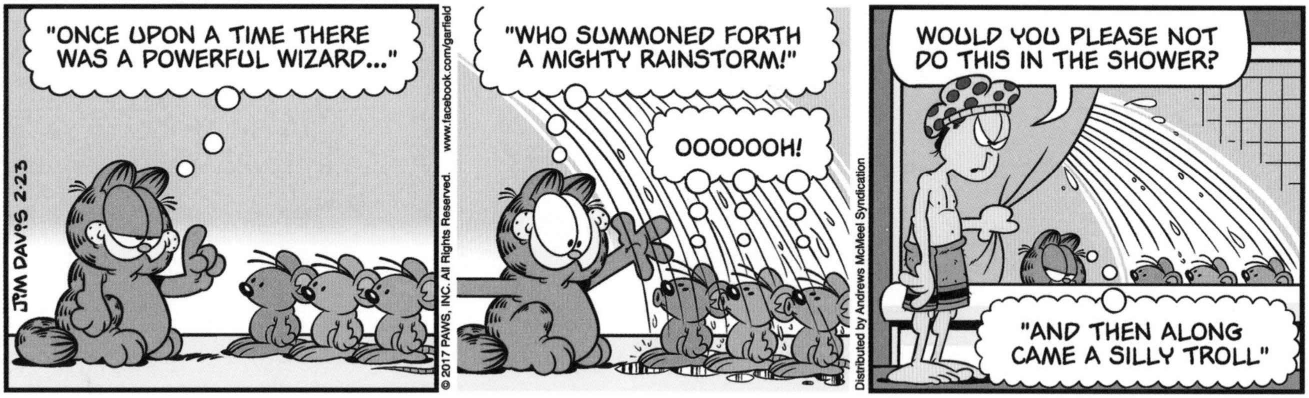
"ONCE UPON A TIME THERE WAS A POWERFUL WIZARD..."
JIM DAVIS 2·23
© 2017 PAWS, INC. All Rights Reserved. www.facebook.com/garfield
"WHO SUMMONED FORTH A MIGHTY RAINSTORM!"
OOOOOOH!
Distributed by Andrews McMeel Syndication
WOULD YOU PLEASE NOT DO THIS IN THE SHOWER?
"AND THEN ALONG CAME A SILLY TROLL"

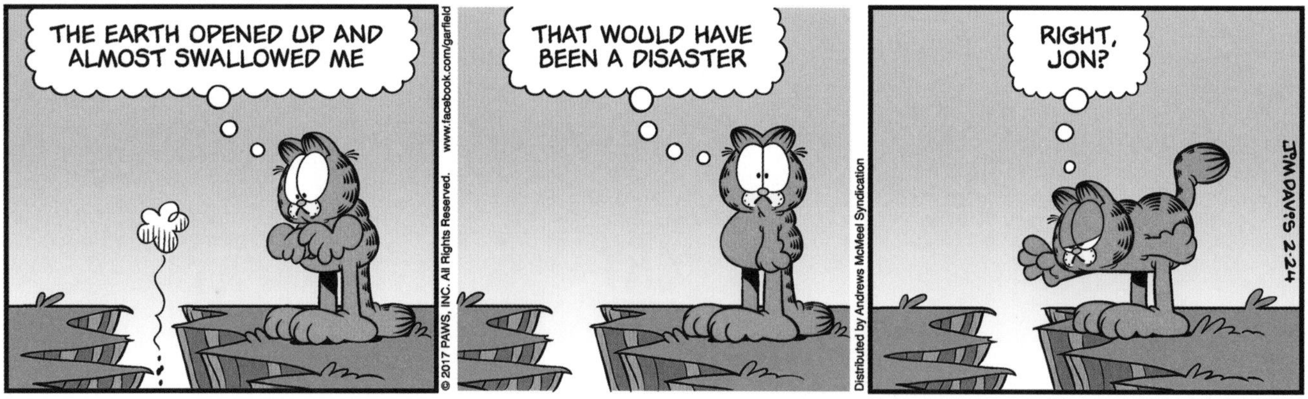
THE EARTH OPENED UP AND ALMOST SWALLOWED ME
© 2017 PAWS, INC. All Rights Reserved. www.facebook.com/garfield
THAT WOULD HAVE BEEN A DISASTER
Distributed by Andrews McMeel Syndication
RIGHT, JON?
JIM DAVIS 2·24

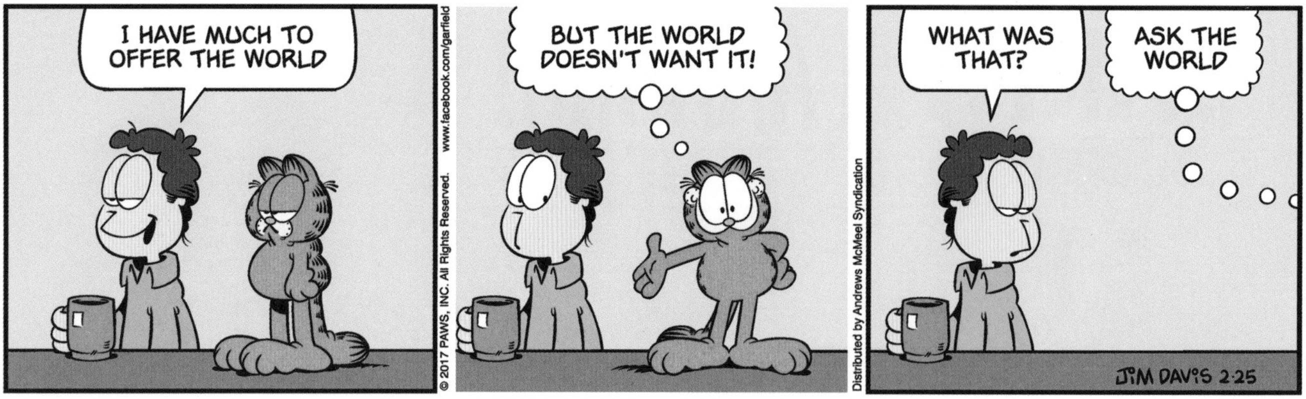
I HAVE MUCH TO OFFER THE WORLD
© 2017 PAWS, INC. All Rights Reserved. www.facebook.com/garfield
BUT THE WORLD DOESN'T WANT IT!
Distributed by Andrews McMeel Syndication
WHAT WAS THAT?
ASK THE WORLD
JIM DAVIS 2·25

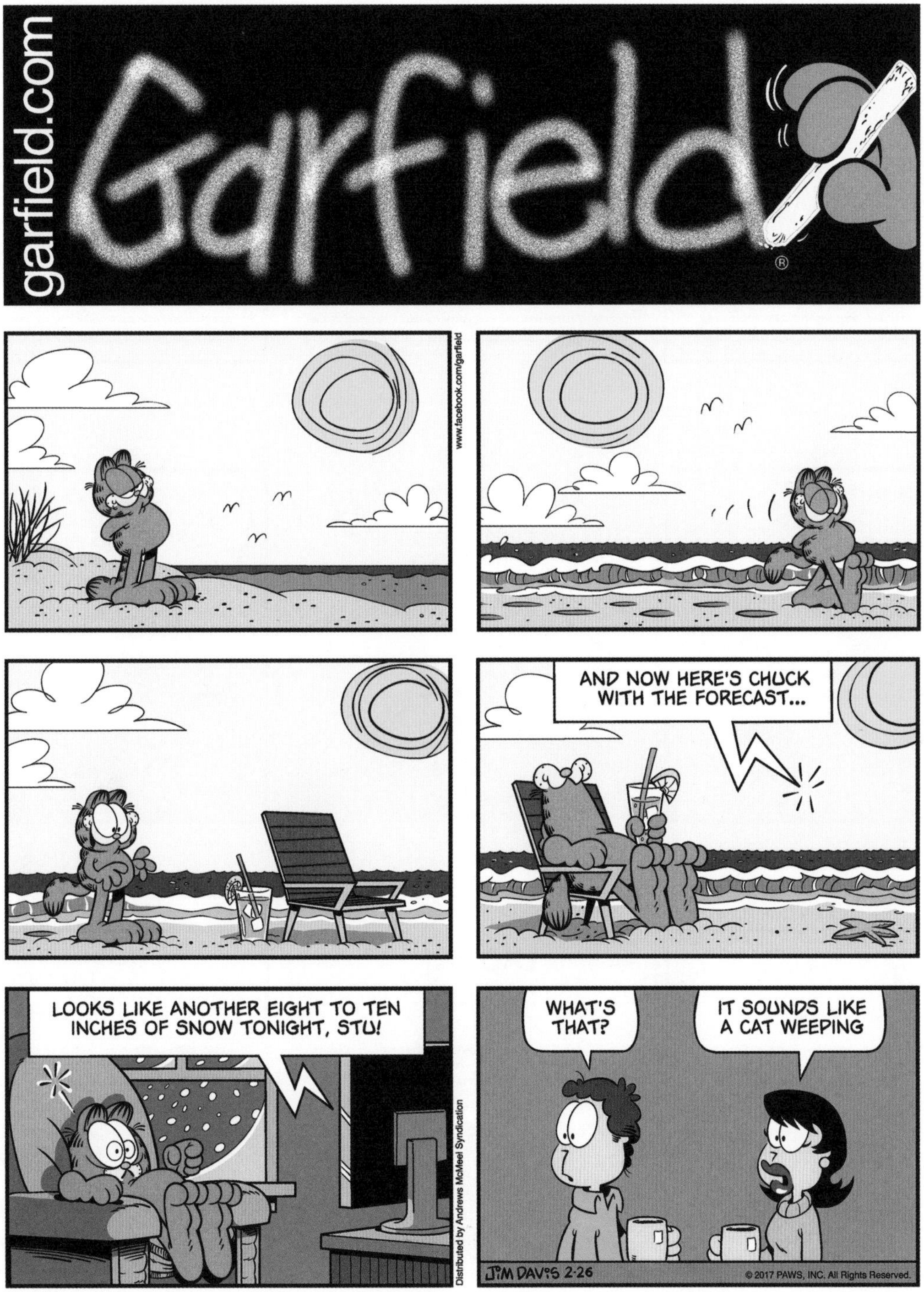
garfield.com
Garfield
www.facebook.com/garfield
AND NOW HERE'S CHUCK WITH THE FORECAST...
LOOKS LIKE ANOTHER EIGHT TO TEN INCHES OF SNOW TONIGHT, STU!
WHAT'S THAT?
IT SOUNDS LIKE A CAT WEEPING
Distributed by Andrews McMeel Syndication
JIM DAVIS 2-26
© 2017 PAWS, INC. All Rights Reserved.

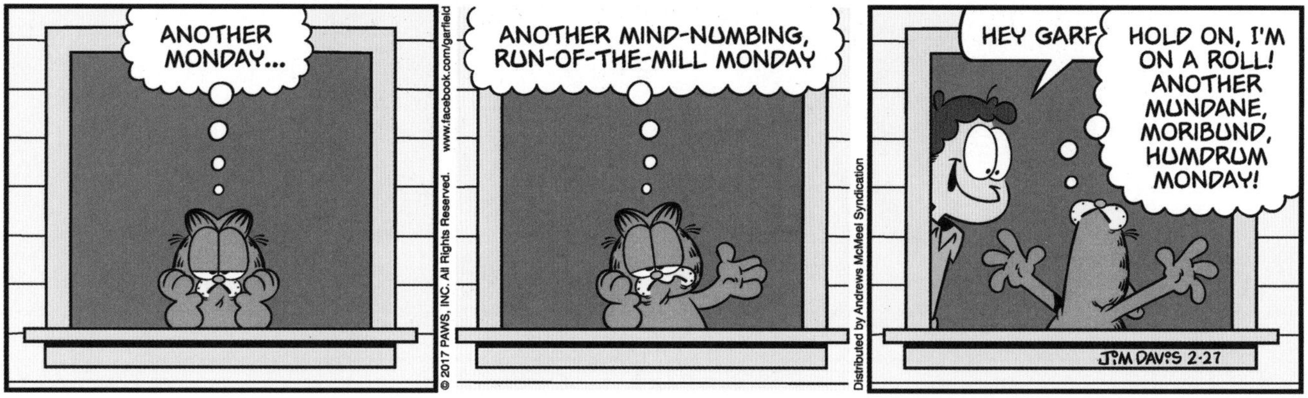
ANOTHER MONDAY...
ANOTHER MIND-NUMBING, RUN-OF-THE-MILL MONDAY
HEY GARF
HOLD ON, I'M ON A ROLL! ANOTHER MUNDANE, MORIBUND, HUMDRUM MONDAY!
JIM DAVIS 2-27
© 2017 PAWS, INC. All Rights Reserved. www.facebook.com/garfield
Distributed by Andrews McMeel Syndication

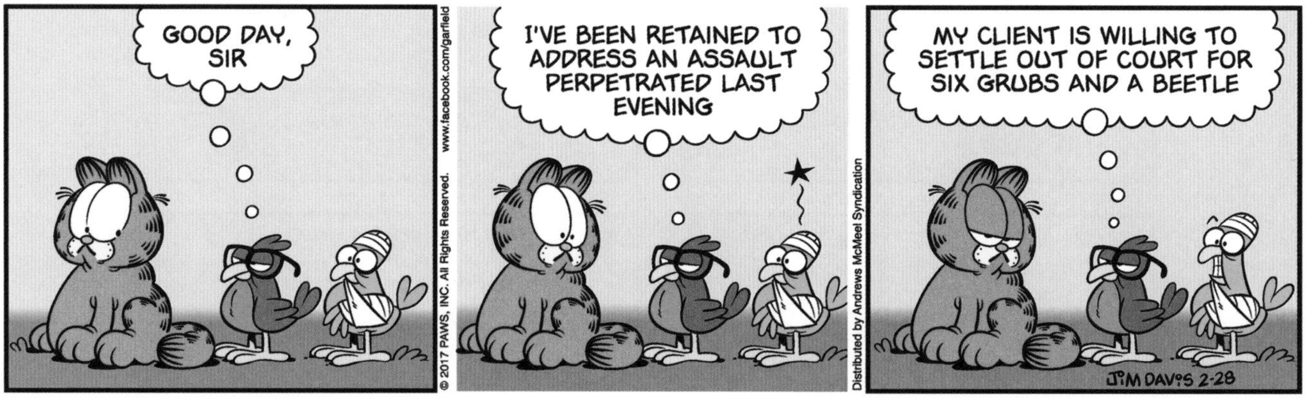
GOOD DAY, SIR
I'VE BEEN RETAINED TO ADDRESS AN ASSAULT PERPETRATED LAST EVENING
MY CLIENT IS WILLING TO SETTLE OUT OF COURT FOR SIX GRUBS AND A BEETLE
JIM DAVIS 2-28
© 2017 PAWS, INC. All Rights Reserved. www.facebook.com/garfield
Distributed by Andrews McMeel Syndication

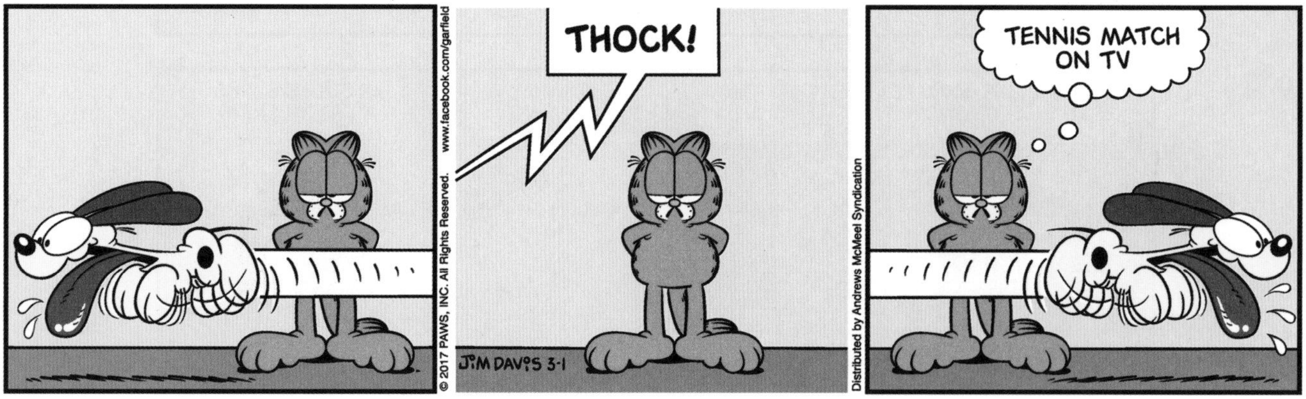
THOCK!
TENNIS MATCH ON TV
JIM DAVIS 3-1
© 2017 PAWS, INC. All Rights Reserved. www.facebook.com/garfield
Distributed by Andrews McMeel Syndication

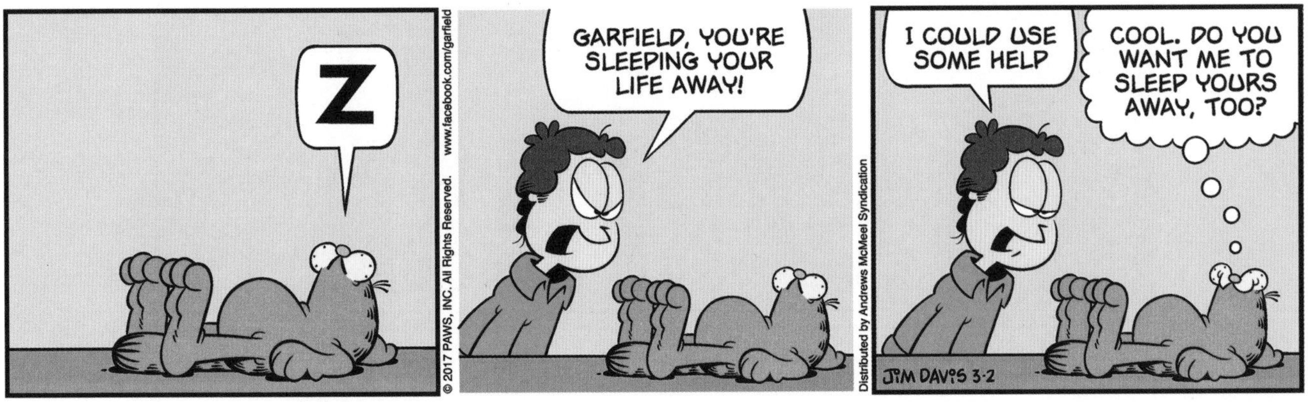
Z
GARFIELD, YOU'RE SLEEPING YOUR LIFE AWAY!
I COULD USE SOME HELP
COOL. DO YOU WANT ME TO SLEEP YOURS AWAY, TOO?
JIM DAVIS 3-2
© 2017 PAWS, INC. All Rights Reserved. www.facebook.com/garfield
Distributed by Andrews McMeel Syndication

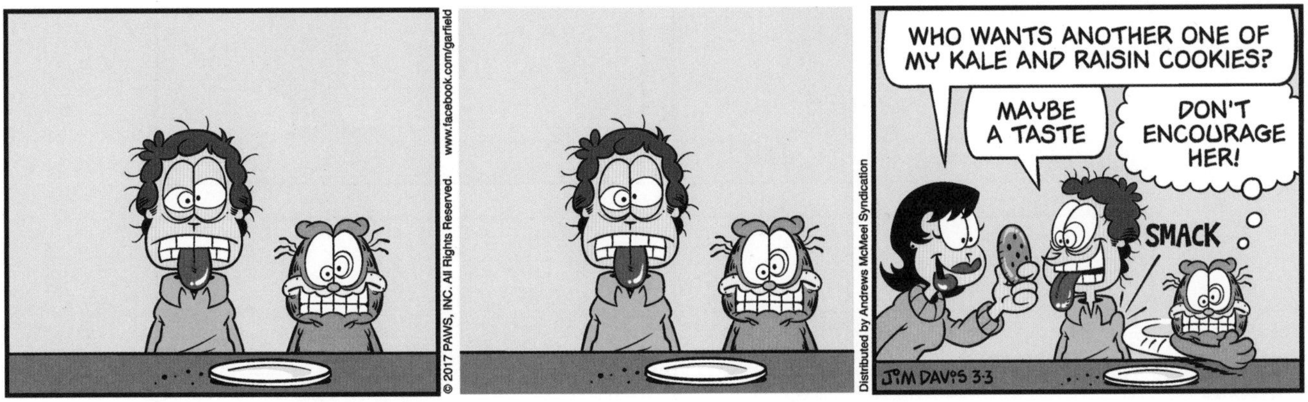
WHO WANTS ANOTHER ONE OF MY KALE AND RAISIN COOKIES?
MAYBE A TASTE
DON'T ENCOURAGE HER!
SMACK
JIM DAVIS 3-3
© 2017 PAWS, INC. All Rights Reserved. www.facebook.com/garfield
Distributed by Andrews McMeel Syndication

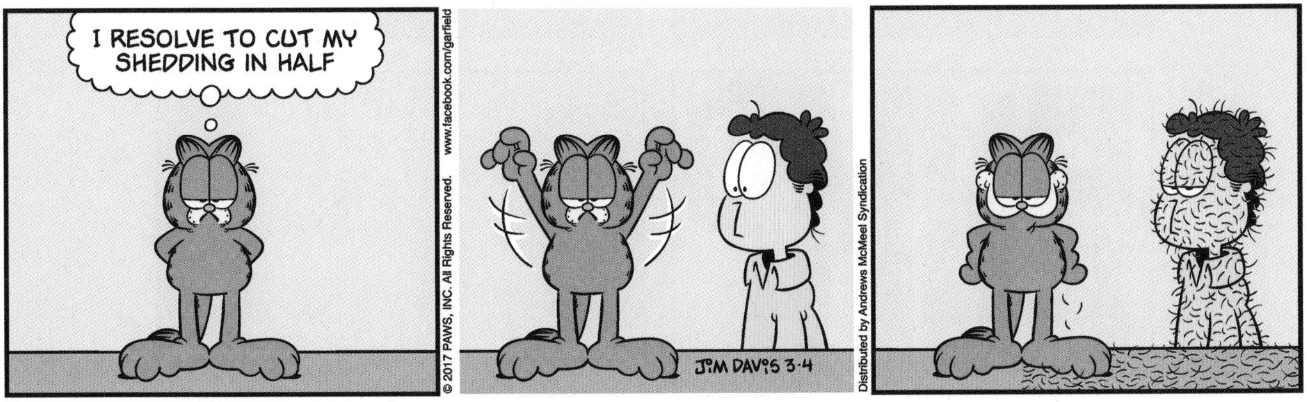
I RESOLVE TO CUT MY SHEDDING IN HALF
JIM DAVIS 3-4
© 2017 PAWS, INC. All Rights Reserved. www.facebook.com/garfield
Distributed by Andrews McMeel Syndication

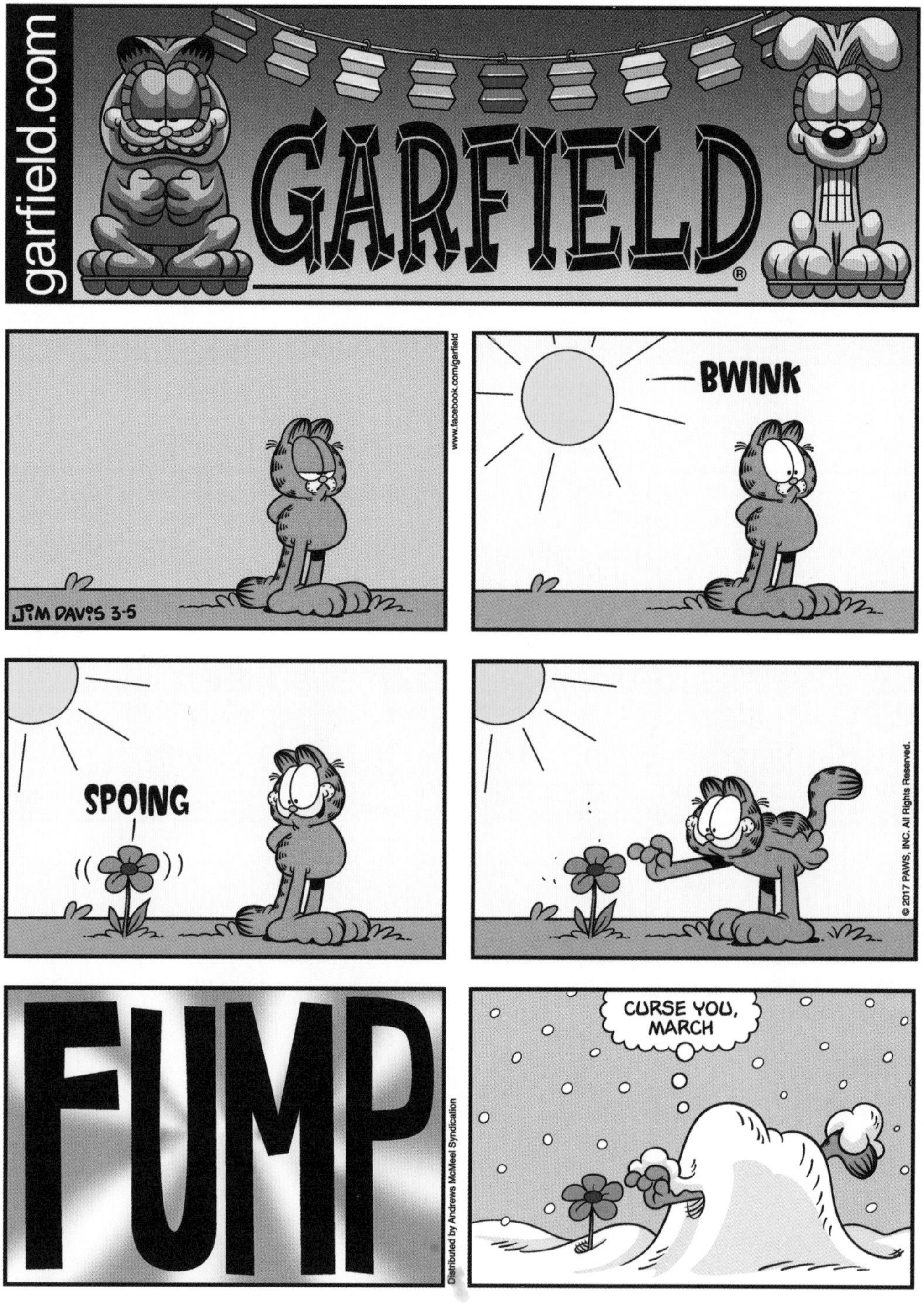
garfield.com
GARFIELD®
JIM DAVIS 3-5
www.facebook.com/garfield
BWINK
SPOING
© 2017 PAWS, INC. All Rights Reserved.
FUMP
Distributed by Andrews McMeel Syndication
CURSE YOU, MARCH

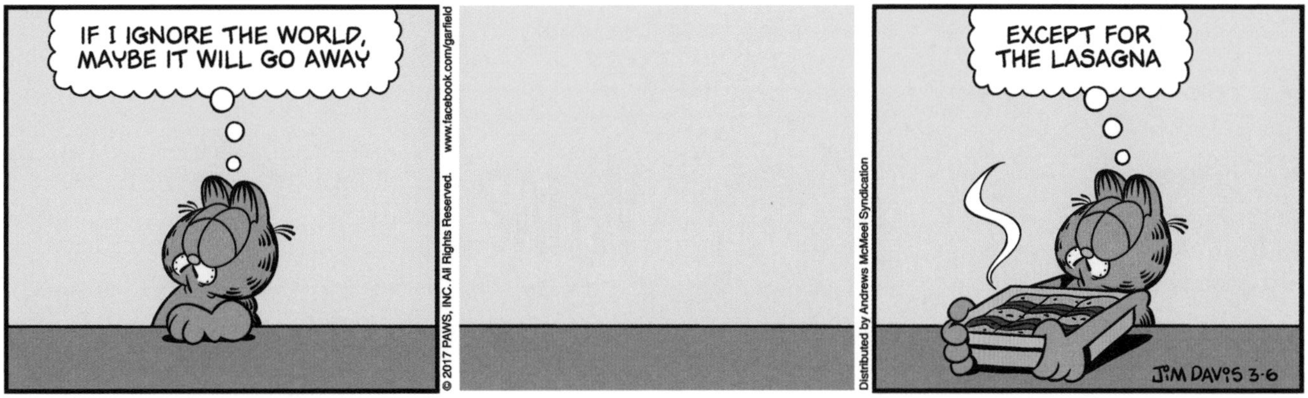
IF I IGNORE THE WORLD, MAYBE IT WILL GO AWAY
© 2017 PAWS, INC. All Rights Reserved. www.facebook.com/garfield
Distributed by Andrews McMeel Syndication
EXCEPT FOR THE LASAGNA
JIM DAVIS 3-6

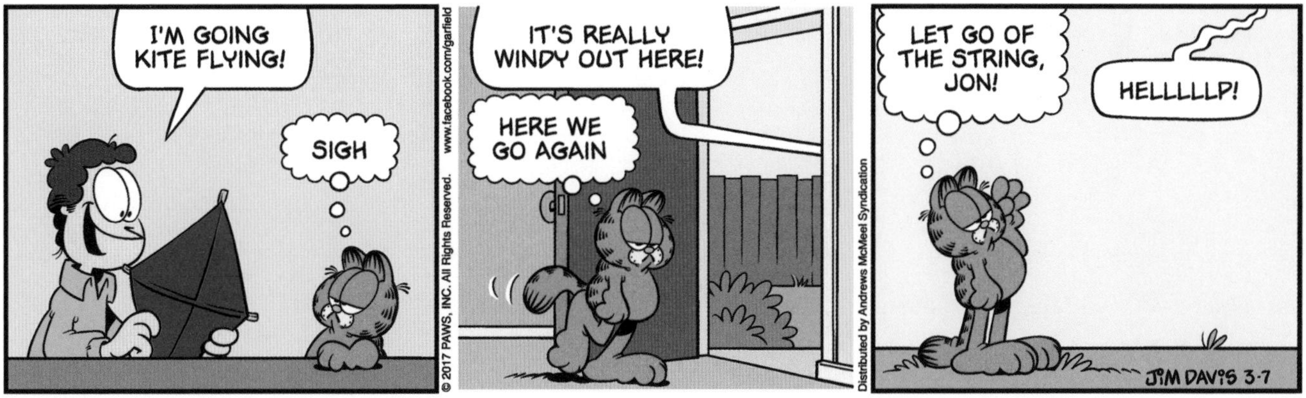
I'M GOING KITE FLYING!
SIGH
© 2017 PAWS, INC. All Rights Reserved. www.facebook.com/garfield
IT'S REALLY WINDY OUT HERE!
HERE WE GO AGAIN
Distributed by Andrews McMeel Syndication
LET GO OF THE STRING, JON!
HELLLLLP!
JIM DAVIS 3-7

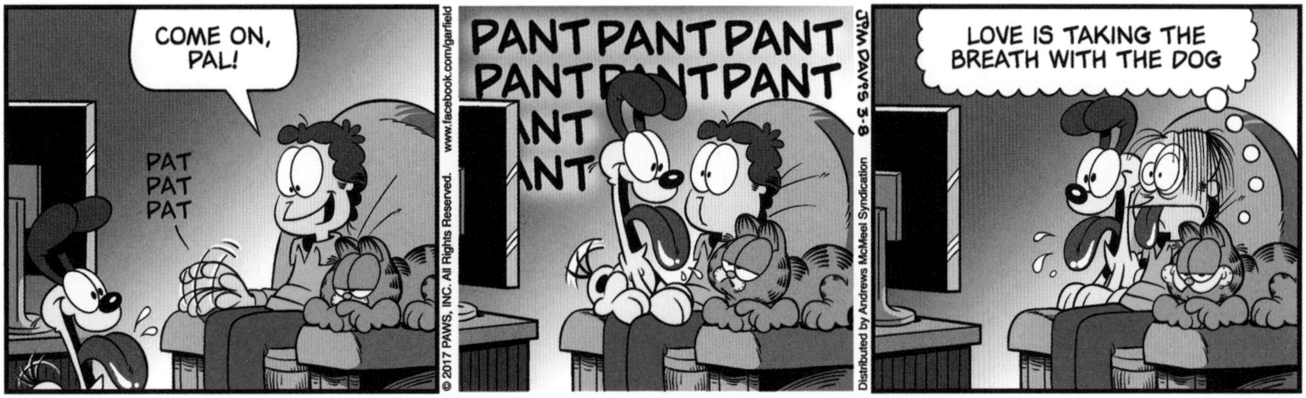
COME ON, PAL!
PAT PAT PAT
© 2017 PAWS, INC. All Rights Reserved. www.facebook.com/garfield
PANT PANT PANT
PANT PANT PANT
JIM DAVIS 3-8
Distributed by Andrews McMeel Syndication
LOVE IS TAKING THE BREATH WITH THE DOG

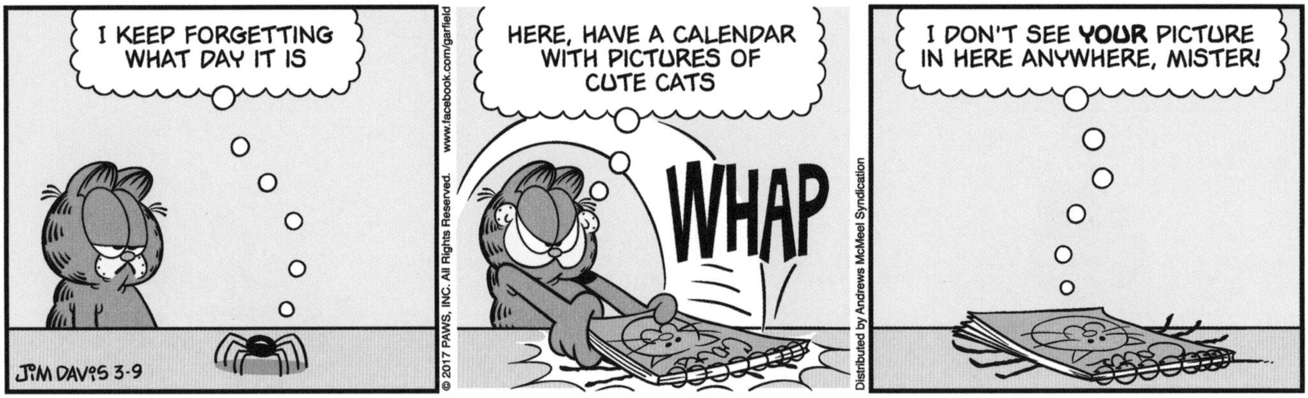
I KEEP FORGETTING WHAT DAY IT IS
JIM DAVIS 3-9
HERE, HAVE A CALENDAR WITH PICTURES OF CUTE CATS
WHAP
I DON'T SEE **YOUR** PICTURE IN HERE ANYWHERE, MISTER!
© 2017 PAWS, INC. All Rights Reserved. www.facebook.com/garfield
Distributed by Andrews McMeel Syndication

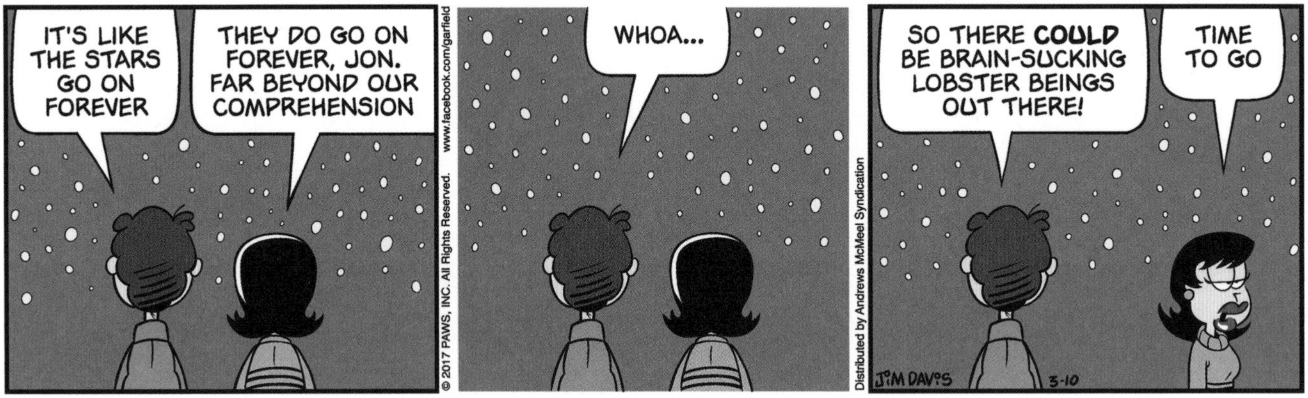
IT'S LIKE THE STARS GO ON FOREVER
THEY DO GO ON FOREVER, JON. FAR BEYOND OUR COMPREHENSION
WHOA...
SO THERE **COULD** BE BRAIN-SUCKING LOBSTER BEINGS OUT THERE!
TIME TO GO
JIM DAVIS 3-10
© 2017 PAWS, INC. All Rights Reserved. www.facebook.com/garfield
Distributed by Andrews McMeel Syndication

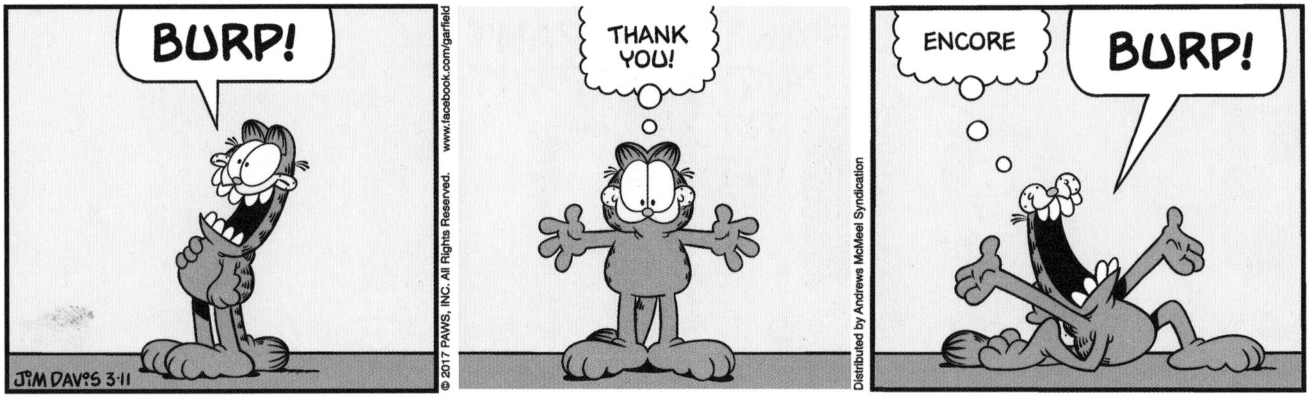
BURP!
JIM DAVIS 3-11
THANK YOU!
ENCORE
BURP!
© 2017 PAWS, INC. All Rights Reserved. www.facebook.com/garfield
Distributed by Andrews McMeel Syndication

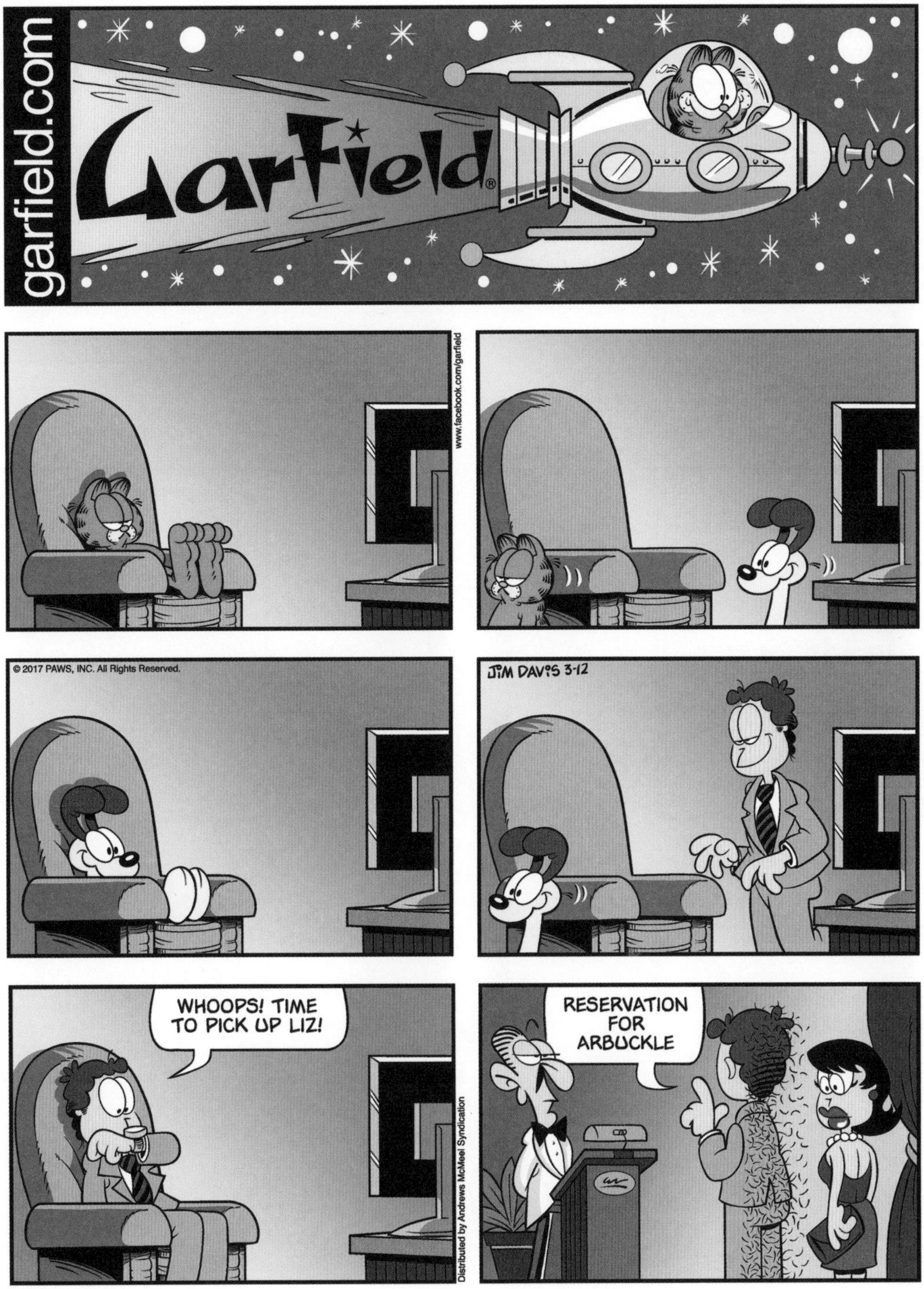
garfield.com
Garfield
www.facebook.com/garfield
© 2017 PAWS, INC. All Rights Reserved.
JIM DAVIS 3-12
WHOOPS! TIME TO PICK UP LIZ!
Distributed by Andrews McMeel Syndication
RESERVATION FOR ARBUCKLE

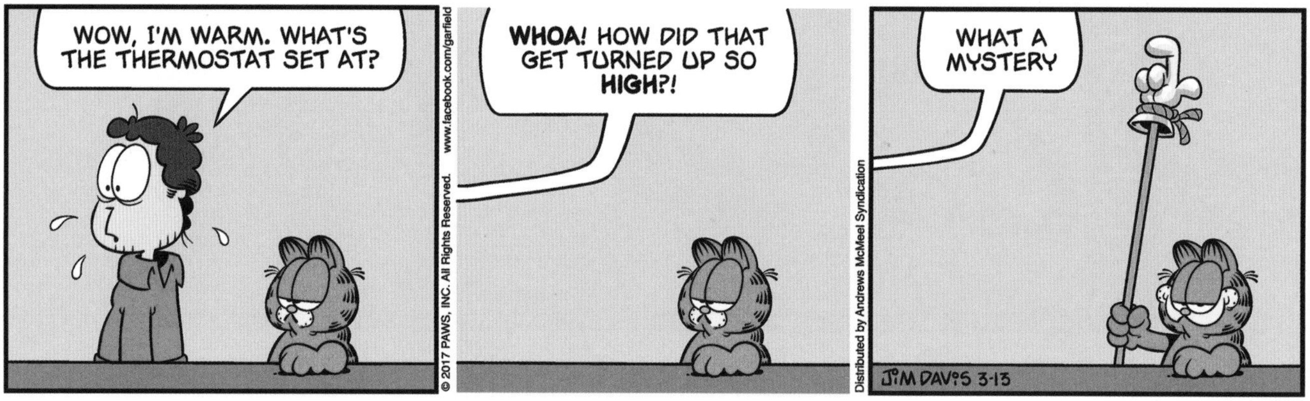
WOW, I'M WARM. WHAT'S THE THERMOSTAT SET AT?
© 2017 PAWS, INC. All Rights Reserved. www.facebook.com/garfield
WHOA! HOW DID THAT GET TURNED UP SO HIGH?!
Distributed by Andrews McMeel Syndication
WHAT A MYSTERY
JIM DAVIS 3-13

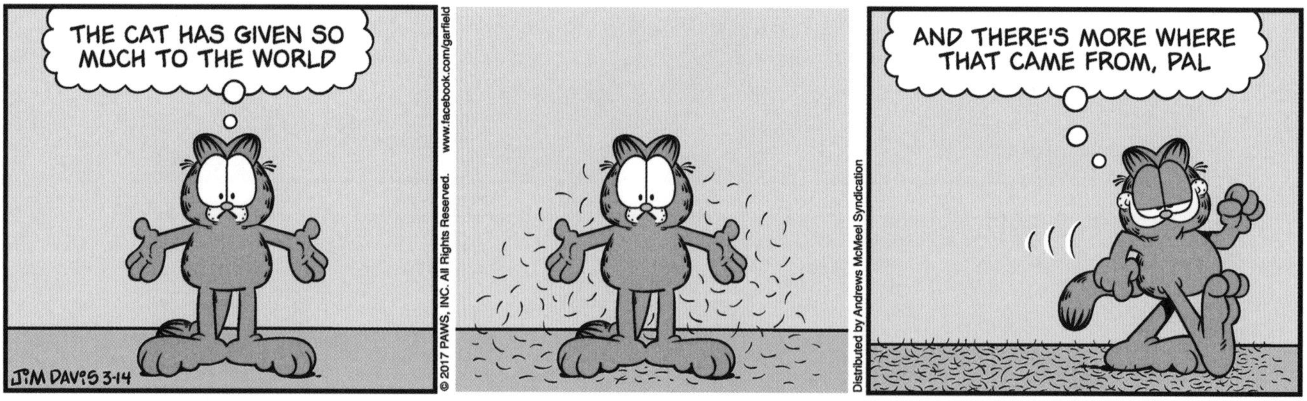
THE CAT HAS GIVEN SO MUCH TO THE WORLD
JIM DAVIS 3-14
© 2017 PAWS, INC. All Rights Reserved. www.facebook.com/garfield
Distributed by Andrews McMeel Syndication
AND THERE'S MORE WHERE THAT CAME FROM, PAL

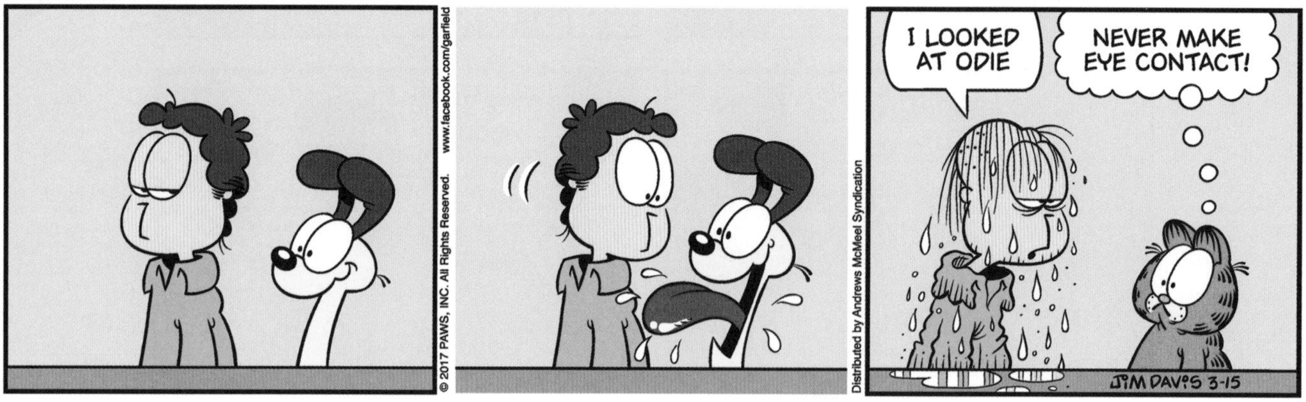
© 2017 PAWS, INC. All Rights Reserved. www.facebook.com/garfield
Distributed by Andrews McMeel Syndication
I LOOKED AT ODIE
NEVER MAKE EYE CONTACT!
JIM DAVIS 3-15

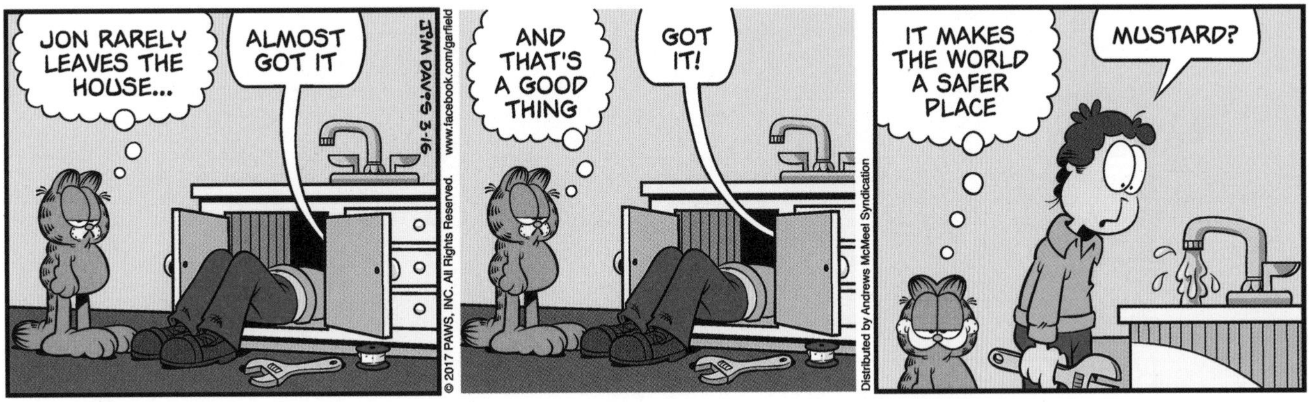
JON RARELY LEAVES THE HOUSE...
ALMOST GOT IT
JIM DAVIS 3-16
© 2017 PAWS, INC. All Rights Reserved. www.facebook.com/garfield
AND THAT'S A GOOD THING
GOT IT!
Distributed by Andrews McMeel Syndication
IT MAKES THE WORLD A SAFER PLACE
MUSTARD?

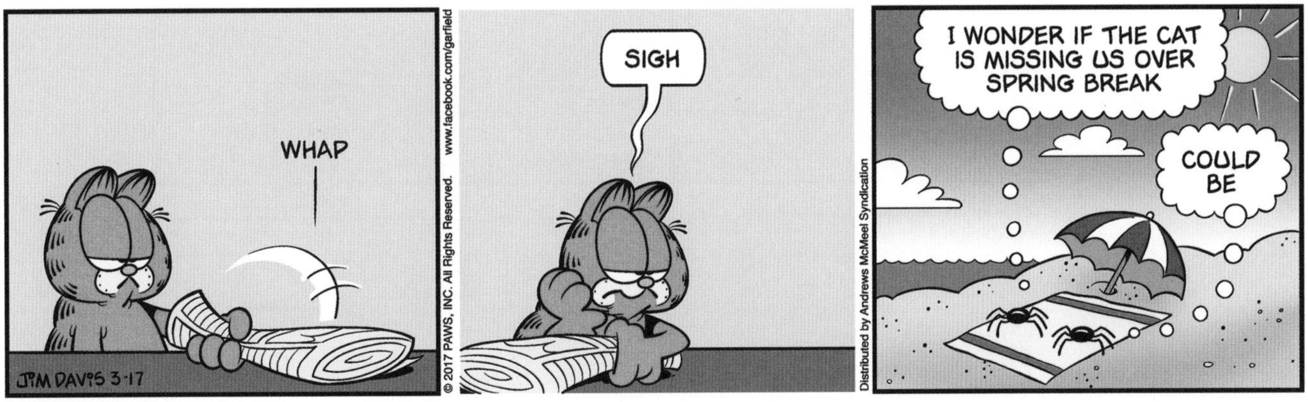
WHAP
JIM DAVIS 3-17
© 2017 PAWS, INC. All Rights Reserved. www.facebook.com/garfield
SIGH
Distributed by Andrews McMeel Syndication
I WONDER IF THE CAT IS MISSING US OVER SPRING BREAK
COULD BE

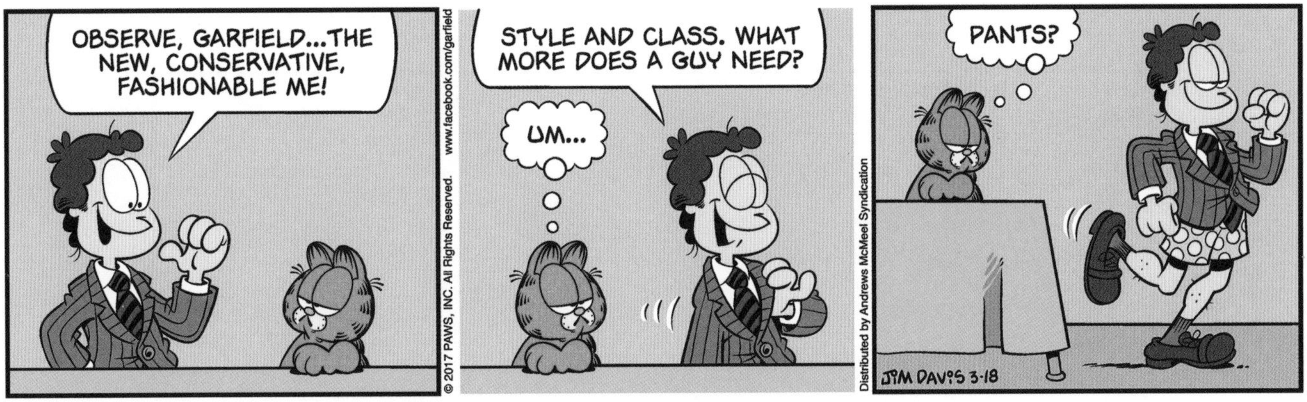
OBSERVE, GARFIELD...THE NEW, CONSERVATIVE, FASHIONABLE ME!
© 2017 PAWS, INC. All Rights Reserved. www.facebook.com/garfield
STYLE AND CLASS. WHAT MORE DOES A GUY NEED?
UM...
Distributed by Andrews McMeel Syndication
PANTS?
JIM DAVIS 3-18

garfield.com
www.facebook.com/garfield
GARFIELD! LUNCHTIME!
Z
Z
© 2017 PAWS, INC. All Rights Reserved.
ARE YOU EVER GOING TO GET HERE?
GARFIELD
HOLD ON. ONLY TWO NAPS AWAY
JIM DAVIS 3-19
Distributed by Andrews McMeel Syndication

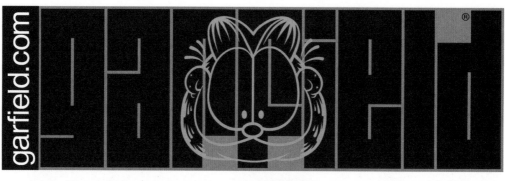

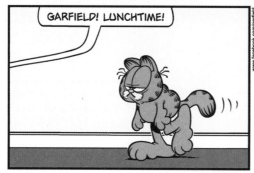

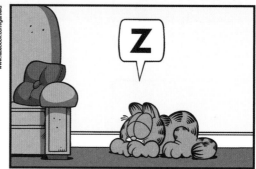

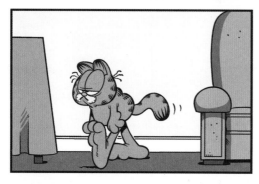

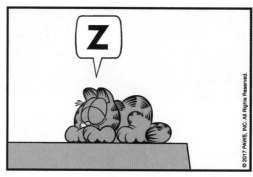

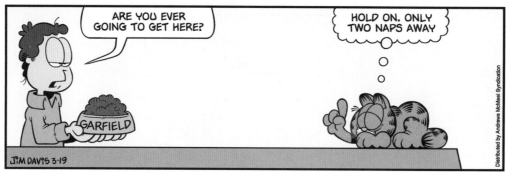

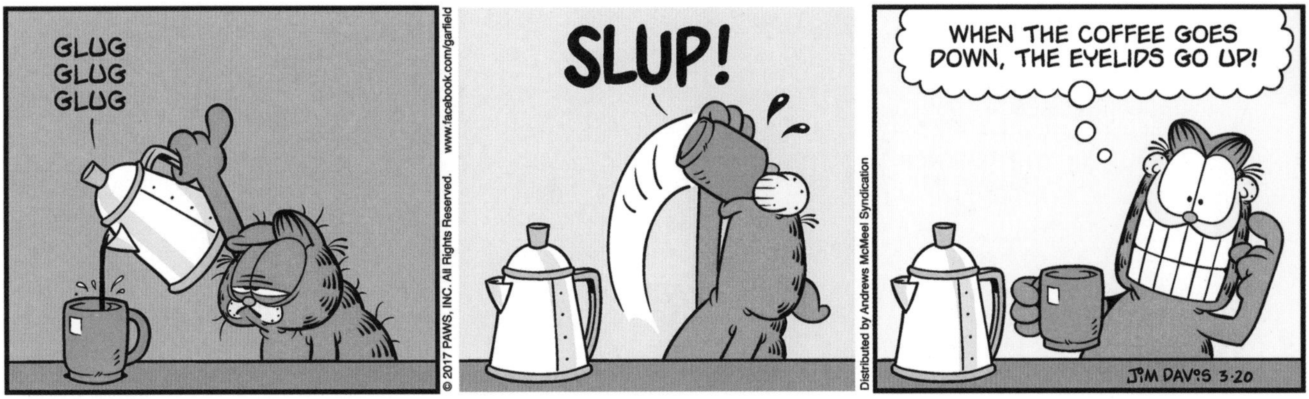
GLUG GLUG GLUG
© 2017 PAWS, INC. All Rights Reserved. www.facebook.com/garfield
SLUP!
Distributed by Andrews McMeel Syndication
WHEN THE COFFEE GOES DOWN, THE EYELIDS GO UP!
JIM DAVIS 3-20

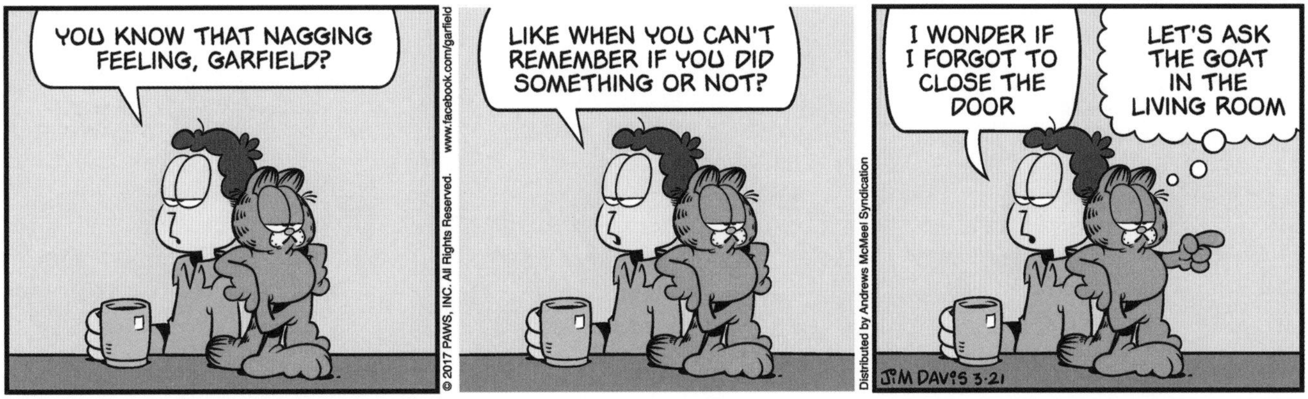
YOU KNOW THAT NAGGING FEELING, GARFIELD?
© 2017 PAWS, INC. All Rights Reserved. www.facebook.com/garfield
LIKE WHEN YOU CAN'T REMEMBER IF YOU DID SOMETHING OR NOT?
Distributed by Andrews McMeel Syndication
I WONDER IF I FORGOT TO CLOSE THE DOOR
LET'S ASK THE GOAT IN THE LIVING ROOM
JIM DAVIS 3-21

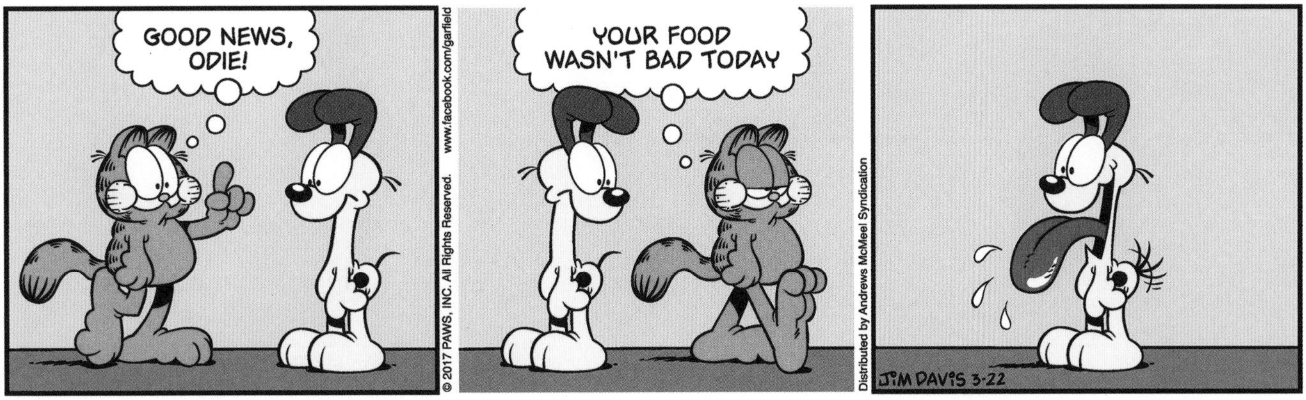
GOOD NEWS, ODIE!
© 2017 PAWS, INC. All Rights Reserved. www.facebook.com/garfield
YOUR FOOD WASN'T BAD TODAY
Distributed by Andrews McMeel Syndication
JIM DAVIS 3-22

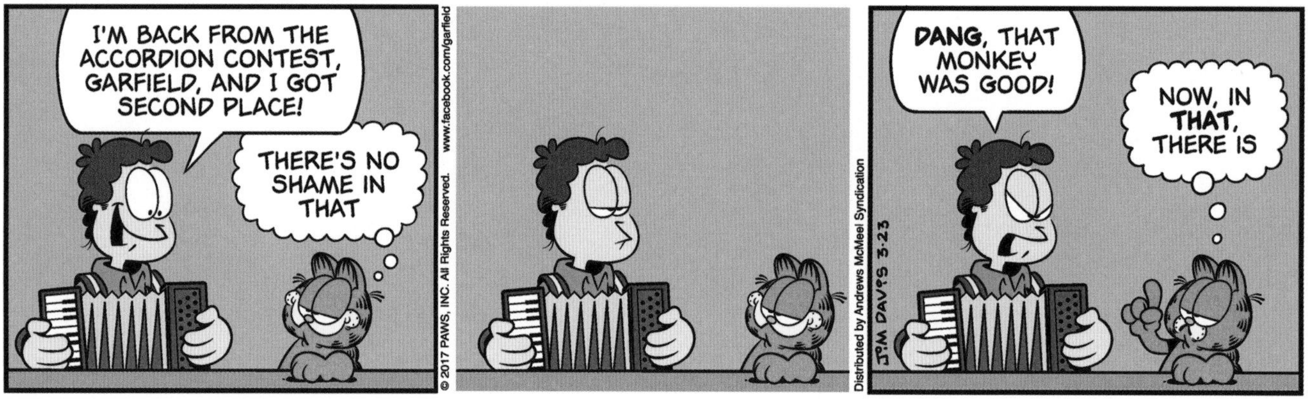
I'M BACK FROM THE ACCORDION CONTEST, GARFIELD, AND I GOT SECOND PLACE!
THERE'S NO SHAME IN THAT
© 2017 PAWS, INC. All Rights Reserved. www.facebook.com/garfield
DANG, THAT MONKEY WAS GOOD!
NOW, IN THAT, THERE IS
Distributed by Andrews McMeel Syndication
JIM DAVIS 3-23

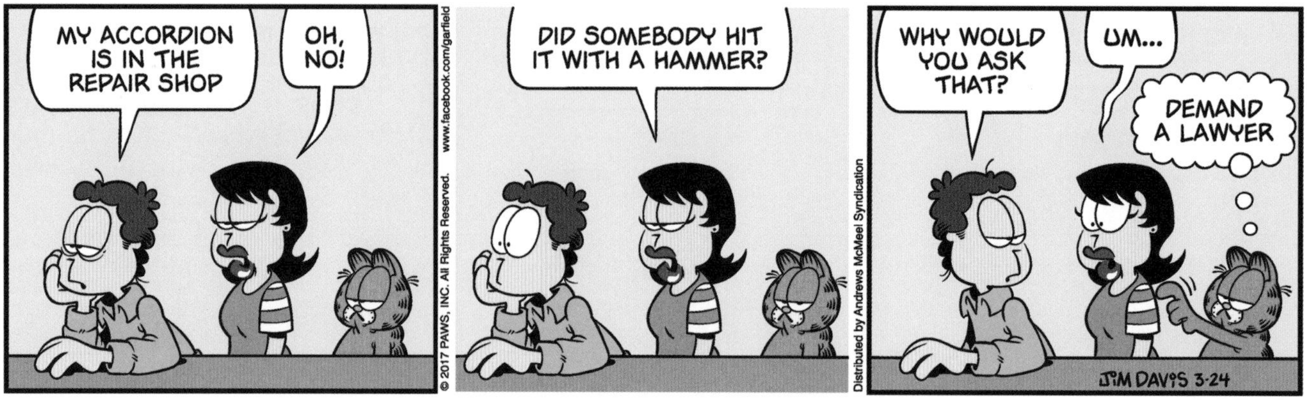
MY ACCORDION IS IN THE REPAIR SHOP
OH, NO!
© 2017 PAWS, INC. All Rights Reserved. www.facebook.com/garfield
DID SOMEBODY HIT IT WITH A HAMMER?
WHY WOULD YOU ASK THAT?
UM...
DEMAND A LAWYER
Distributed by Andrews McMeel Syndication
JIM DAVIS 3-24

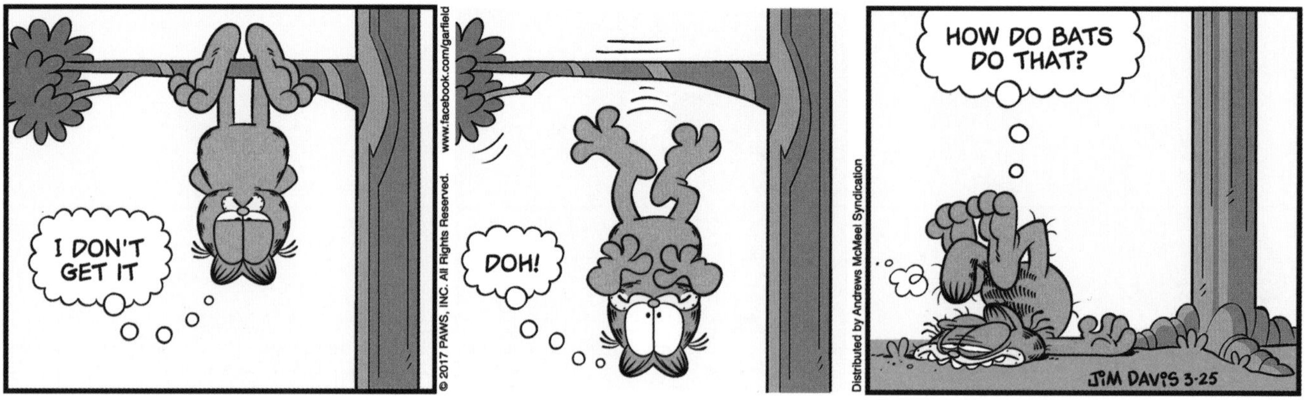
I DON'T GET IT
© 2017 PAWS, INC. All Rights Reserved. www.facebook.com/garfield
DOH!
HOW DO BATS DO THAT?
Distributed by Andrews McMeel Syndication
JIM DAVIS 3-25

garfield.com
www.facebook.com/garfield
Camera
TAP
TAP
CLICK
© 2017 PAWS, INC. All Rights Reserved.
CLICK
CLICK
JIM DAVIS 3-26
ODIE
Distributed by Andrews McMeel Syndication
CLICK
CLICK
MAR

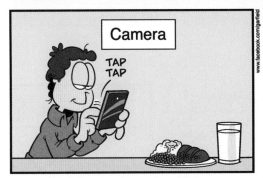

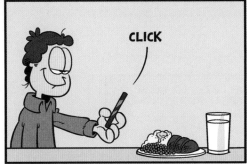

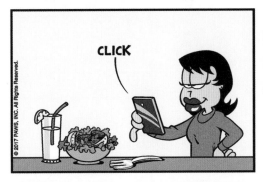

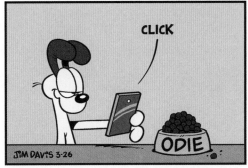

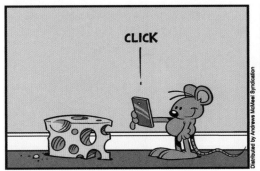

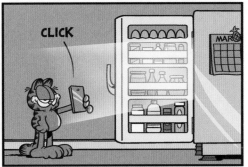

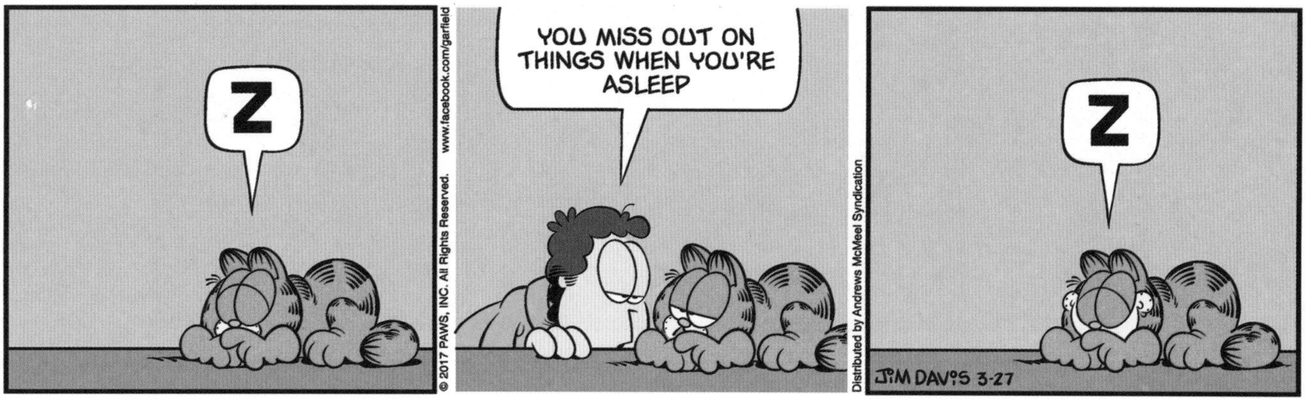
Z
© 2017 PAWS, INC. All Rights Reserved. www.facebook.com/garfield
YOU MISS OUT ON THINGS WHEN YOU'RE ASLEEP
Distributed by Andrews McMeel Syndication
Z
JIM DAVIS 3-27

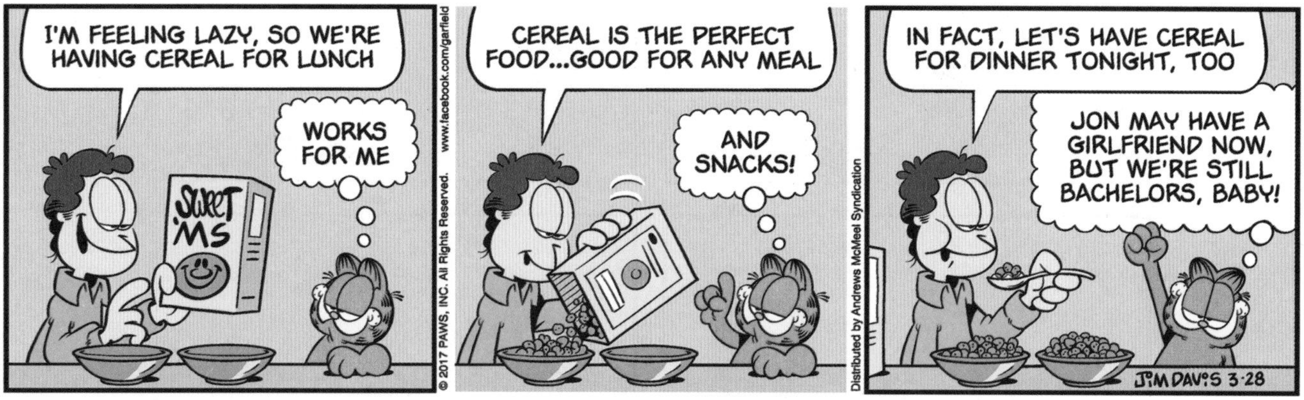
I'M FEELING LAZY, SO WE'RE HAVING CEREAL FOR LUNCH
WORKS FOR ME
SWEET 'MS
© 2017 PAWS, INC. All Rights Reserved. www.facebook.com/garfield
CEREAL IS THE PERFECT FOOD...GOOD FOR ANY MEAL
AND SNACKS!
Distributed by Andrews McMeel Syndication
IN FACT, LET'S HAVE CEREAL FOR DINNER TONIGHT, TOO
JON MAY HAVE A GIRLFRIEND NOW, BUT WE'RE STILL BACHELORS, BABY!
JIM DAVIS 3-28

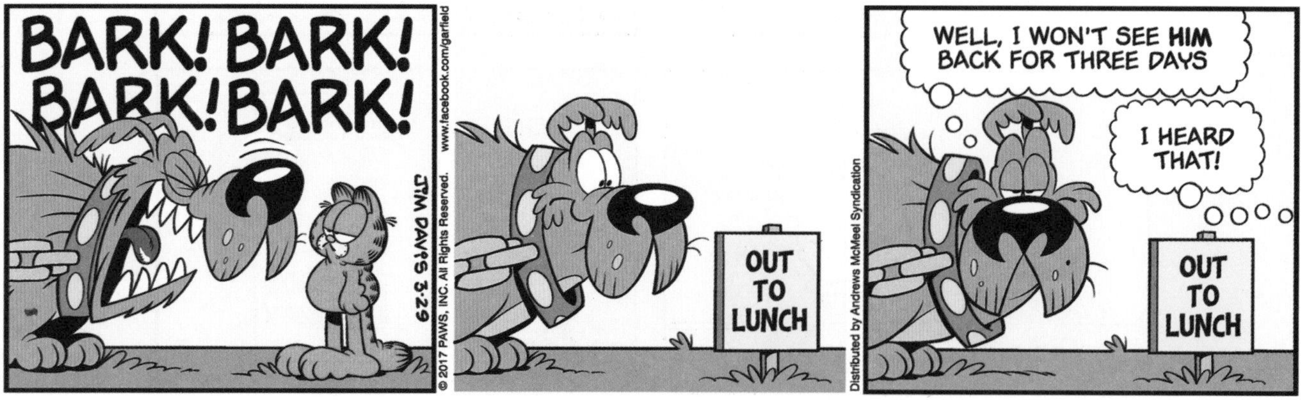
BARK! BARK! BARK! BARK!
JIM DAVIS 3-29
© 2017 PAWS, INC. All Rights Reserved. www.facebook.com/garfield
OUT TO LUNCH
Distributed by Andrews McMeel Syndication
WELL, I WON'T SEE HIM BACK FOR THREE DAYS
I HEARD THAT!
OUT TO LUNCH

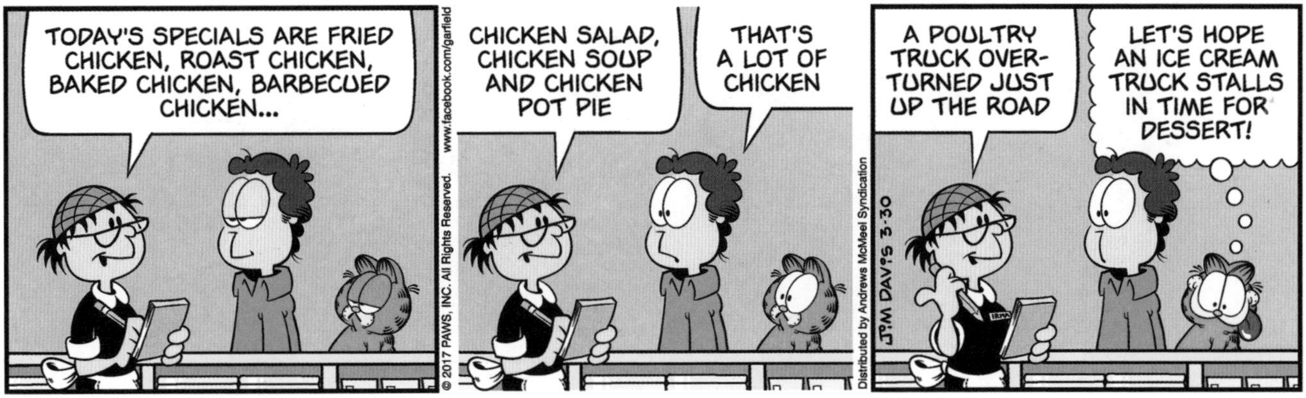
TODAY'S SPECIALS ARE FRIED CHICKEN, ROAST CHICKEN, BAKED CHICKEN, BARBECUED CHICKEN...
CHICKEN SALAD, CHICKEN SOUP AND CHICKEN POT PIE
THAT'S A LOT OF CHICKEN
A POULTRY TRUCK OVER-TURNED JUST UP THE ROAD
LET'S HOPE AN ICE CREAM TRUCK STALLS IN TIME FOR DESSERT!
© 2017 PAWS, INC. All Rights Reserved. www.facebook.com/garfield
Distributed by Andrews McMeel Syndication
JIM DAVIS 3-30

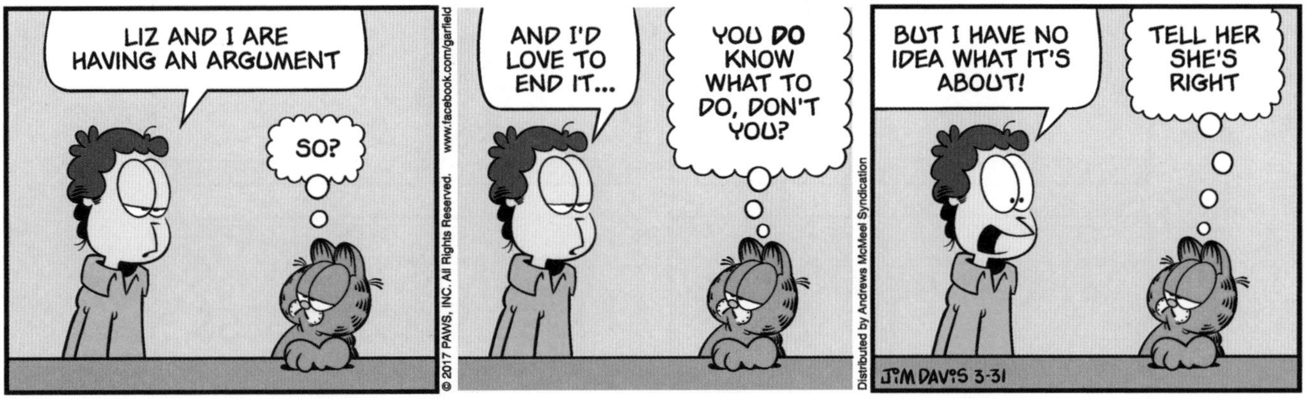
LIZ AND I ARE HAVING AN ARGUMENT
SO?
AND I'D LOVE TO END IT...
YOU DO KNOW WHAT TO DO, DON'T YOU?
BUT I HAVE NO IDEA WHAT IT'S ABOUT!
TELL HER SHE'S RIGHT
© 2017 PAWS, INC. All Rights Reserved. www.facebook.com/garfield
Distributed by Andrews McMeel Syndication
JIM DAVIS 3-31

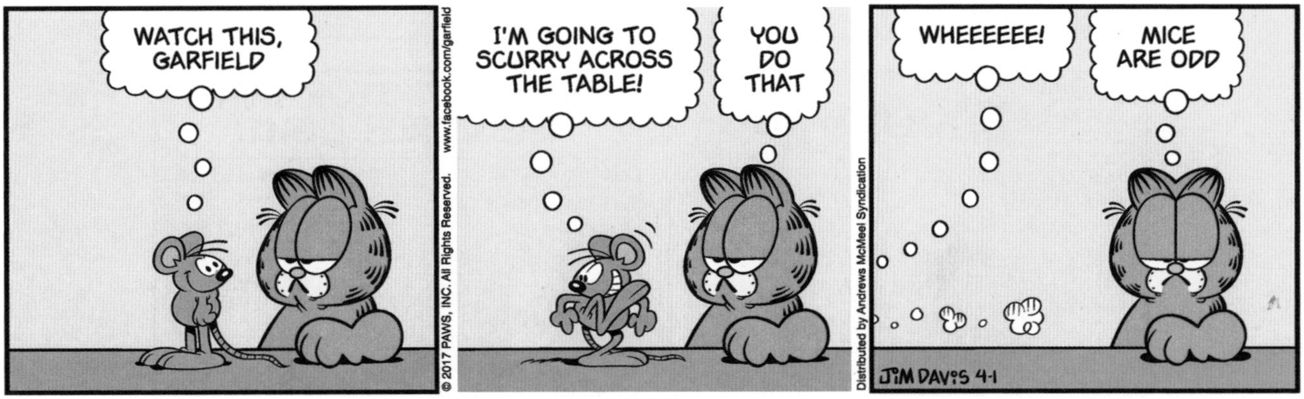
WATCH THIS, GARFIELD
I'M GOING TO SCURRY ACROSS THE TABLE!
YOU DO THAT
WHEEEEEE!
MICE ARE ODD
© 2017 PAWS, INC. All Rights Reserved. www.facebook.com/garfield
Distributed by Andrews McMeel Syndication
JIM DAVIS 4-1

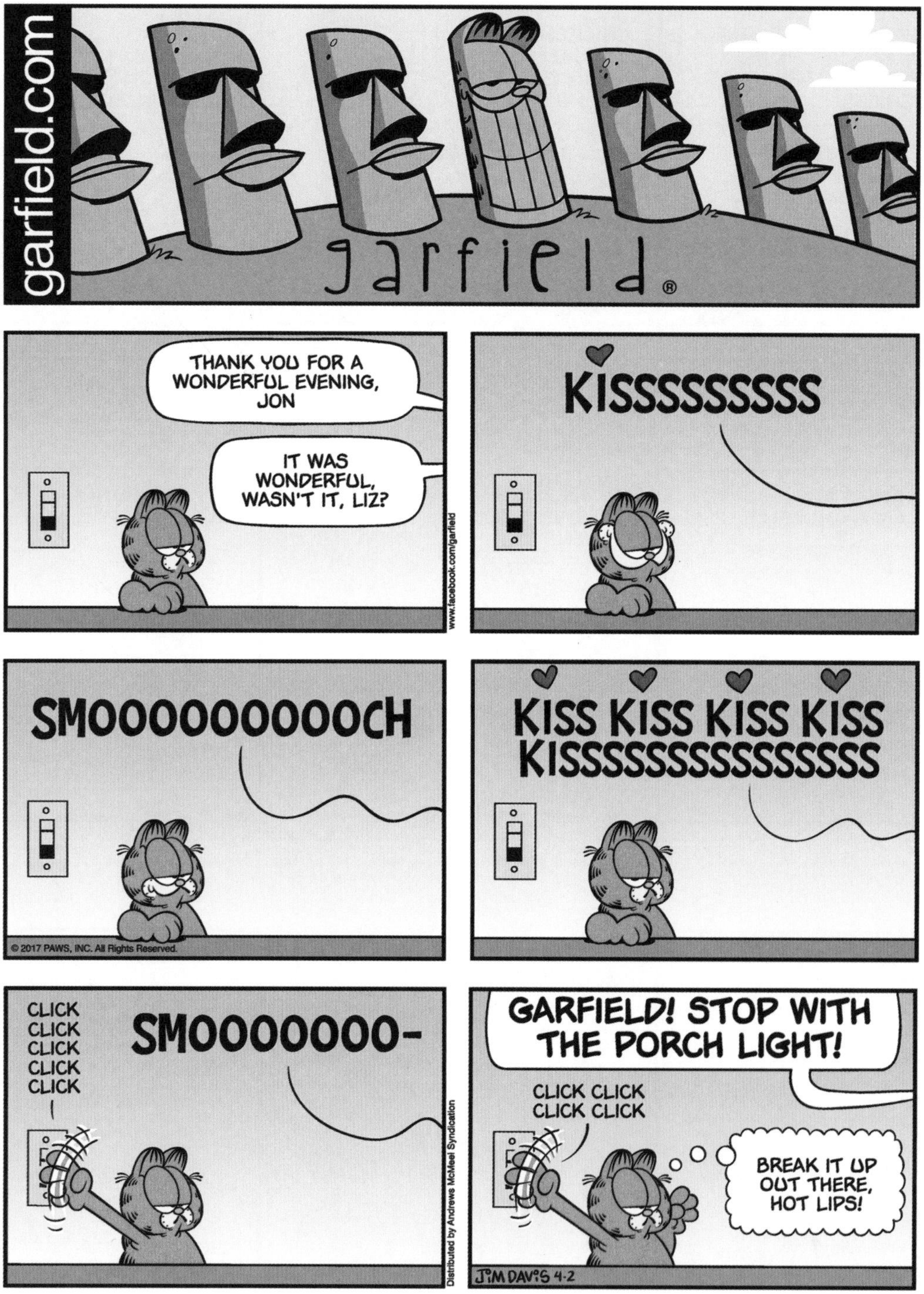
garfield.com
garfield®
THANK YOU FOR A WONDERFUL EVENING, JON
IT WAS WONDERFUL, WASN'T IT, LIZ?
www.facebook.com/garfield
KISSSSSSSSS
SMOOOOOOOOOCH
© 2017 PAWS, INC. All Rights Reserved.
KISS KISS KISS KISS KISSSSSSSSSSSSSSS
CLICK CLICK CLICK CLICK CLICK
SMOOOOOOO-
Distributed by Andrews McMeel Syndication
GARFIELD! STOP WITH THE PORCH LIGHT!
CLICK CLICK CLICK CLICK
BREAK IT UP OUT THERE, HOT LIPS!
JIM DAVIS 4-2

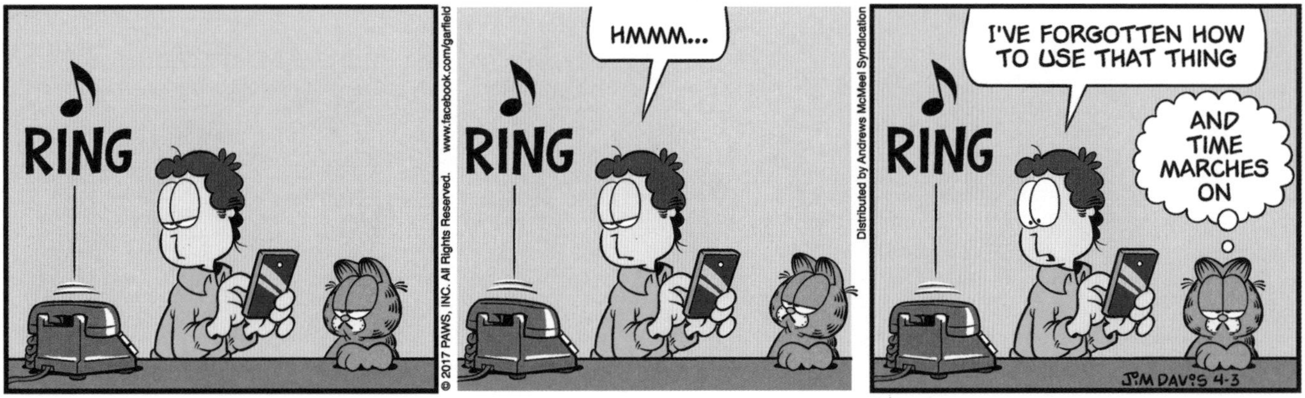
RING
RING
HMMM...
RING
I'VE FORGOTTEN HOW TO USE THAT THING
AND TIME MARCHES ON
JIM DAVIS 4-3
© 2017 PAWS, INC. All Rights Reserved. www.facebook.com/garfield
Distributed by Andrews McMeel Syndication

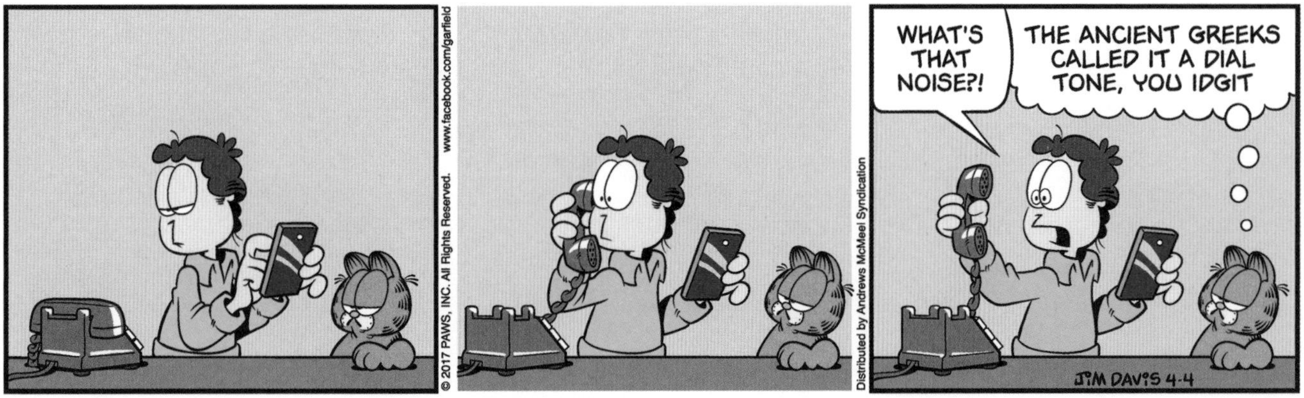
WHAT'S THAT NOISE?!
THE ANCIENT GREEKS CALLED IT A DIAL TONE, YOU IDGIT
JIM DAVIS 4-4
© 2017 PAWS, INC. All Rights Reserved. www.facebook.com/garfield
Distributed by Andrews McMeel Syndication

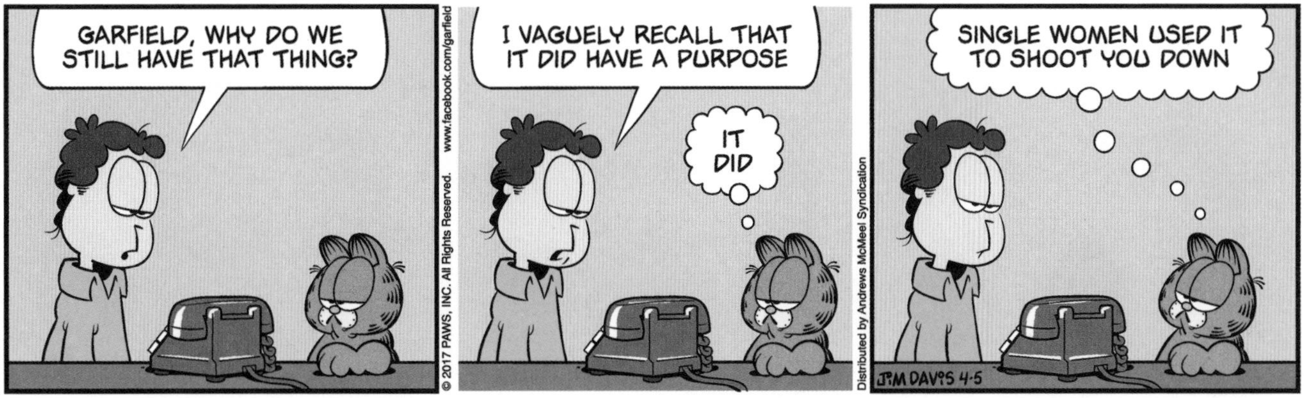
GARFIELD, WHY DO WE STILL HAVE THAT THING?
I VAGUELY RECALL THAT IT DID HAVE A PURPOSE
IT DID
SINGLE WOMEN USED IT TO SHOOT YOU DOWN
JIM DAVIS 4-5
© 2017 PAWS, INC. All Rights Reserved. www.facebook.com/garfield
Distributed by Andrews McMeel Syndication

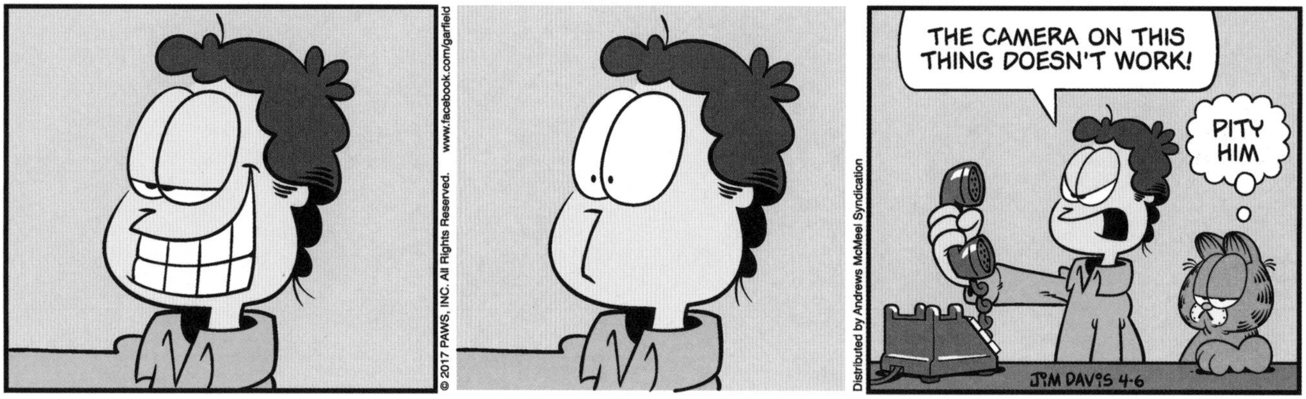
THE CAMERA ON THIS THING DOESN'T WORK!
PITY HIM
© 2017 PAWS, INC. All Rights Reserved. www.facebook.com/garfield
Distributed by Andrews McMeel Syndication
JIM DAVIS 4-6

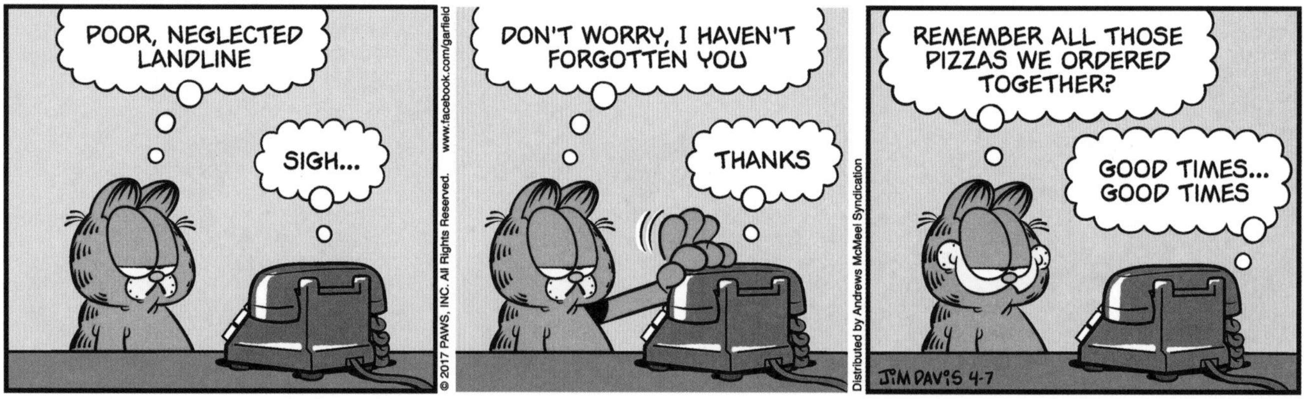
POOR, NEGLECTED LANDLINE
SIGH...
DON'T WORRY, I HAVEN'T FORGOTTEN YOU
THANKS
REMEMBER ALL THOSE PIZZAS WE ORDERED TOGETHER?
GOOD TIMES... GOOD TIMES
© 2017 PAWS, INC. All Rights Reserved. www.facebook.com/garfield
Distributed by Andrews McMeel Syndication
JIM DAVIS 4-7

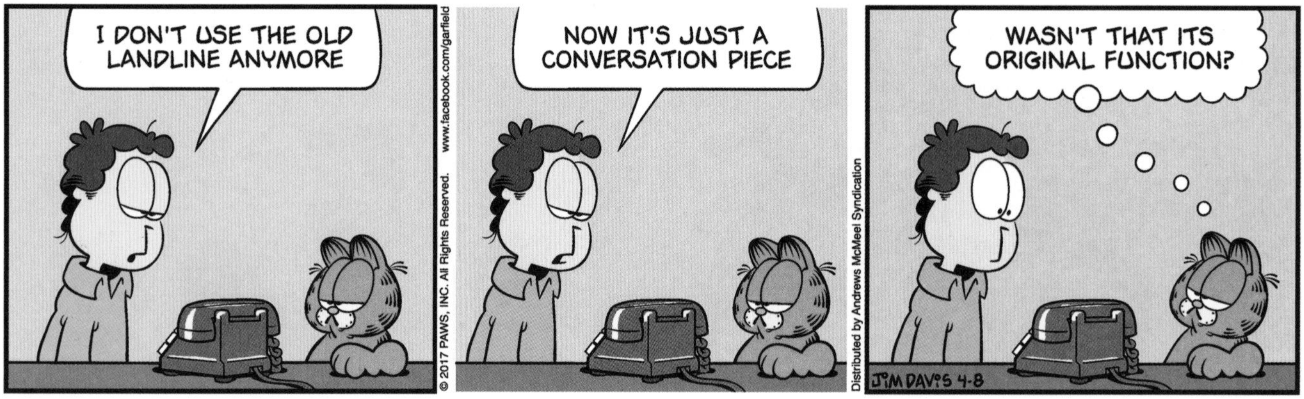
I DON'T USE THE OLD LANDLINE ANYMORE
NOW IT'S JUST A CONVERSATION PIECE
WASN'T THAT ITS ORIGINAL FUNCTION?
© 2017 PAWS, INC. All Rights Reserved. www.facebook.com/garfield
Distributed by Andrews McMeel Syndication
JIM DAVIS 4-8

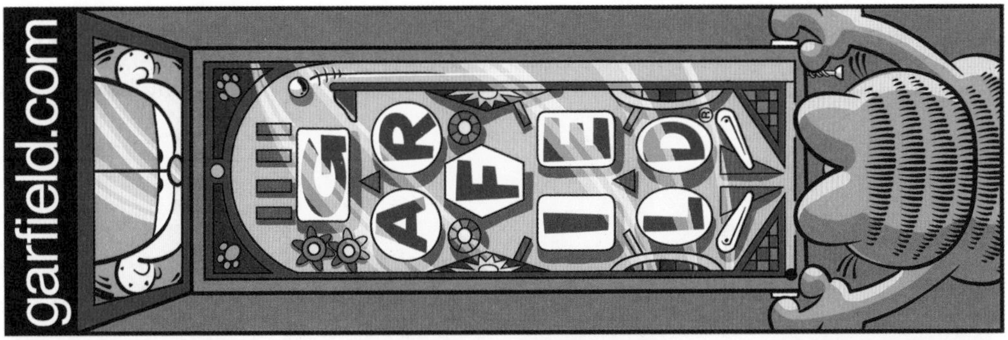
garfield.com
GARFIELD

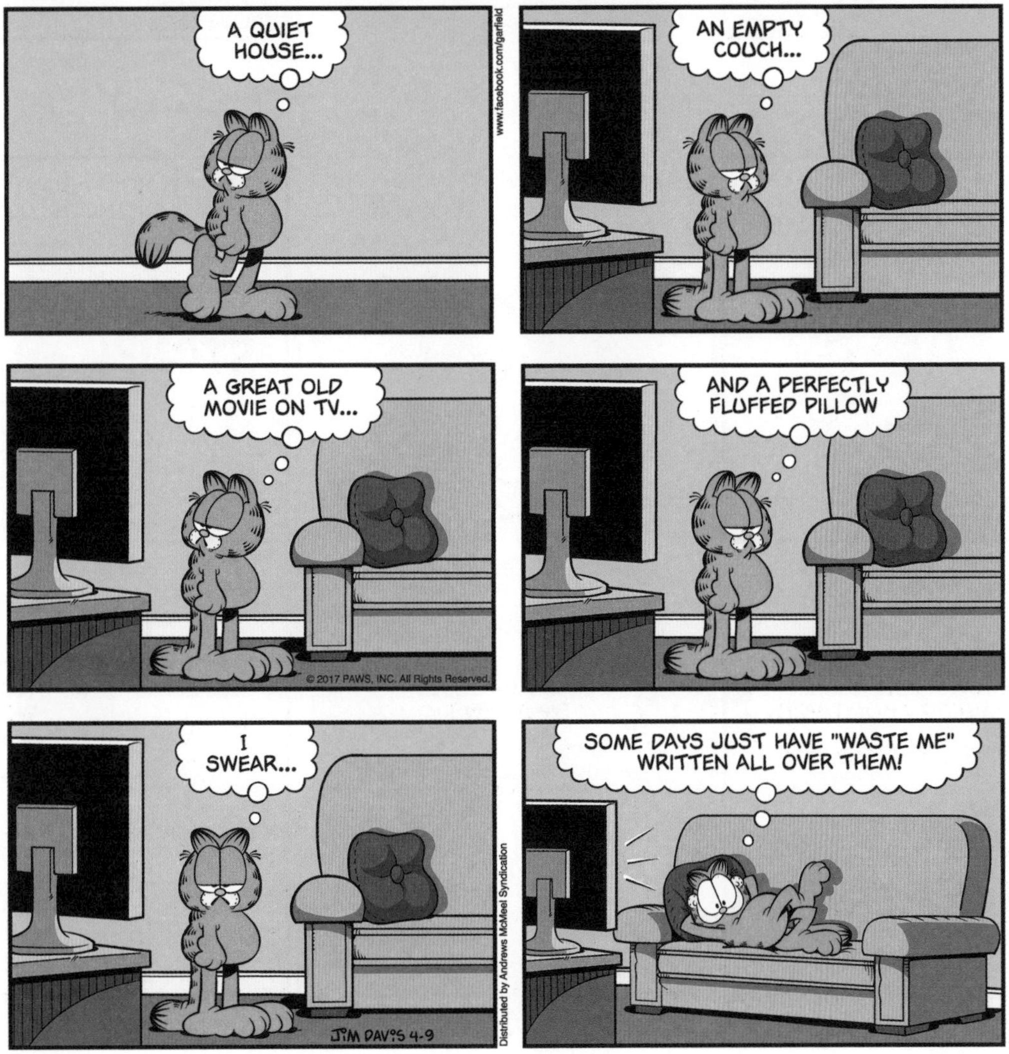
A QUIET HOUSE...
AN EMPTY COUCH...
A GREAT OLD MOVIE ON TV...
AND A PERFECTLY FLUFFED PILLOW
I SWEAR...
SOME DAYS JUST HAVE "WASTE ME" WRITTEN ALL OVER THEM!
JIM DAVIS 4-9
www.facebook.com/garfield
© 2017 PAWS, INC. All Rights Reserved.
Distributed by Andrews McMeel Syndication

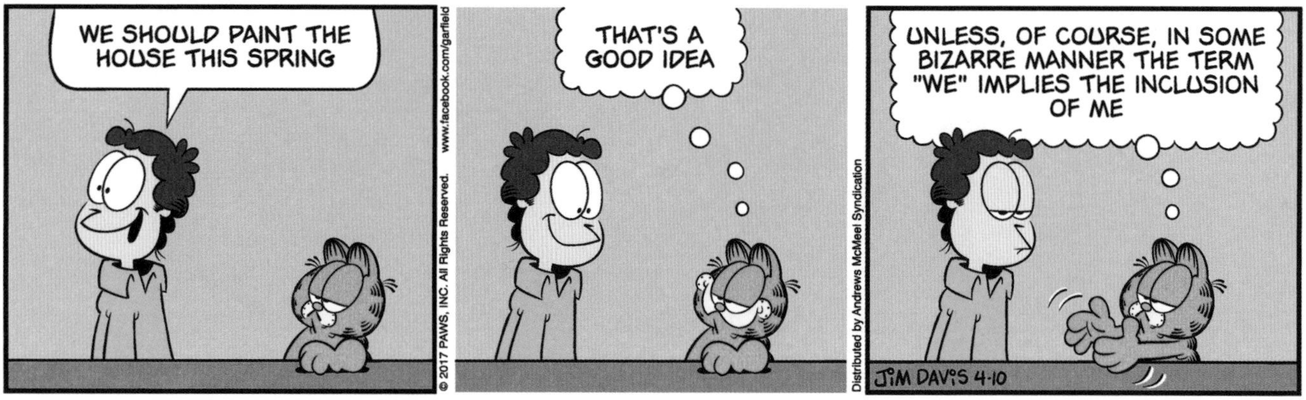
WE SHOULD PAINT THE HOUSE THIS SPRING
© 2017 PAWS, INC. All Rights Reserved. www.facebook.com/garfield
THAT'S A GOOD IDEA
Distributed by Andrews McMeel Syndication
UNLESS, OF COURSE, IN SOME BIZARRE MANNER THE TERM "WE" IMPLIES THE INCLUSION OF ME
JIM DAVIS 4-10

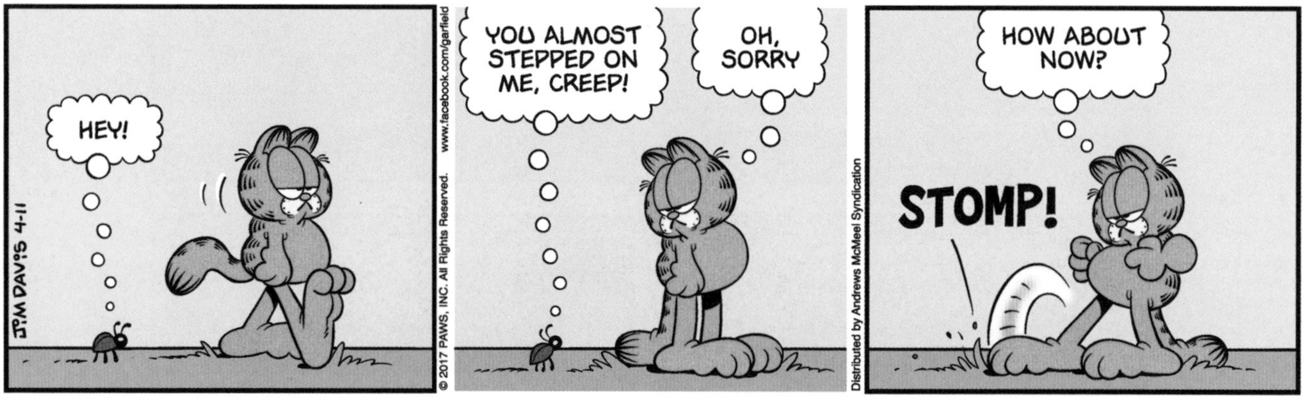
HEY!
JIM DAVIS 4-11
© 2017 PAWS, INC. All Rights Reserved. www.facebook.com/garfield
YOU ALMOST STEPPED ON ME, CREEP!
OH, SORRY
Distributed by Andrews McMeel Syndication
STOMP!
HOW ABOUT NOW?

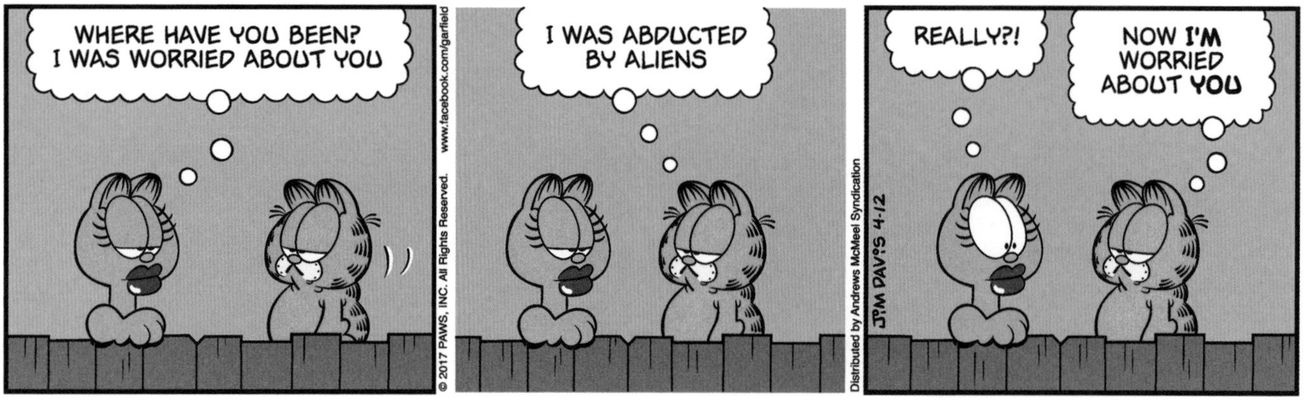
WHERE HAVE YOU BEEN? I WAS WORRIED ABOUT YOU
© 2017 PAWS, INC. All Rights Reserved. www.facebook.com/garfield
I WAS ABDUCTED BY ALIENS
Distributed by Andrews McMeel Syndication
JIM DAVIS 4-12
REALLY?!
NOW I'M WORRIED ABOUT YOU

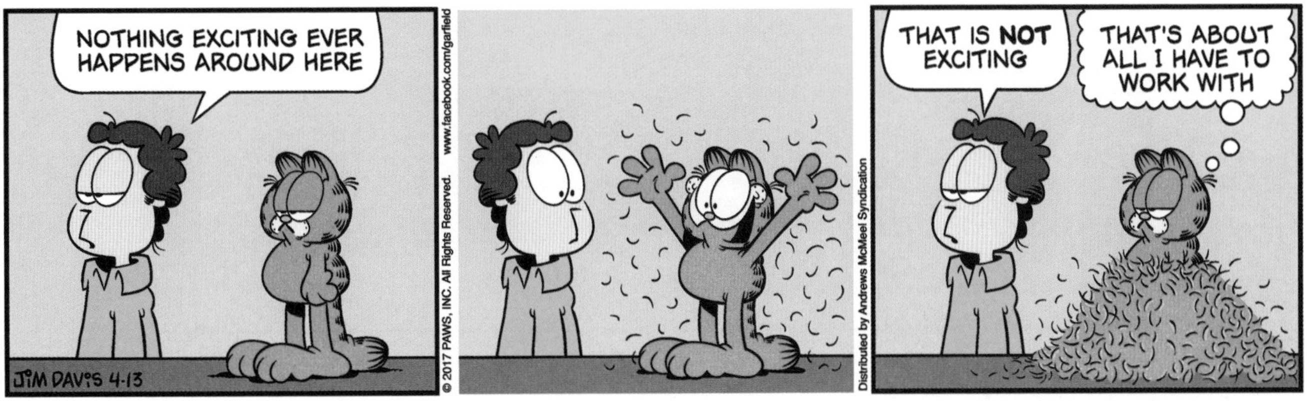
NOTHING EXCITING EVER HAPPENS AROUND HERE
JIM DAVIS 4-13
© 2017 PAWS, INC. All Rights Reserved. www.facebook.com/garfield
THAT IS **NOT** EXCITING
THAT'S ABOUT ALL I HAVE TO WORK WITH
Distributed by Andrews McMeel Syndication

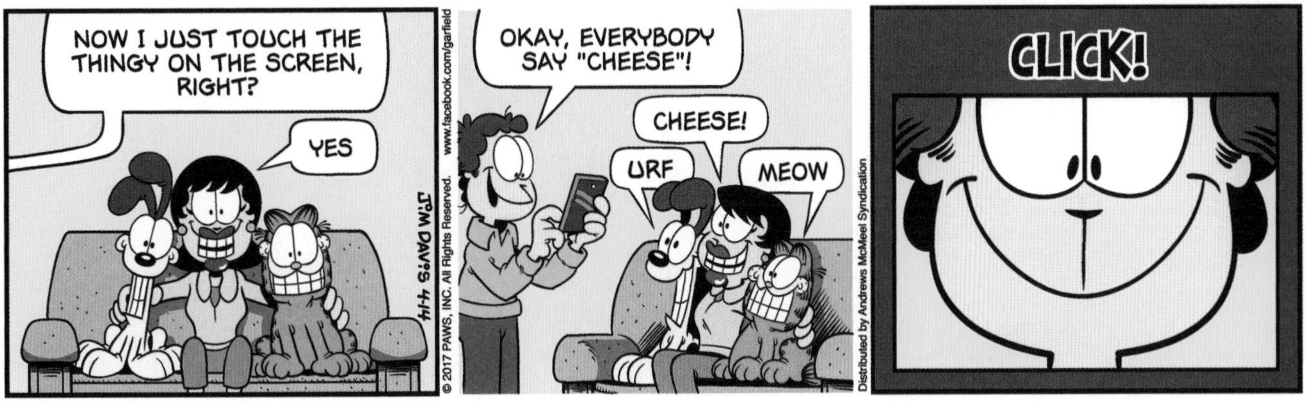
NOW I JUST TOUCH THE THINGY ON THE SCREEN, RIGHT?
YES
JIM DAVIS 4-14
© 2017 PAWS, INC. All Rights Reserved. www.facebook.com/garfield
OKAY, EVERYBODY SAY "CHEESE"!
CHEESE!
URF
MEOW
Distributed by Andrews McMeel Syndication
CLICK!

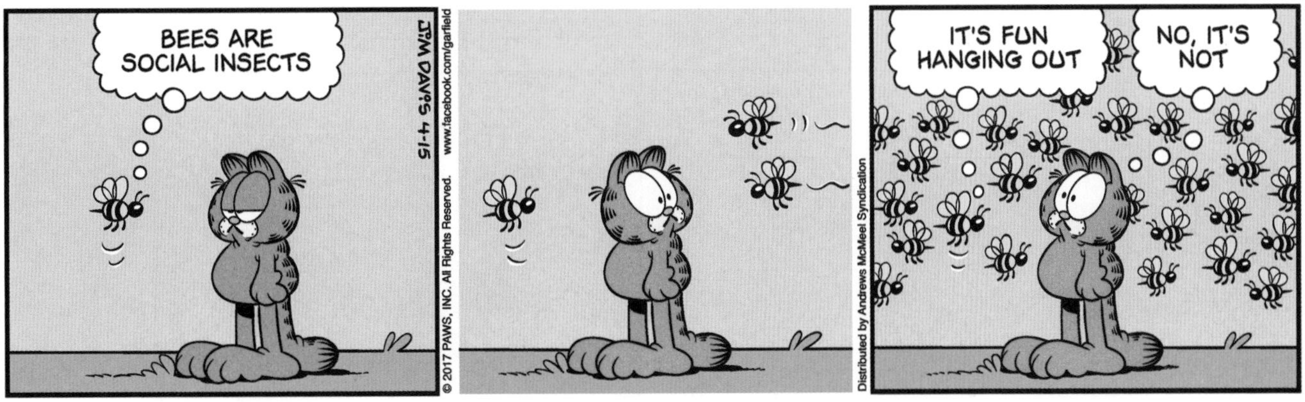
BEES ARE SOCIAL INSECTS
JIM DAVIS 4-15
© 2017 PAWS, INC. All Rights Reserved. www.facebook.com/garfield
Distributed by Andrews McMeel Syndication
IT'S FUN HANGING OUT
NO, IT'S NOT

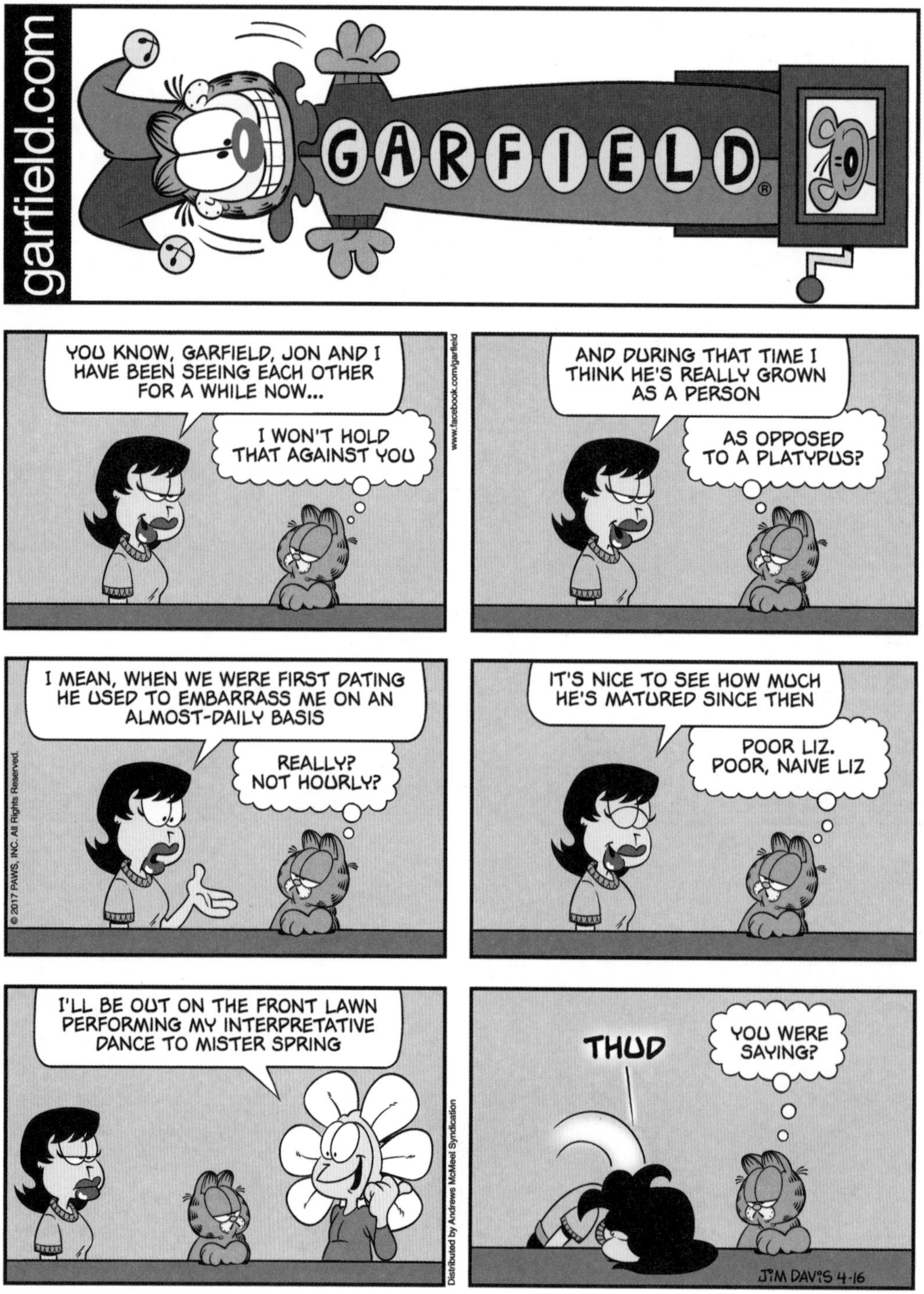

garfield.com
GARFIELD®
YOU KNOW, GARFIELD, JON AND I HAVE BEEN SEEING EACH OTHER FOR A WHILE NOW...
I WON'T HOLD THAT AGAINST YOU
www.facebook.com/garfield
AND DURING THAT TIME I THINK HE'S REALLY GROWN AS A PERSON
AS OPPOSED TO A PLATYPUS?
I MEAN, WHEN WE WERE FIRST DATING HE USED TO EMBARRASS ME ON AN ALMOST-DAILY BASIS
REALLY? NOT HOURLY?
© 2017 PAWS, INC. All Rights Reserved.
IT'S NICE TO SEE HOW MUCH HE'S MATURED SINCE THEN
POOR LIZ. POOR, NAIVE LIZ
I'LL BE OUT ON THE FRONT LAWN PERFORMING MY INTERPRETATIVE DANCE TO MISTER SPRING
Distributed by Andrews McMeel Syndication
THUD
YOU WERE SAYING?
JIM DAVIS 4-16

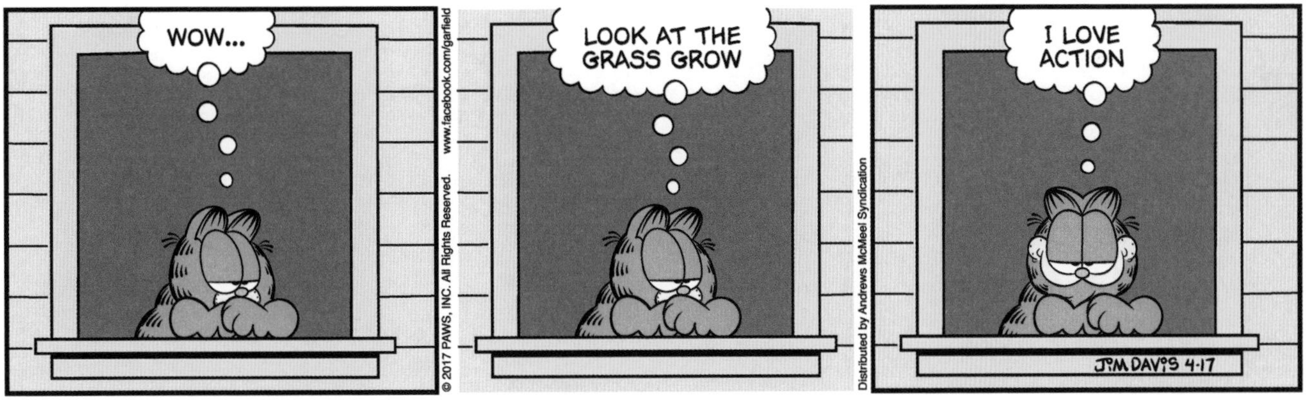
WOW...
LOOK AT THE GRASS GROW
I LOVE ACTION
JIM DAVIS 4-17
© 2017 PAWS, INC. All Rights Reserved. www.facebook.com/garfield
Distributed by Andrews McMeel Syndication

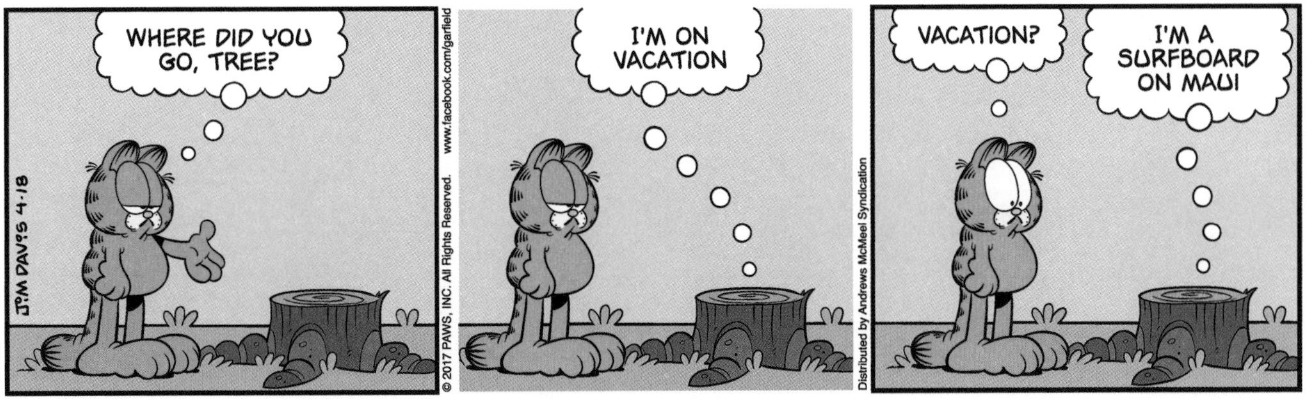
WHERE DID YOU GO, TREE?
JIM DAVIS 4-18
I'M ON VACATION
VACATION?
I'M A SURFBOARD ON MAUI
© 2017 PAWS, INC. All Rights Reserved. www.facebook.com/garfield
Distributed by Andrews McMeel Syndication

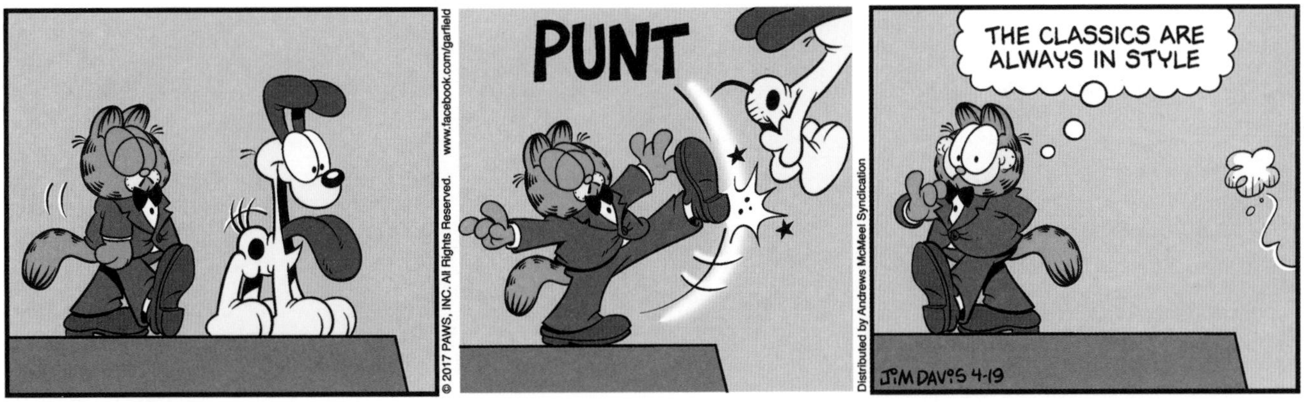
PUNT
THE CLASSICS ARE ALWAYS IN STYLE
JIM DAVIS 4-19
© 2017 PAWS, INC. All Rights Reserved. www.facebook.com/garfield
Distributed by Andrews McMeel Syndication

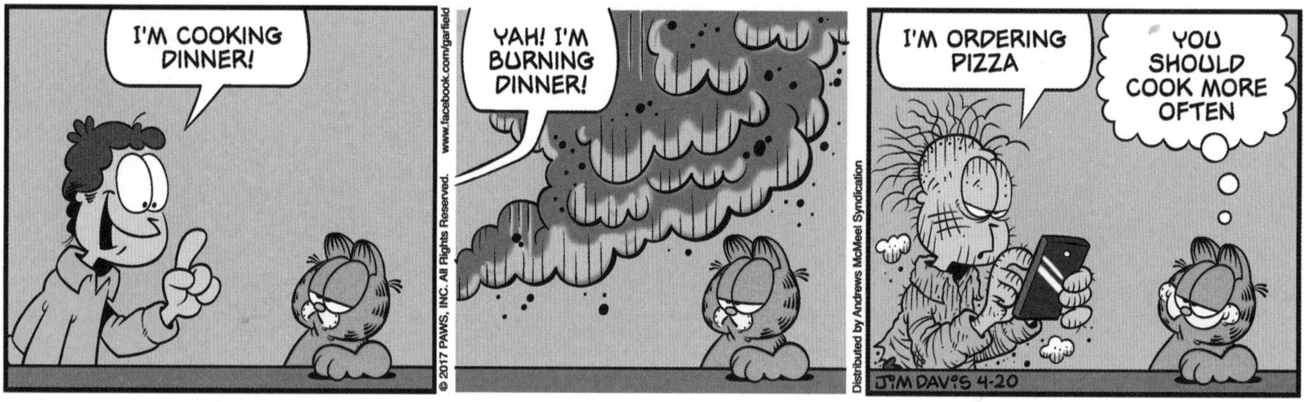
I'M COOKING DINNER!
YAH! I'M BURNING DINNER!
I'M ORDERING PIZZA
YOU SHOULD COOK MORE OFTEN
JIM DAVIS 4-20
© 2017 PAWS, INC. All Rights Reserved. www.facebook.com/garfield
Distributed by Andrews McMeel Syndication

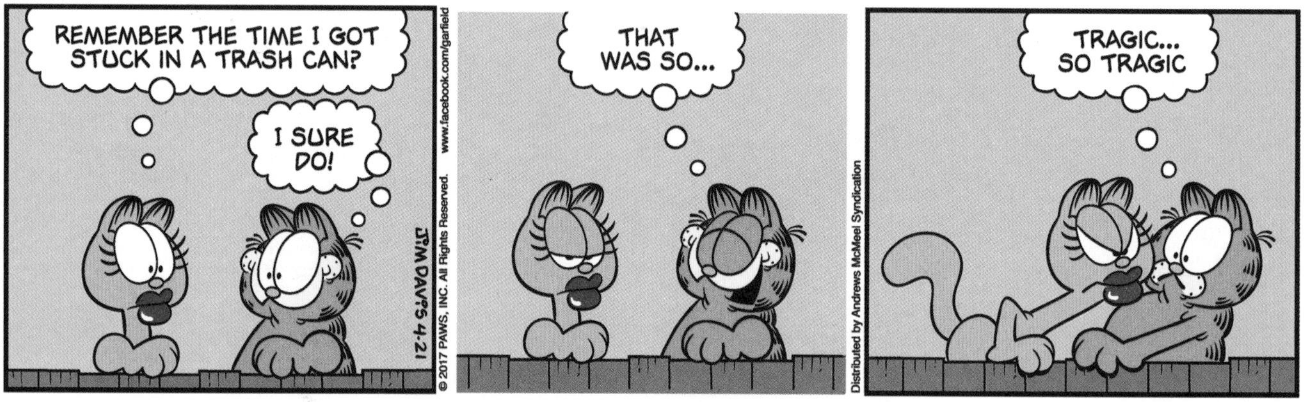
REMEMBER THE TIME I GOT STUCK IN A TRASH CAN?
I SURE DO!
THAT WAS SO...
TRAGIC... SO TRAGIC
JIM DAVIS 4-21
© 2017 PAWS, INC. All Rights Reserved. www.facebook.com/garfield
Distributed by Andrews McMeel Syndication

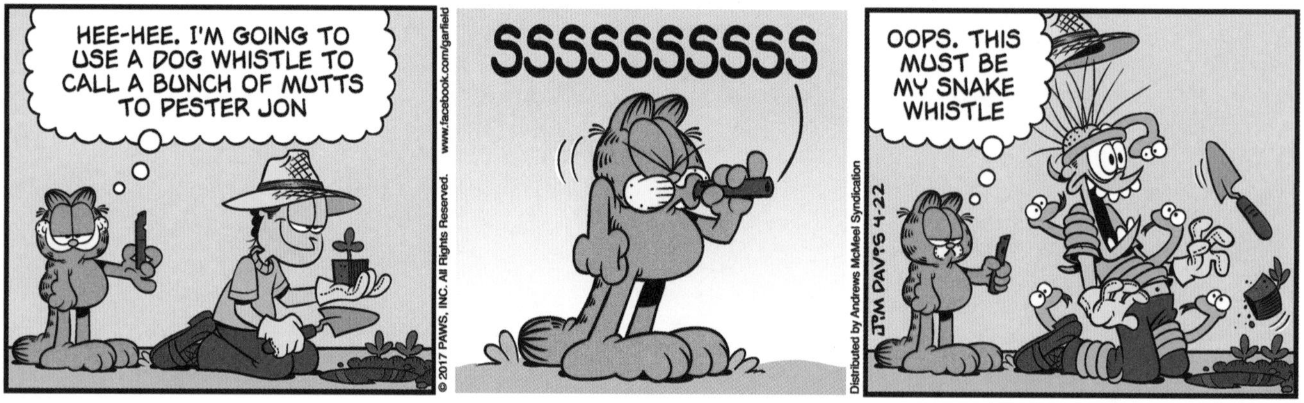
HEE-HEE. I'M GOING TO USE A DOG WHISTLE TO CALL A BUNCH OF MUTTS TO PESTER JON
SSSSSSSSSSS
OOPS. THIS MUST BE MY SNAKE WHISTLE
JIM DAVIS 4-22
© 2017 PAWS, INC. All Rights Reserved. www.facebook.com/garfield
Distributed by Andrews McMeel Syndication

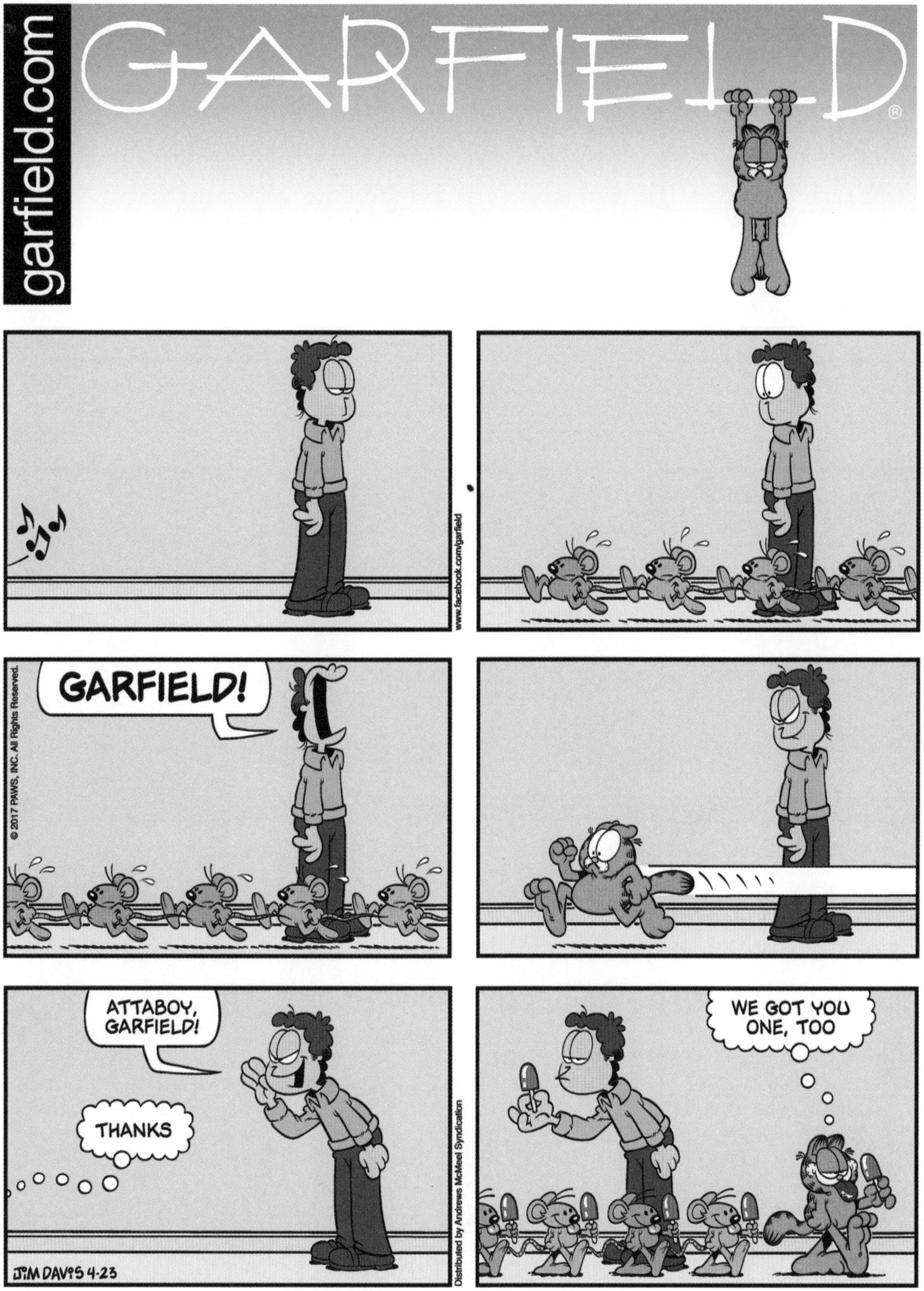

garfield.com
GARFIELD
GARFIELD!
ATTABOY, GARFIELD!
THANKS
WE GOT YOU ONE, TOO
JIM DAVIS 4-23
www.facebook.com/garfield
© 2017 PAWS, INC. All Rights Reserved.
Distributed by Andrews McMeel Syndication

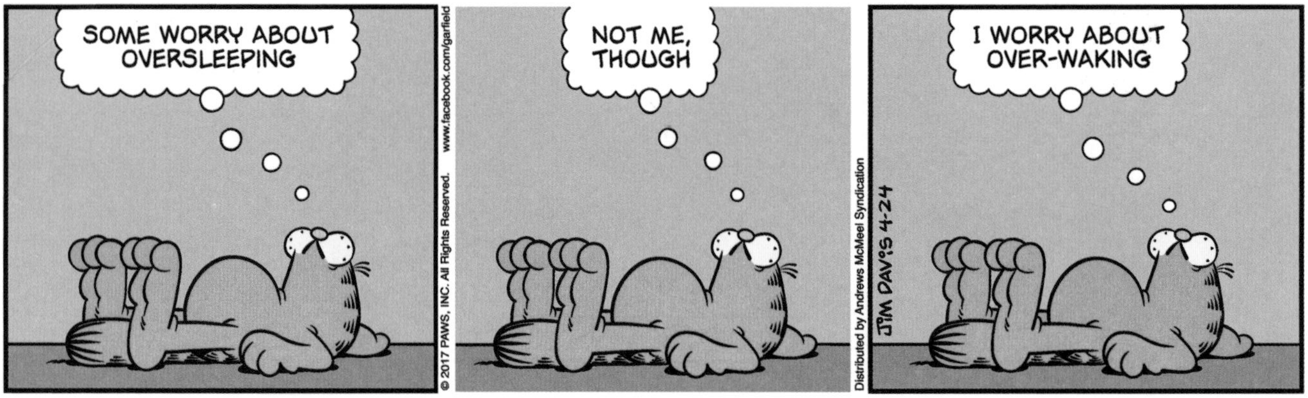
SOME WORRY ABOUT OVERSLEEPING
© 2017 PAWS, INC. All Rights Reserved. www.facebook.com/garfield
NOT ME, THOUGH
Distributed by Andrews McMeel Syndication
JIM DAVIS 4-24
I WORRY ABOUT OVER-WAKING

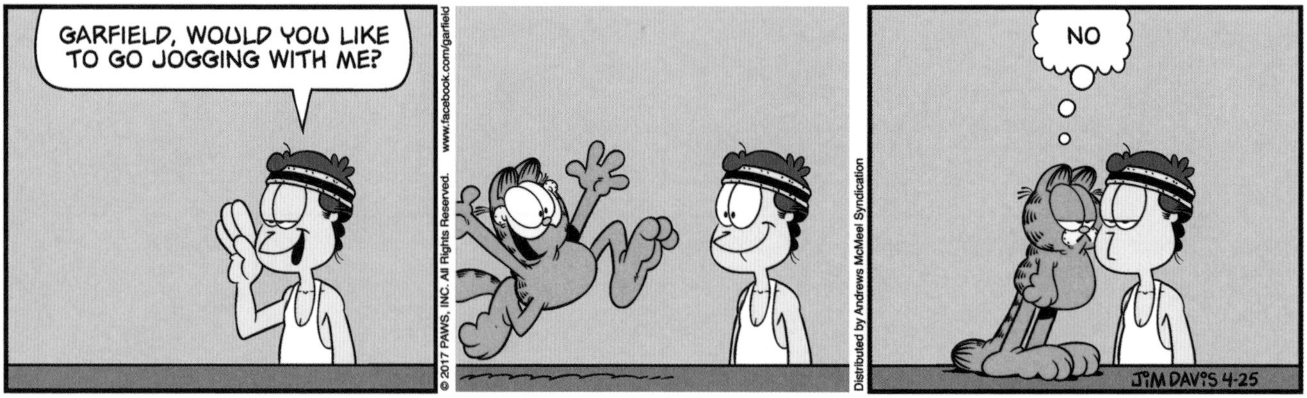
GARFIELD, WOULD YOU LIKE TO GO JOGGING WITH ME?
© 2017 PAWS, INC. All Rights Reserved. www.facebook.com/garfield
Distributed by Andrews McMeel Syndication
NO
JIM DAVIS 4-25

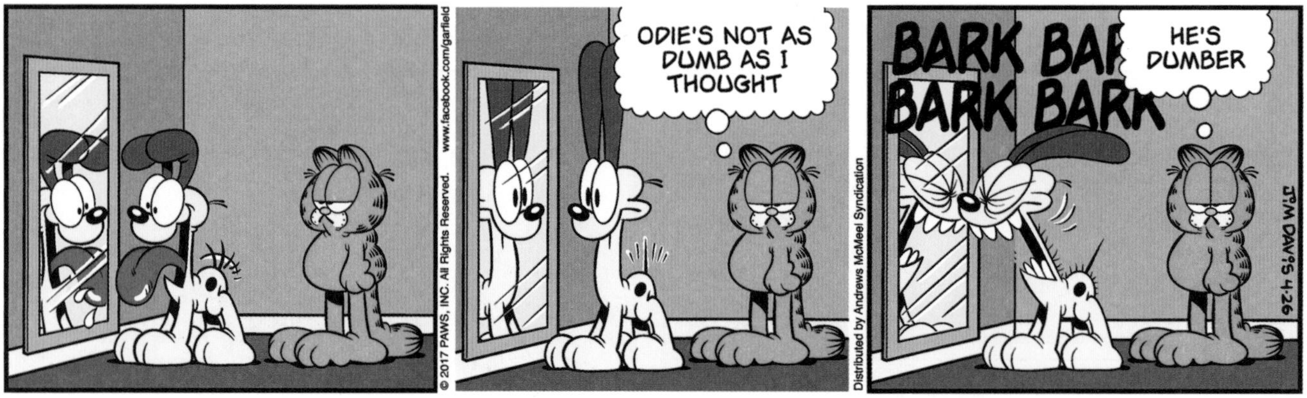
© 2017 PAWS, INC. All Rights Reserved. www.facebook.com/garfield
ODIE'S NOT AS DUMB AS I THOUGHT
Distributed by Andrews McMeel Syndication
BARK BAR
BARK BARK
HE'S DUMBER
JIM DAVIS 4-26

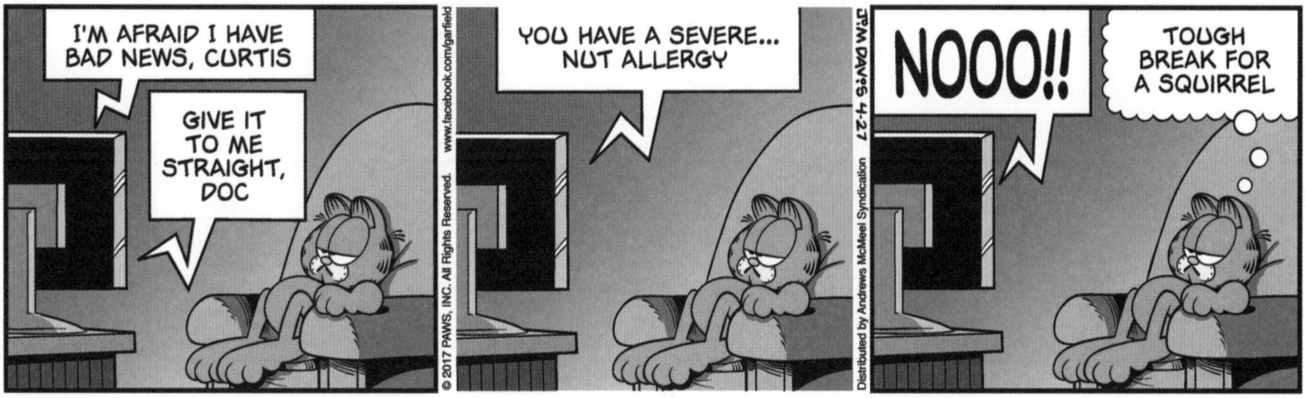
I'M AFRAID I HAVE BAD NEWS, CURTIS
GIVE IT TO ME STRAIGHT, DOC
YOU HAVE A SEVERE... NUT ALLERGY
NOOO!!
TOUGH BREAK FOR A SQUIRREL
JIM DAVIS 4-27
© 2017 PAWS, INC. All Rights Reserved. www.facebook.com/garfield
Distributed by Andrews McMeel Syndication

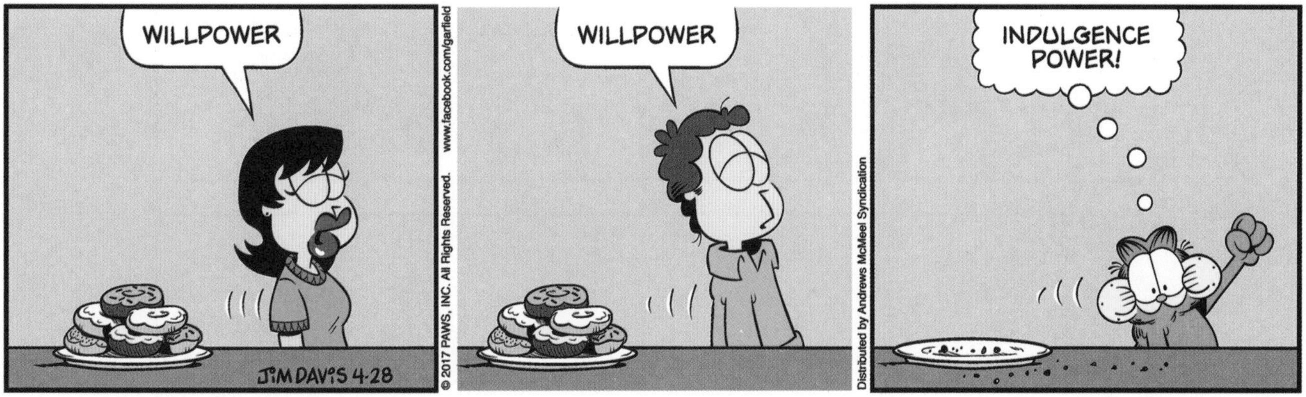
WILLPOWER
WILLPOWER
INDULGENCE POWER!
JIM DAVIS 4-28
© 2017 PAWS, INC. All Rights Reserved. www.facebook.com/garfield
Distributed by Andrews McMeel Syndication

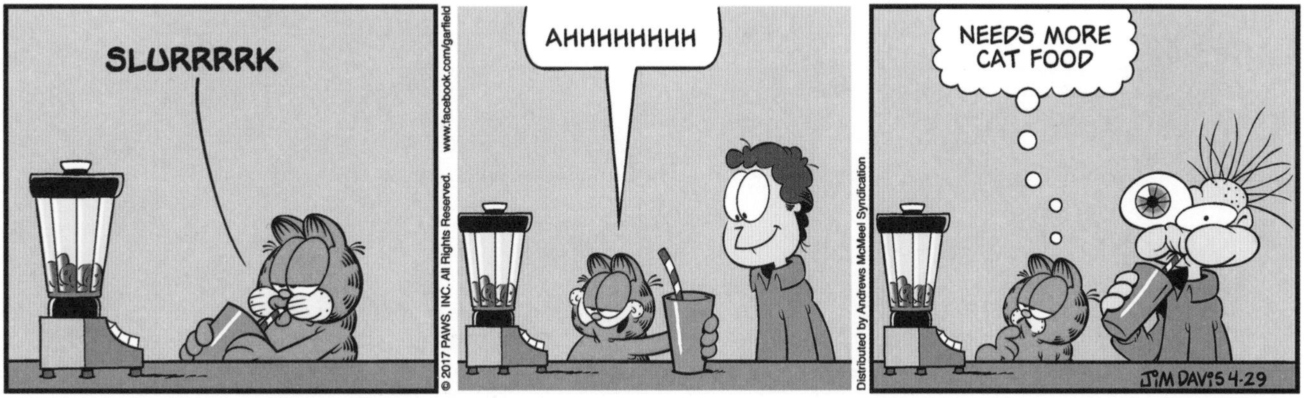
SLURRRRK
AHHHHHHHH
NEEDS MORE CAT FOOD
JIM DAVIS 4-29
© 2017 PAWS, INC. All Rights Reserved. www.facebook.com/garfield
Distributed by Andrews McMeel Syndication

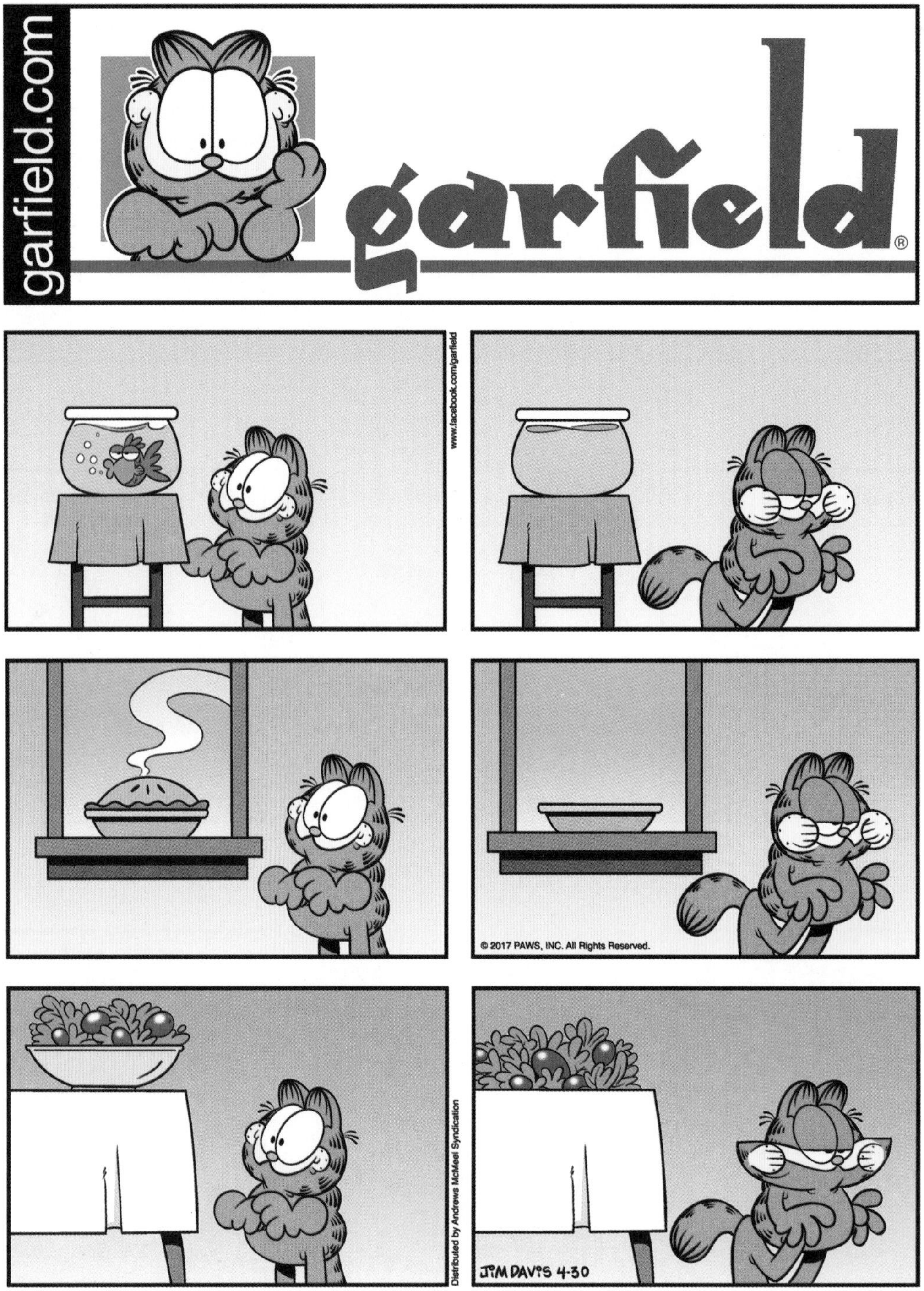
garfield.com
garfield
www.facebook.com/garfield
© 2017 PAWS, INC. All Rights Reserved.
Distributed by Andrews McMeel Syndication
JIM DAVIS 4-30

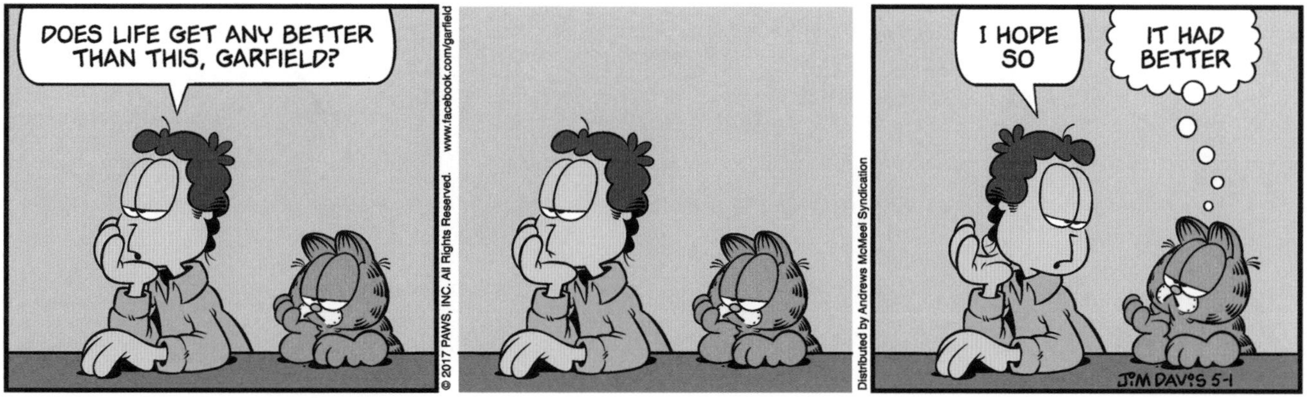
DOES LIFE GET ANY BETTER THAN THIS, GARFIELD?
I HOPE SO
IT HAD BETTER
JIM DAVIS 5-1

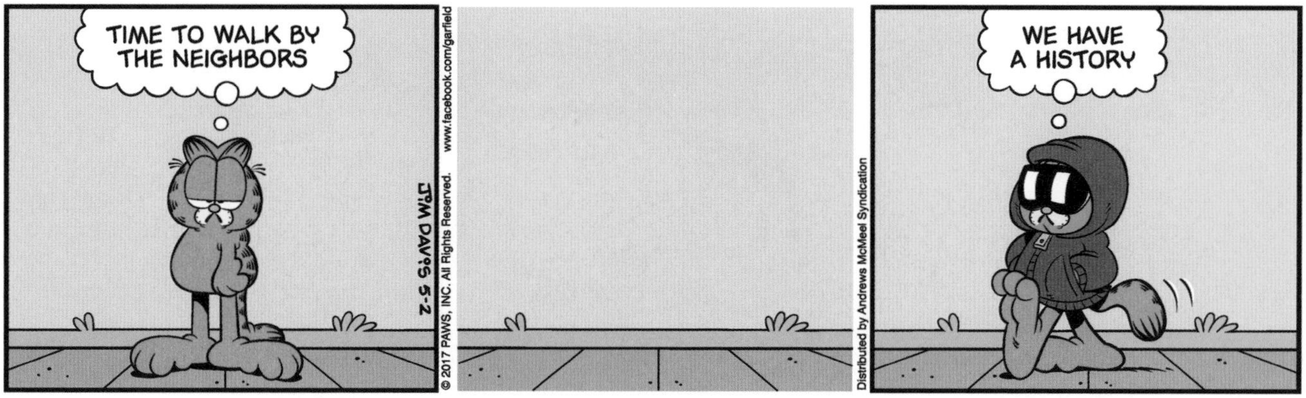
TIME TO WALK BY THE NEIGHBORS
JIM DAVIS 5-2
WE HAVE A HISTORY

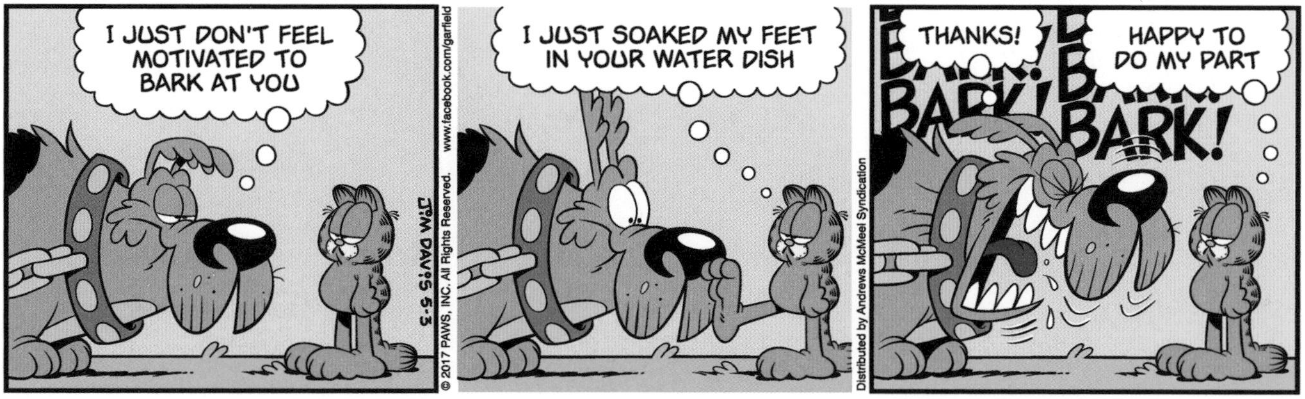
I JUST DON'T FEEL MOTIVATED TO BARK AT YOU
JIM DAVIS 5-3
I JUST SOAKED MY FEET IN YOUR WATER DISH
BARK!
BARK!
THANKS!
HAPPY TO DO MY PART

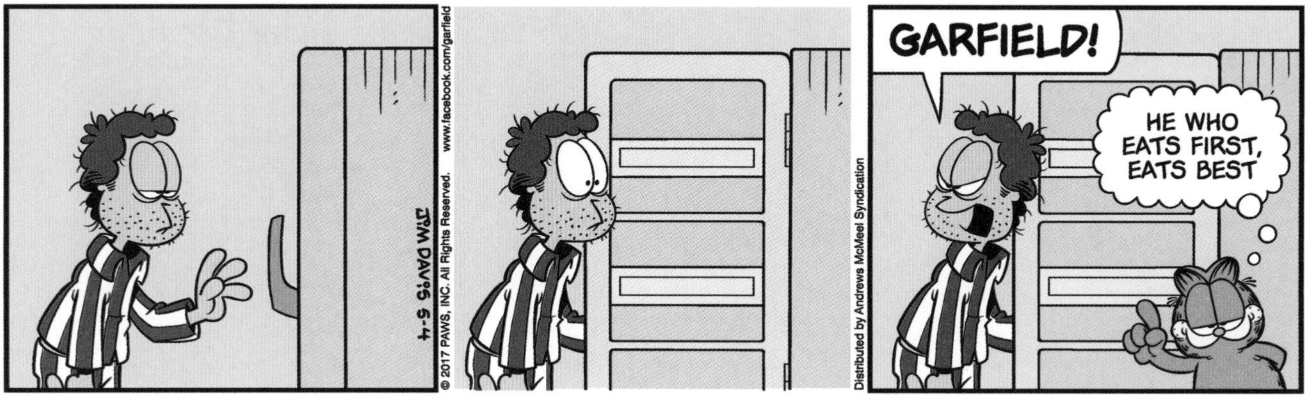
JIM DAVIS 5-4
© 2017 PAWS, INC. All Rights Reserved. www.facebook.com/garfield
GARFIELD!
HE WHO EATS FIRST, EATS BEST
Distributed by Andrews McMeel Syndication

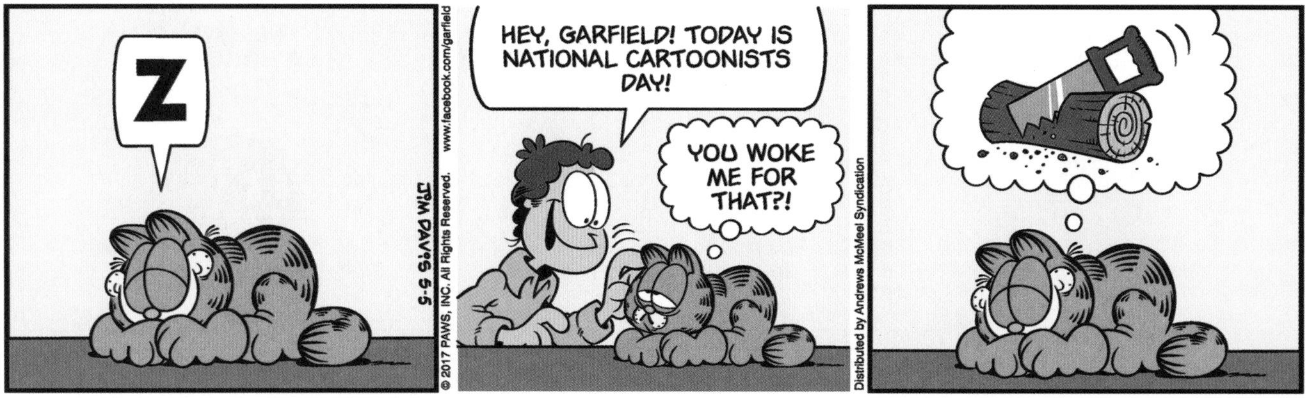
Z
JIM DAVIS 5-5
© 2017 PAWS, INC. All Rights Reserved. www.facebook.com/garfield
HEY, GARFIELD! TODAY IS NATIONAL CARTOONISTS DAY!
YOU WOKE ME FOR THAT?!
Distributed by Andrews McMeel Syndication

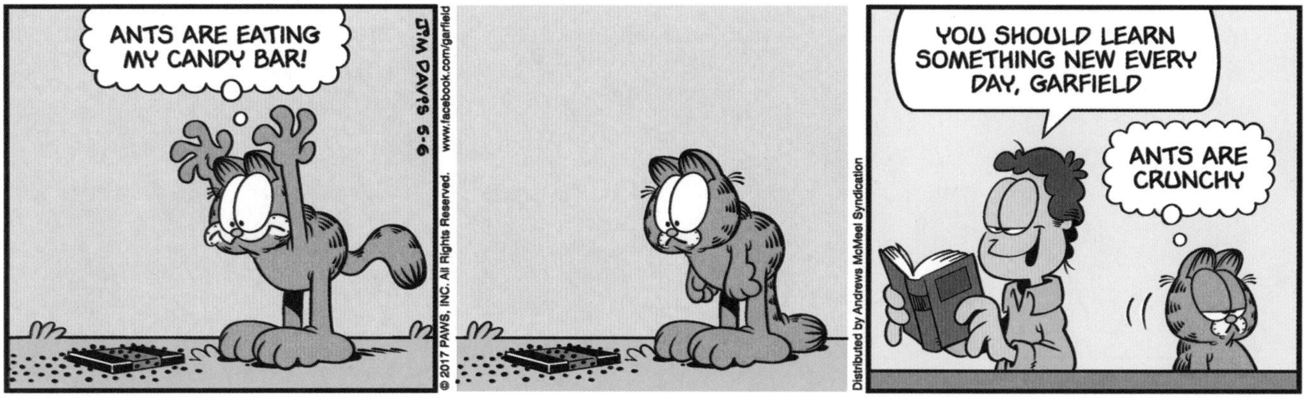
ANTS ARE EATING MY CANDY BAR!
JIM DAVIS 5-6
© 2017 PAWS, INC. All Rights Reserved. www.facebook.com/garfield
YOU SHOULD LEARN SOMETHING NEW EVERY DAY, GARFIELD
ANTS ARE CRUNCHY
Distributed by Andrews McMeel Syndication

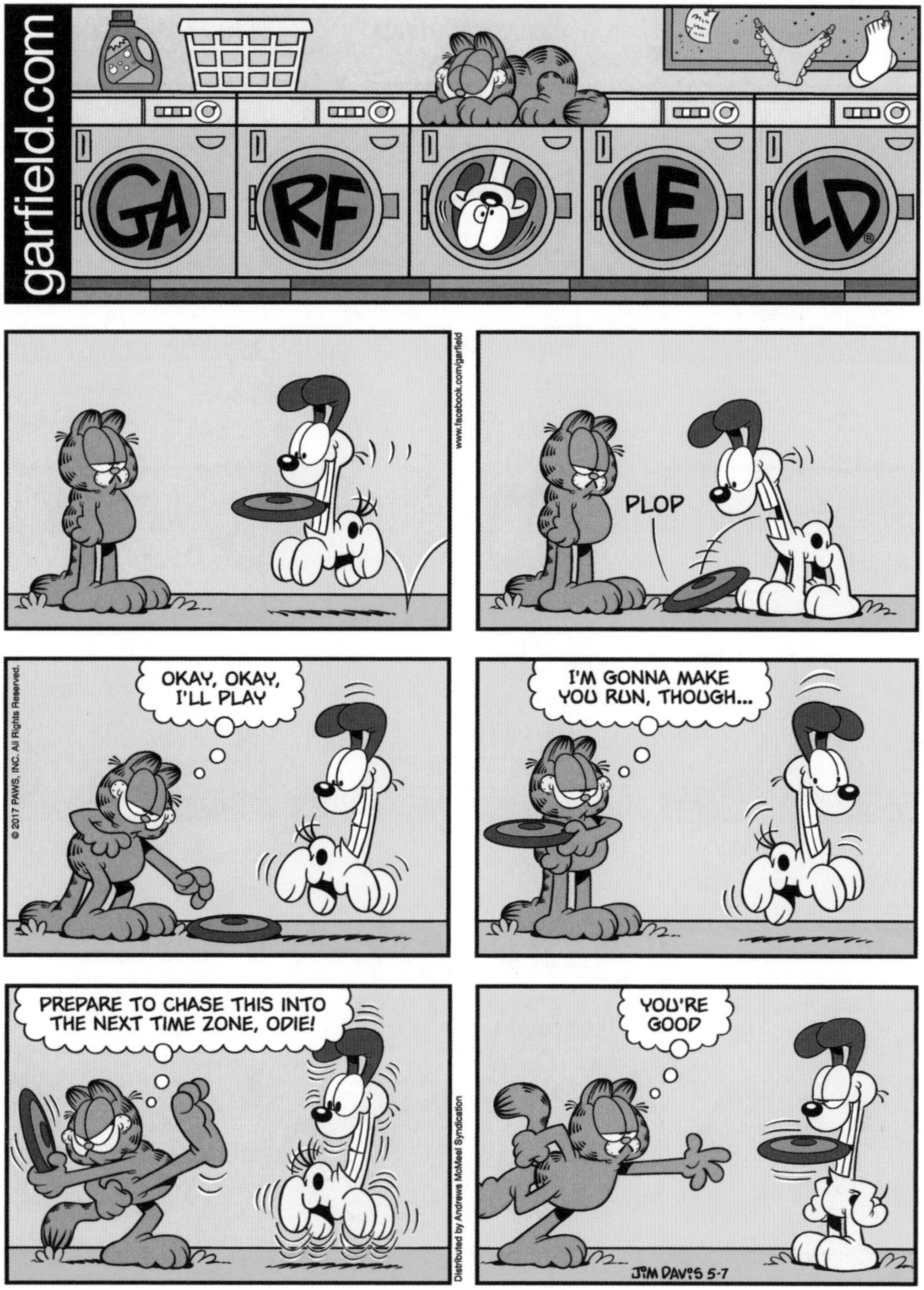
garfield.com
GARFIELD
www.facebook.com/garfield
PLOP
OKAY, OKAY, I'LL PLAY
I'M GONNA MAKE YOU RUN, THOUGH...
PREPARE TO CHASE THIS INTO THE NEXT TIME ZONE, ODIE!
YOU'RE GOOD
© 2017 PAWS, INC. All Rights Reserved.
Distributed by Andrews McMeel Syndication
JIM DAVIS 5-7

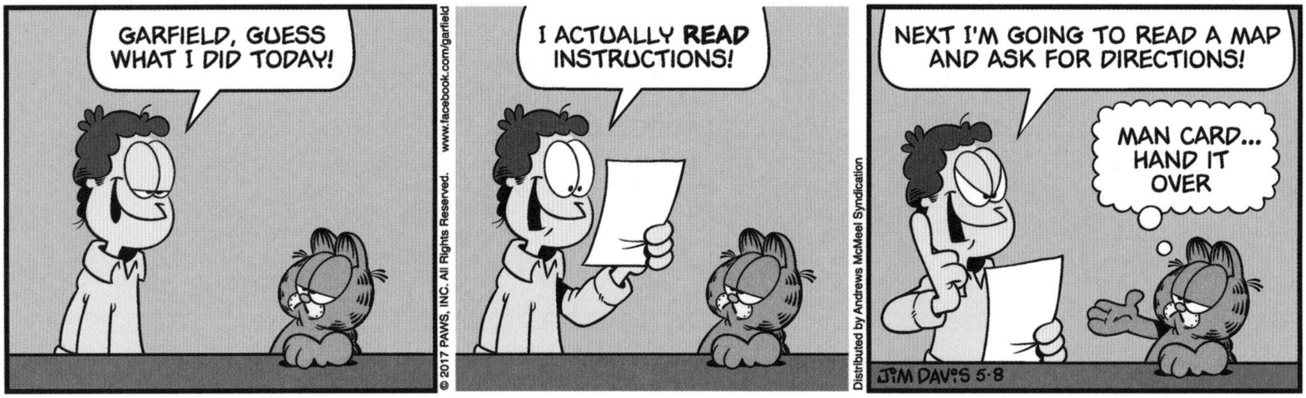
GARFIELD, GUESS WHAT I DID TODAY!
© 2017 PAWS, INC. All Rights Reserved. www.facebook.com/garfield
I ACTUALLY **READ** INSTRUCTIONS!
Distributed by Andrews McMeel Syndication
NEXT I'M GOING TO READ A MAP AND ASK FOR DIRECTIONS!
MAN CARD... HAND IT OVER
JIM DAVIS 5-8

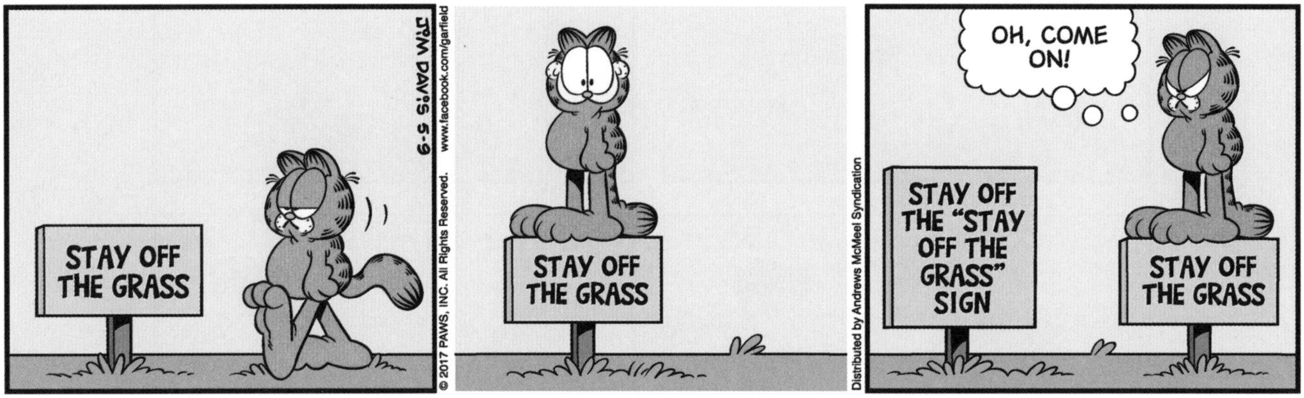
STAY OFF THE GRASS
JIM DAVIS 5-9
© 2017 PAWS, INC. All Rights Reserved. www.facebook.com/garfield
STAY OFF THE GRASS
Distributed by Andrews McMeel Syndication
OH, COME ON!
STAY OFF THE "STAY OFF THE GRASS" SIGN
STAY OFF THE GRASS

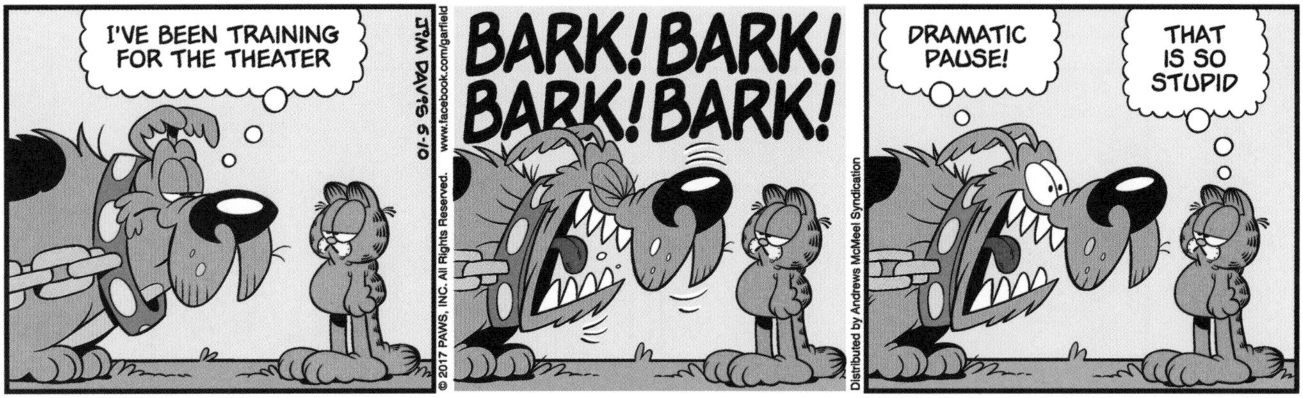
I'VE BEEN TRAINING FOR THE THEATER
JIM DAVIS 5-10
© 2017 PAWS, INC. All Rights Reserved. www.facebook.com/garfield
BARK! BARK! BARK! BARK!
Distributed by Andrews McMeel Syndication
DRAMATIC PAUSE!
THAT IS SO STUPID

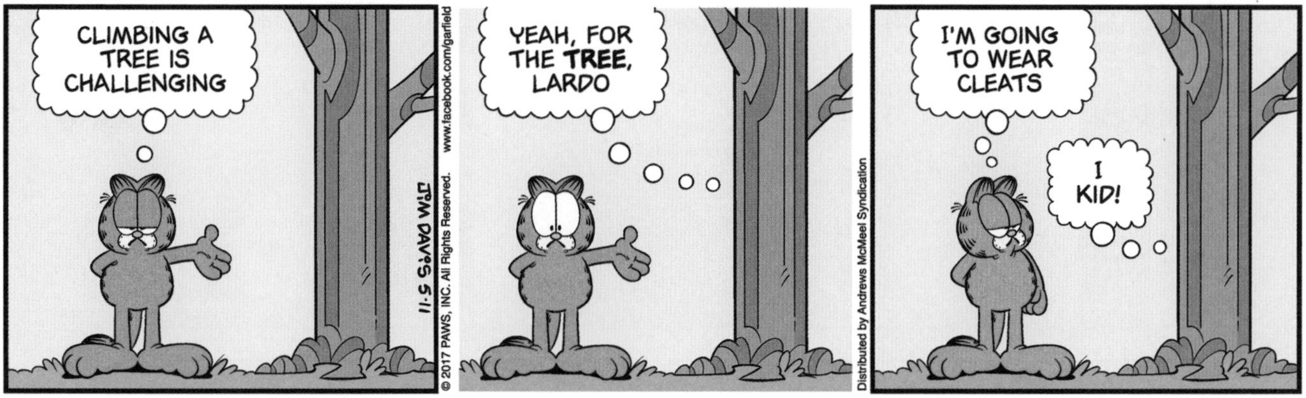
CLIMBING A TREE IS CHALLENGING
JIM DAVIS 5-11
© 2017 PAWS, INC. All Rights Reserved. www.facebook.com/garfield
YEAH, FOR THE **TREE**, LARDO
Distributed by Andrews McMeel Syndication
I'M GOING TO WEAR CLEATS
I KID!

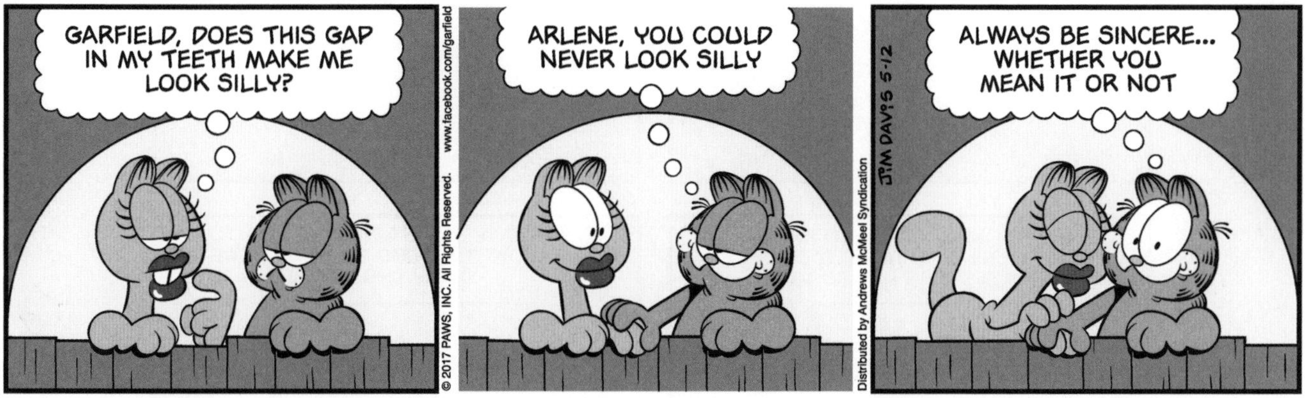
GARFIELD, DOES THIS GAP IN MY TEETH MAKE ME LOOK SILLY?
© 2017 PAWS, INC. All Rights Reserved. www.facebook.com/garfield
ARLENE, YOU COULD NEVER LOOK SILLY
Distributed by Andrews McMeel Syndication
JIM DAVIS 5-12
ALWAYS BE SINCERE... WHETHER YOU MEAN IT OR NOT

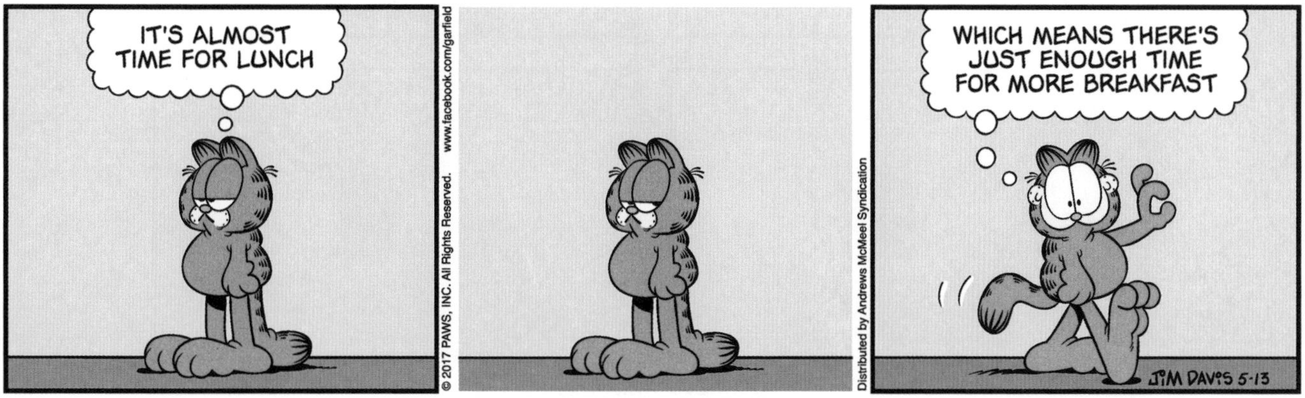
IT'S ALMOST TIME FOR LUNCH
© 2017 PAWS, INC. All Rights Reserved. www.facebook.com/garfield
Distributed by Andrews McMeel Syndication
WHICH MEANS THERE'S JUST ENOUGH TIME FOR MORE BREAKFAST
JIM DAVIS 5-13

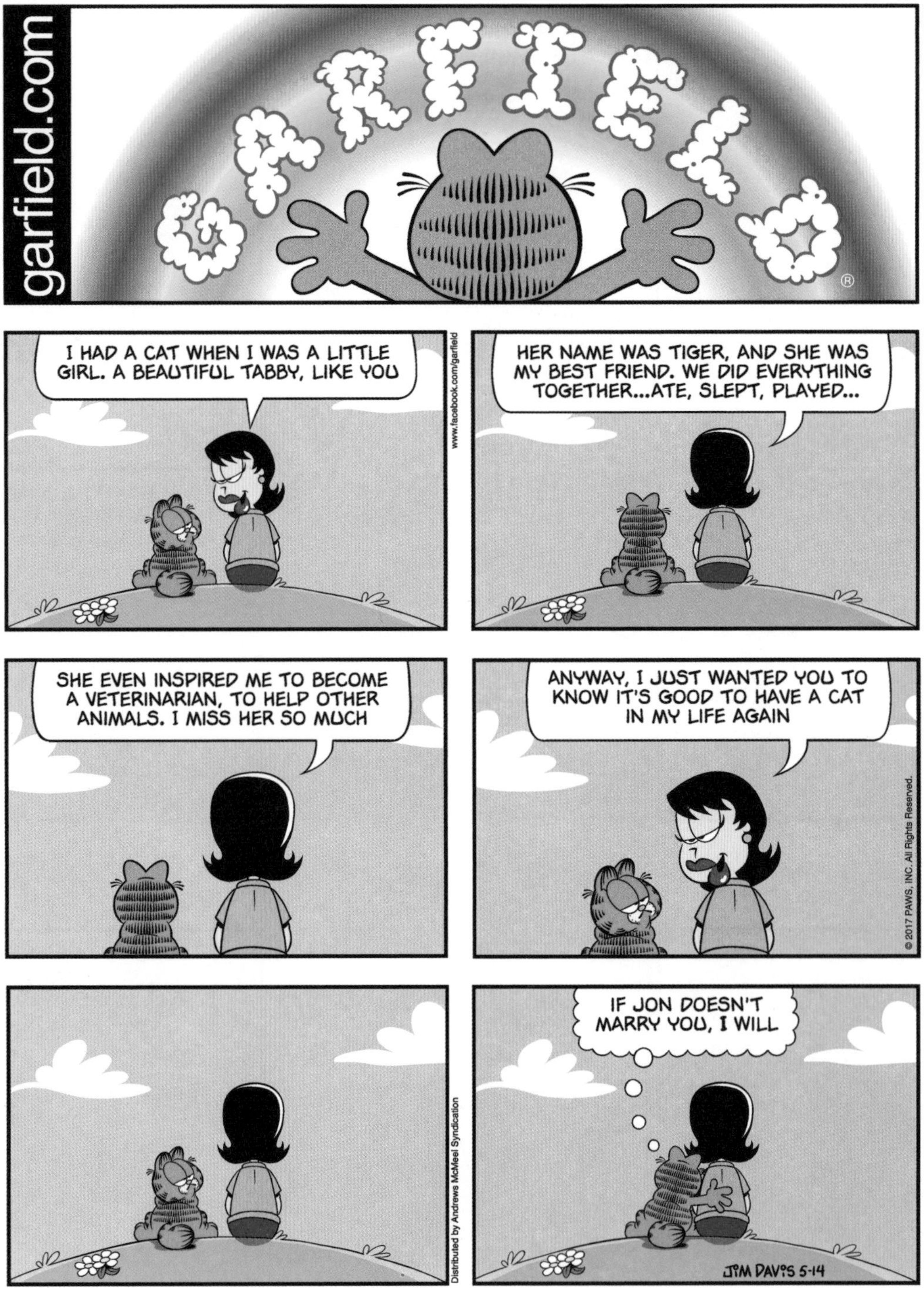
garfield.com
GARFIELD
I HAD A CAT WHEN I WAS A LITTLE GIRL. A BEAUTIFUL TABBY, LIKE YOU
www.facebook.com/garfield
HER NAME WAS TIGER, AND SHE WAS MY BEST FRIEND. WE DID EVERYTHING TOGETHER...ATE, SLEPT, PLAYED...
SHE EVEN INSPIRED ME TO BECOME A VETERINARIAN, TO HELP OTHER ANIMALS. I MISS HER SO MUCH
ANYWAY, I JUST WANTED YOU TO KNOW IT'S GOOD TO HAVE A CAT IN MY LIFE AGAIN
© 2017 PAWS, INC. All Rights Reserved.
Distributed by Andrews McMeel Syndication
IF JON DOESN'T MARRY YOU, I WILL
JIM DAVIS 5-14

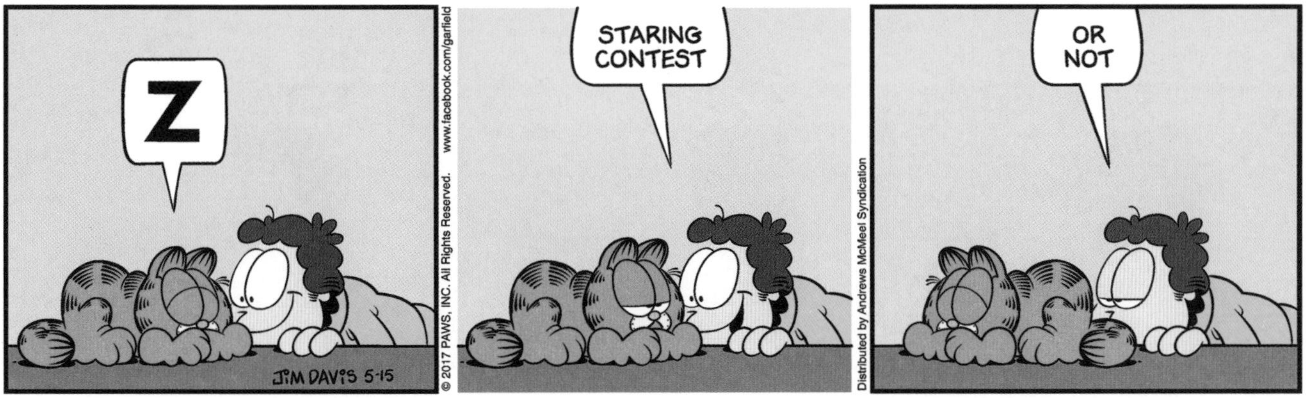
Z
STARING CONTEST
OR NOT
JIM DAVIS 5-15
© 2017 PAWS, INC. All Rights Reserved. www.facebook.com/garfield
Distributed by Andrews McMeel Syndication

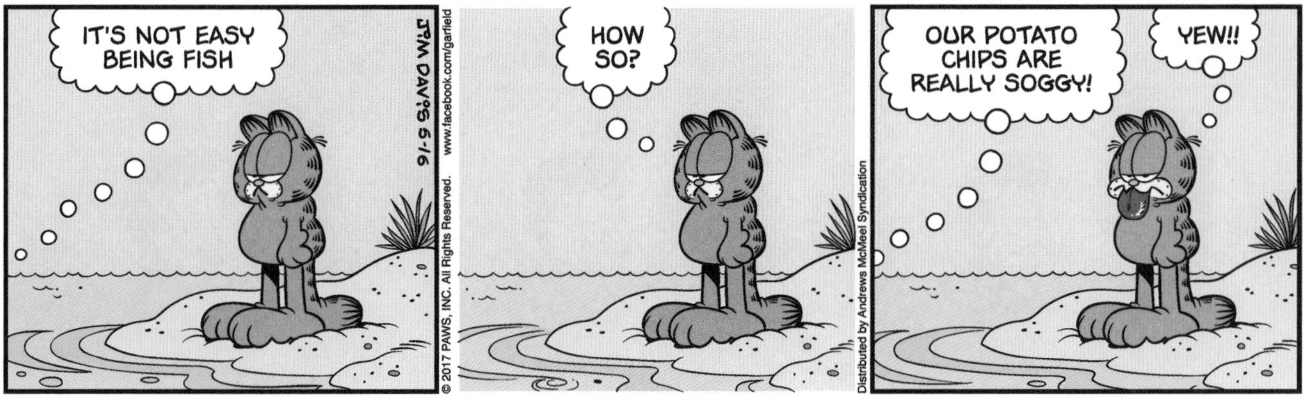
IT'S NOT EASY BEING FISH
HOW SO?
OUR POTATO CHIPS ARE REALLY SOGGY!
YEW!!
JIM DAVIS 5-16
© 2017 PAWS, INC. All Rights Reserved. www.facebook.com/garfield
Distributed by Andrews McMeel Syndication

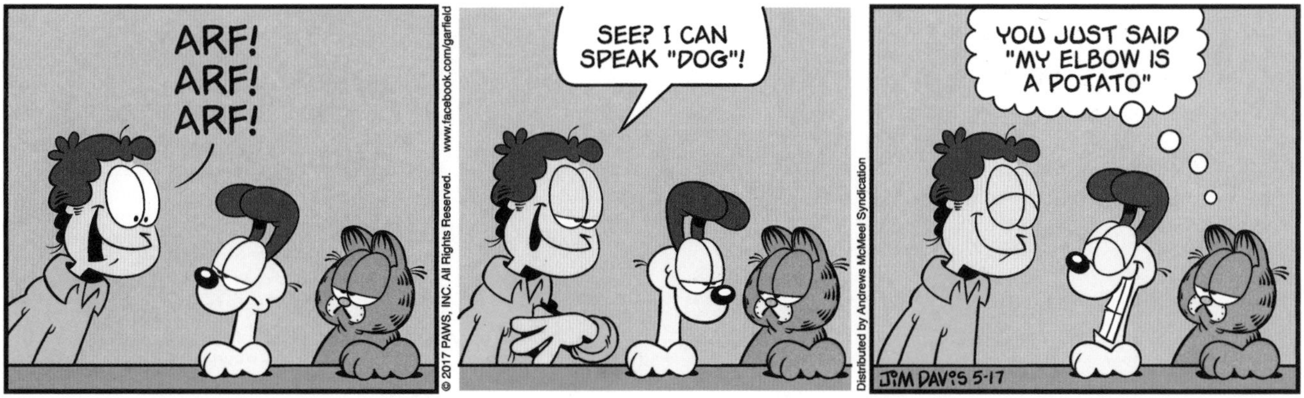
ARF! ARF! ARF!
SEE? I CAN SPEAK "DOG"!
YOU JUST SAID "MY ELBOW IS A POTATO"
JIM DAVIS 5-17
© 2017 PAWS, INC. All Rights Reserved. www.facebook.com/garfield
Distributed by Andrews McMeel Syndication

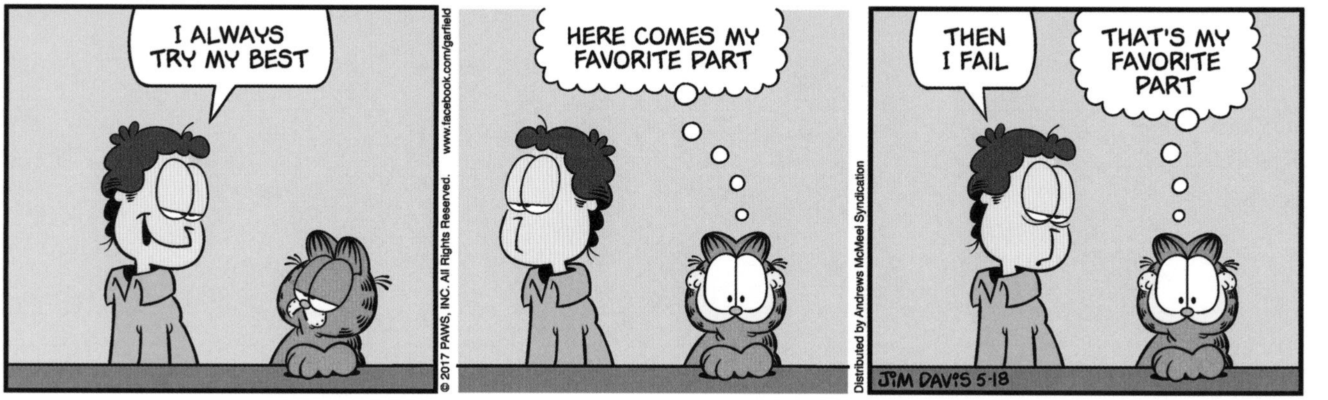
I ALWAYS TRY MY BEST
HERE COMES MY FAVORITE PART
THEN I FAIL
THAT'S MY FAVORITE PART
© 2017 PAWS, INC. All Rights Reserved. www.facebook.com/garfield
Distributed by Andrews McMeel Syndication
JIM DAVIS 5-18

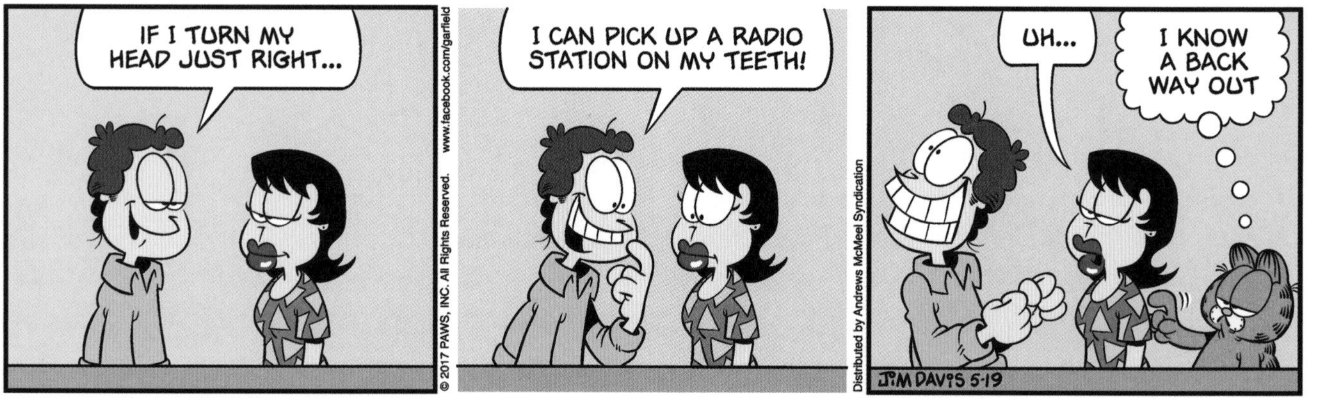
IF I TURN MY HEAD JUST RIGHT...
I CAN PICK UP A RADIO STATION ON MY TEETH!
UH...
I KNOW A BACK WAY OUT
© 2017 PAWS, INC. All Rights Reserved. www.facebook.com/garfield
Distributed by Andrews McMeel Syndication
JIM DAVIS 5-19

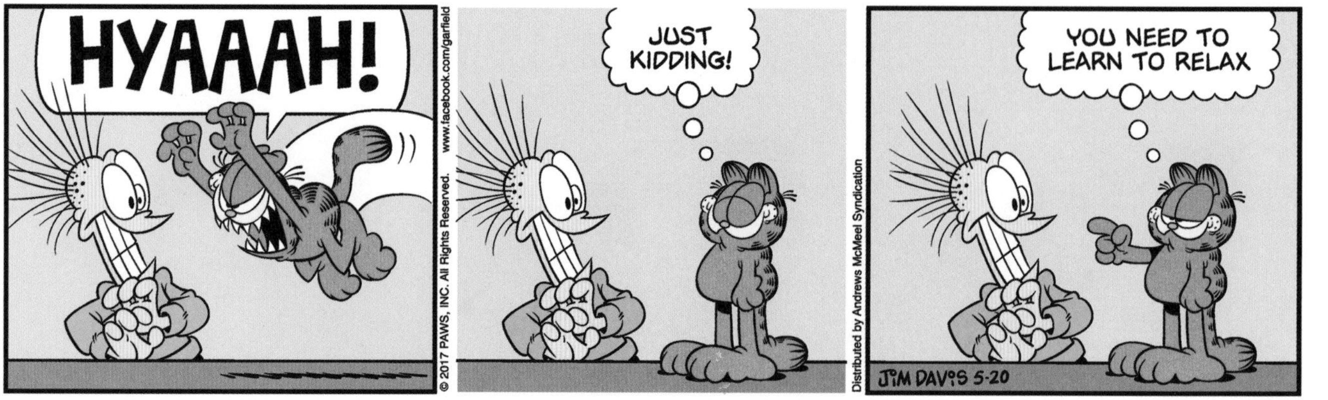
HYAAAH!
JUST KIDDING!
YOU NEED TO LEARN TO RELAX
© 2017 PAWS, INC. All Rights Reserved. www.facebook.com/garfield
Distributed by Andrews McMeel Syndication
JIM DAVIS 5-20

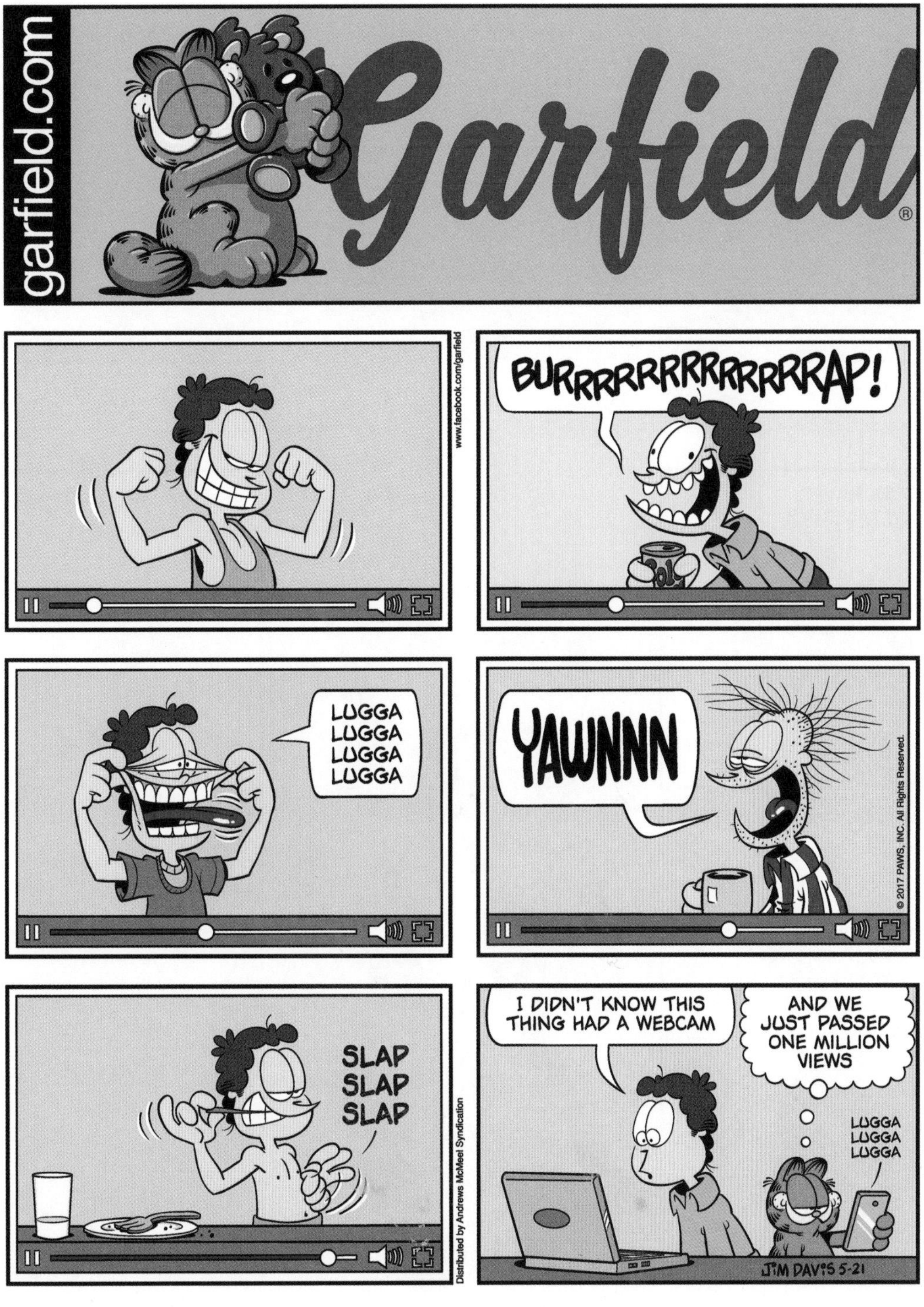
garfield.com
Garfield®
www.facebook.com/garfield
BURRRRRRRRRRRRRAP!
LUGGA
LUGGA
LUGGA
LUGGA
YAWNNN
© 2017 PAWS, INC. All Rights Reserved.
SLAP
SLAP
SLAP
Distributed by Andrews McMeel Syndication
I DIDN'T KNOW THIS THING HAD A WEBCAM
AND WE JUST PASSED ONE MILLION VIEWS
LUGGA
LUGGA
LUGGA
JIM DAVIS 5-21

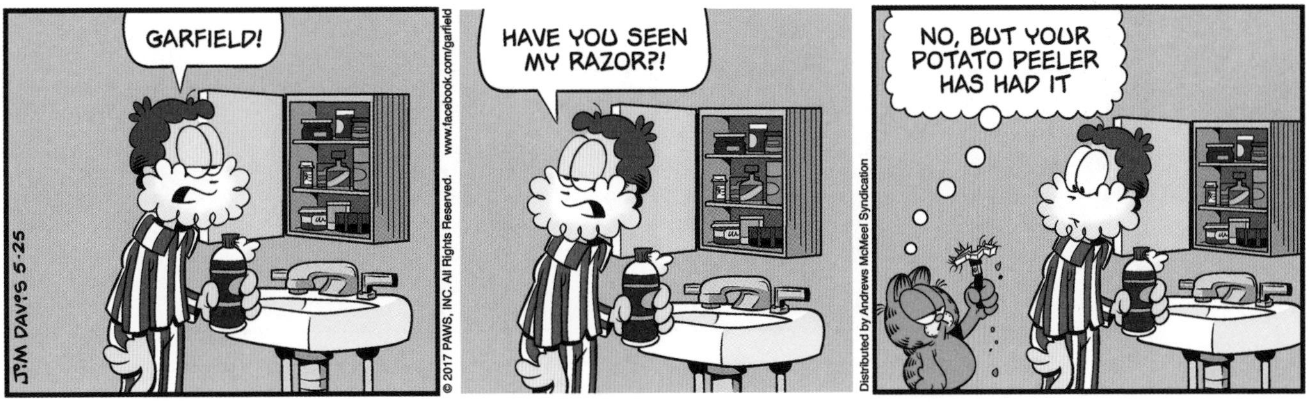
JIM DAVIS 5-25
GARFIELD!
© 2017 PAWS, INC. All Rights Reserved. www.facebook.com/garfield
HAVE YOU SEEN MY RAZOR?!
Distributed by Andrews McMeel Syndication
NO, BUT YOUR POTATO PEELER HAS HAD IT

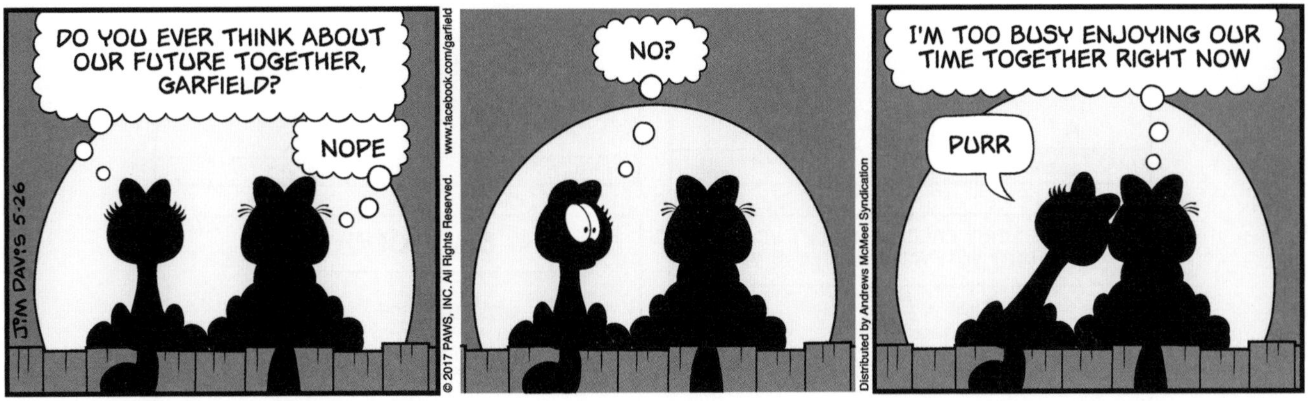
JIM DAVIS 5-26
DO YOU EVER THINK ABOUT OUR FUTURE TOGETHER, GARFIELD?
NOPE
© 2017 PAWS, INC. All Rights Reserved. www.facebook.com/garfield
NO?
Distributed by Andrews McMeel Syndication
I'M TOO BUSY ENJOYING OUR TIME TOGETHER RIGHT NOW
PURR

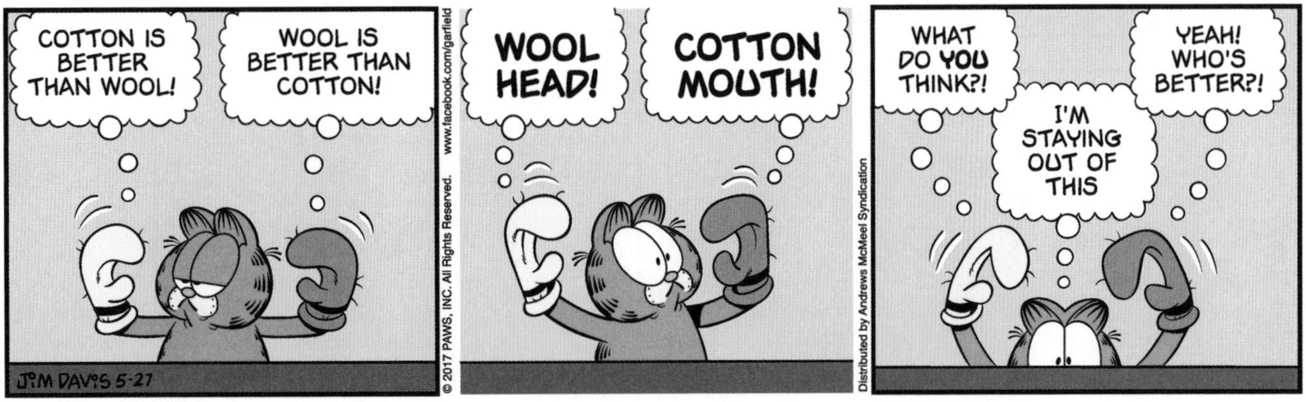
COTTON IS BETTER THAN WOOL!
WOOL IS BETTER THAN COTTON!
JIM DAVIS 5-27
© 2017 PAWS, INC. All Rights Reserved. www.facebook.com/garfield
WOOL HEAD!
COTTON MOUTH!
Distributed by Andrews McMeel Syndication
WHAT DO **YOU** THINK?!
YEAH! WHO'S BETTER?!
I'M STAYING OUT OF THIS

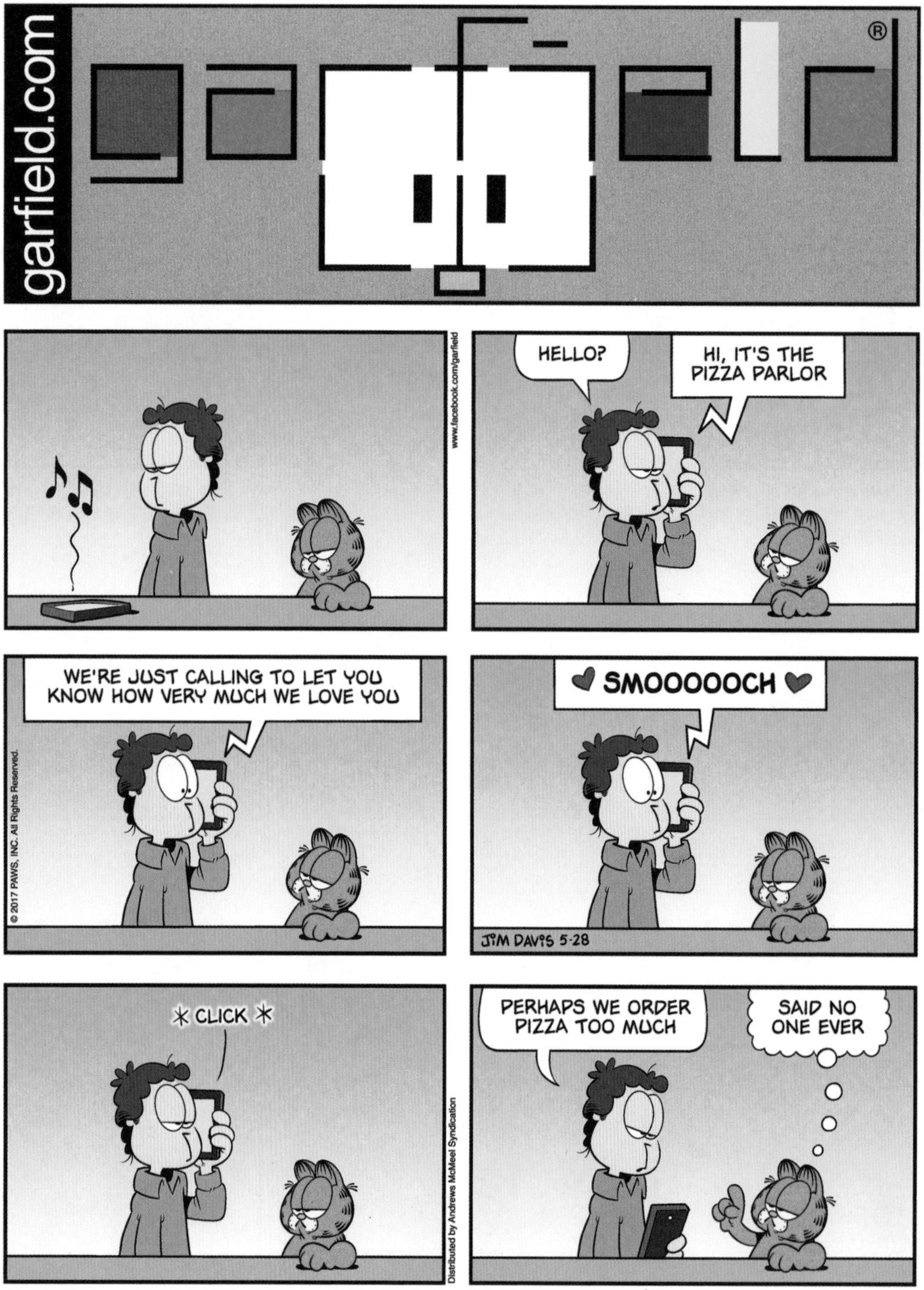
garfield.com
www.facebook.com/garfield
HELLO?
HI, IT'S THE PIZZA PARLOR
WE'RE JUST CALLING TO LET YOU KNOW HOW VERY MUCH WE LOVE YOU
© 2017 PAWS, INC. All Rights Reserved.
SMOOOOOCH
JIM DAVIS 5-28
* CLICK *
Distributed by Andrews McMeel Syndication
PERHAPS WE ORDER PIZZA TOO MUCH
SAID NO ONE EVER

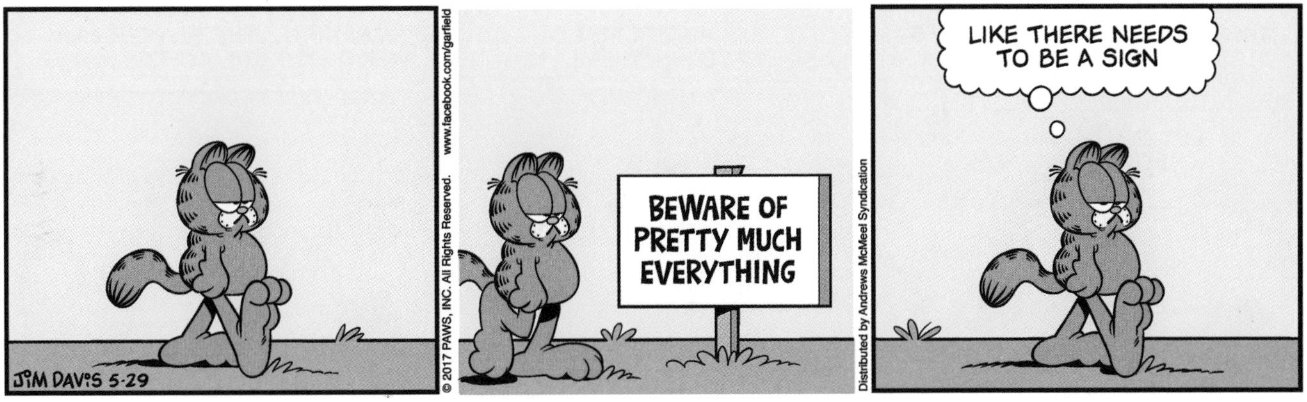
JIM DAVIS 5-29
© 2017 PAWS, INC. All Rights Reserved. www.facebook.com/garfield
BEWARE OF PRETTY MUCH EVERYTHING
Distributed by Andrews McMeel Syndication
LIKE THERE NEEDS TO BE A SIGN

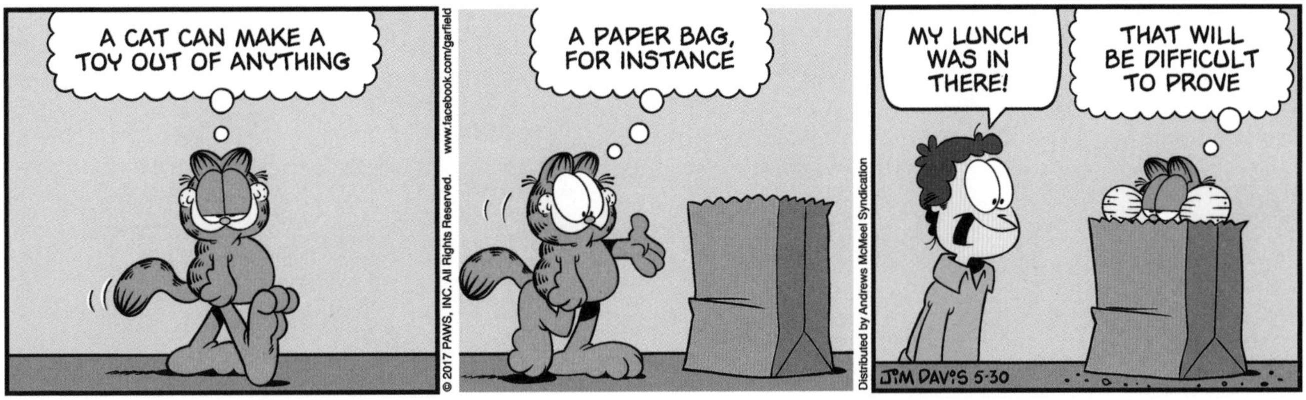
A CAT CAN MAKE A TOY OUT OF ANYTHING
© 2017 PAWS, INC. All Rights Reserved. www.facebook.com/garfield
A PAPER BAG, FOR INSTANCE
Distributed by Andrews McMeel Syndication
MY LUNCH WAS IN THERE!
THAT WILL BE DIFFICULT TO PROVE
JIM DAVIS 5-30

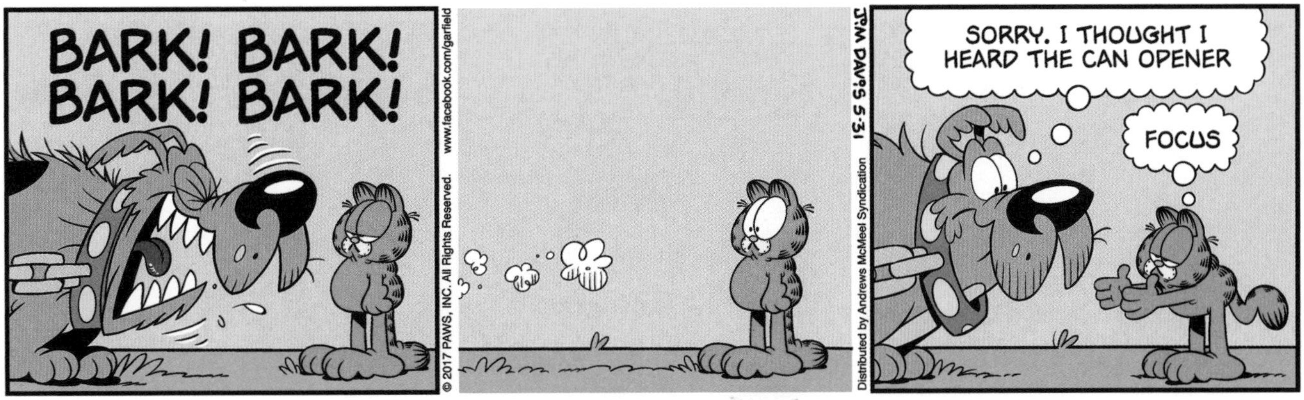
BARK! BARK! BARK! BARK!
© 2017 PAWS, INC. All Rights Reserved. www.facebook.com/garfield
JIM DAVIS 5-31
Distributed by Andrews McMeel Syndication
SORRY. I THOUGHT I HEARD THE CAN OPENER
FOCUS

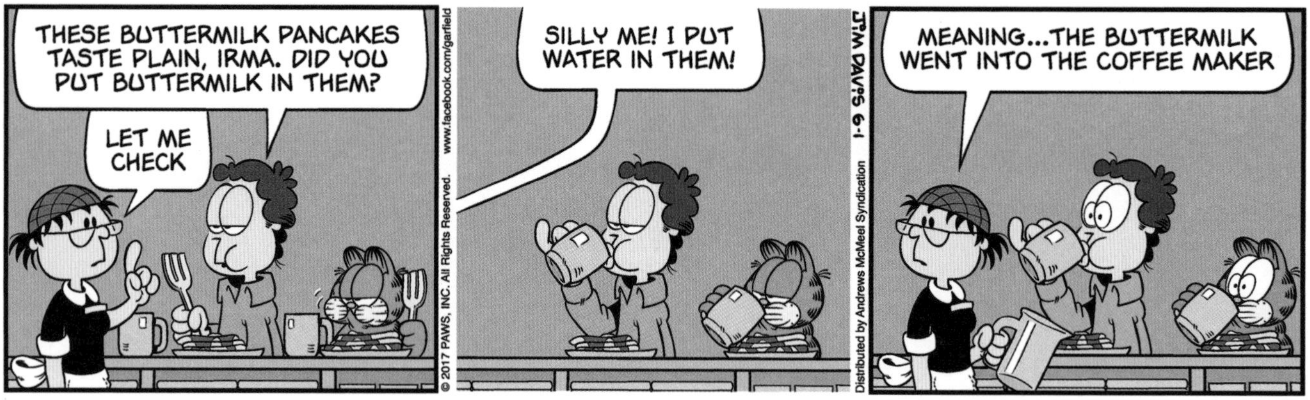
THESE BUTTERMILK PANCAKES TASTE PLAIN, IRMA. DID YOU PUT BUTTERMILK IN THEM?
LET ME CHECK
© 2017 PAWS, INC. All Rights Reserved. www.facebook.com/garfield
SILLY ME! I PUT WATER IN THEM!
JIM DAVIS 6-1
Distributed by Andrews McMeel Syndication
MEANING...THE BUTTERMILK WENT INTO THE COFFEE MAKER

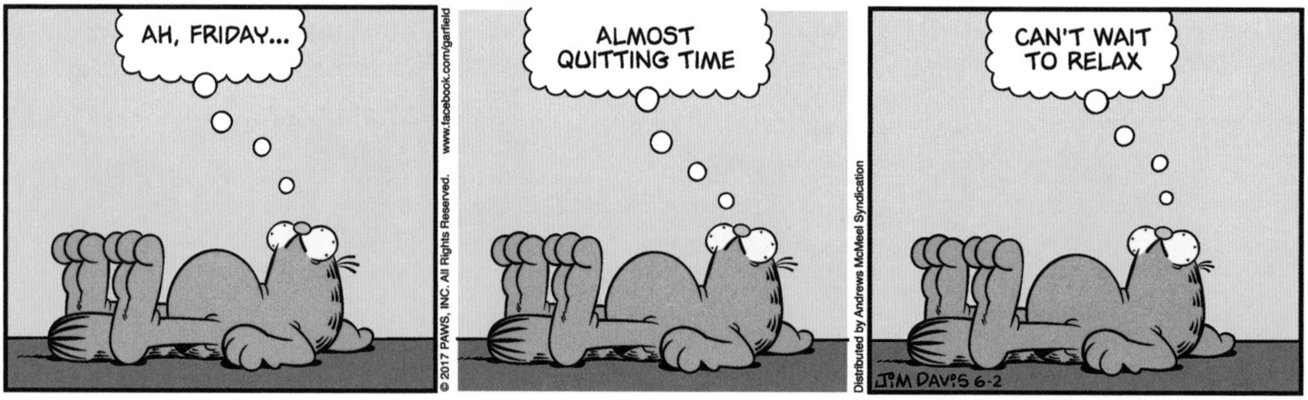
AH, FRIDAY...
© 2017 PAWS, INC. All Rights Reserved. www.facebook.com/garfield
ALMOST QUITTING TIME
Distributed by Andrews McMeel Syndication
CAN'T WAIT TO RELAX
JIM DAVIS 6-2

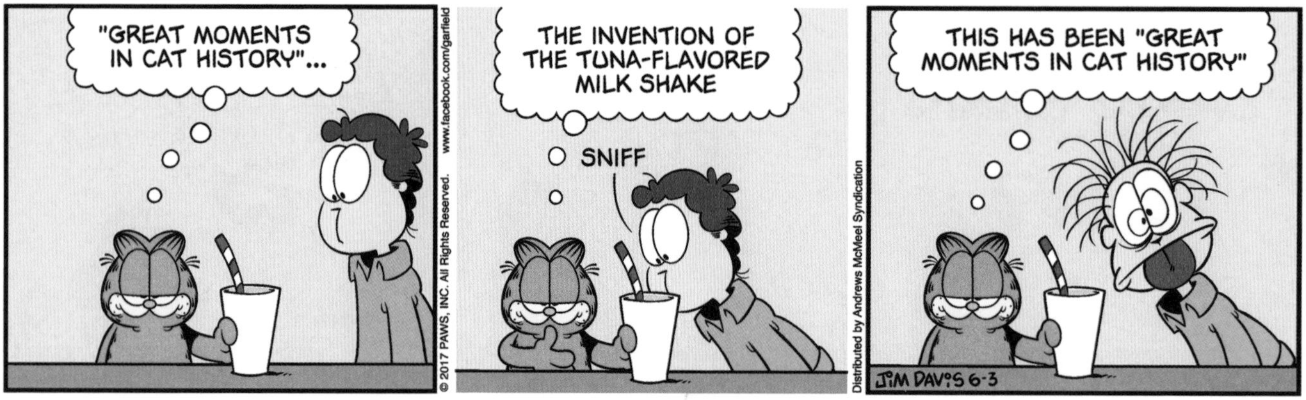
"GREAT MOMENTS IN CAT HISTORY"...
© 2017 PAWS, INC. All Rights Reserved. www.facebook.com/garfield
THE INVENTION OF THE TUNA-FLAVORED MILK SHAKE
SNIFF
Distributed by Andrews McMeel Syndication
THIS HAS BEEN "GREAT MOMENTS IN CAT HISTORY"
JIM DAVIS 6-3

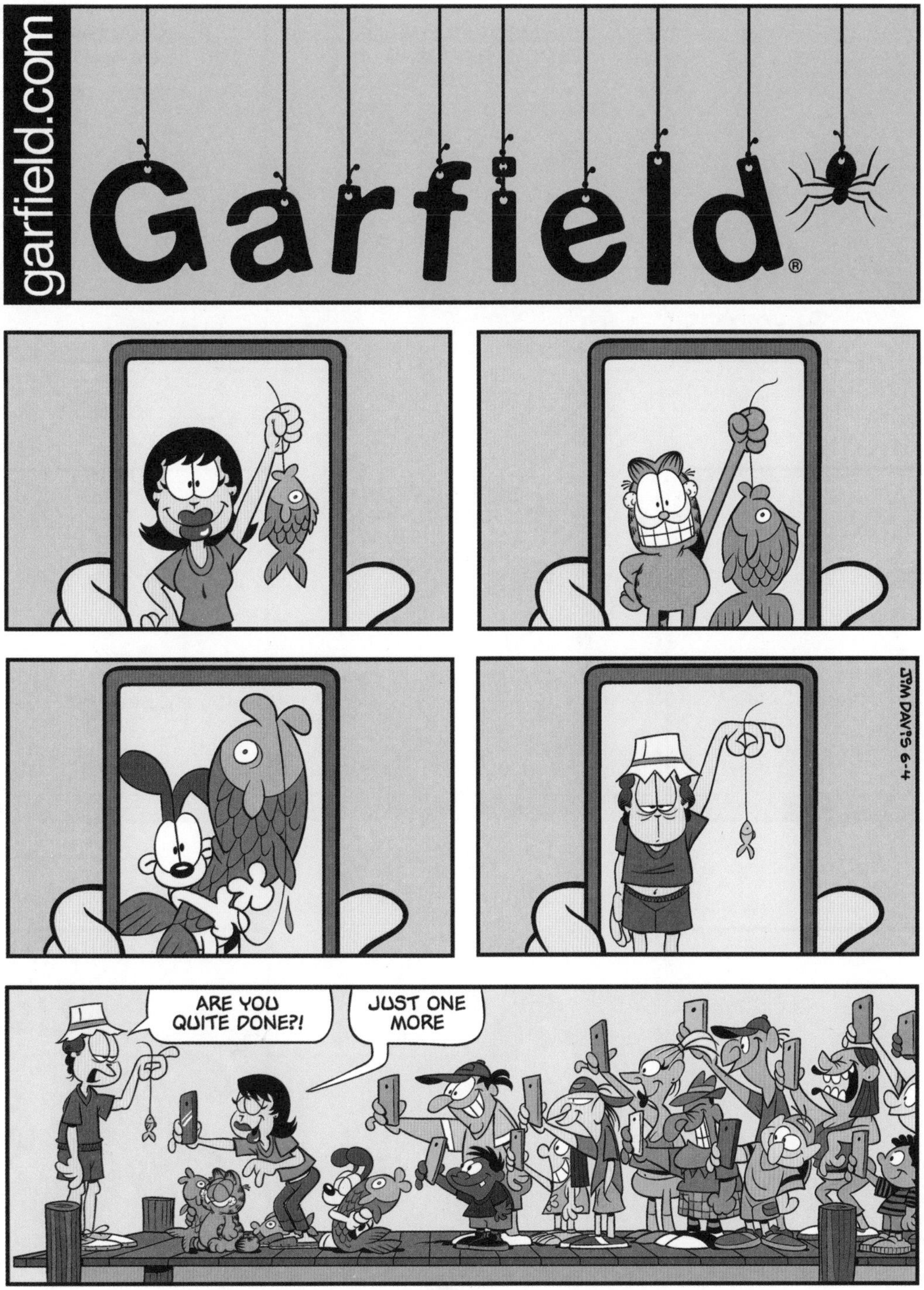
garfield.com
Garfield®
JIM DAVIS 6-4
ARE YOU QUITE DONE?!
JUST ONE MORE

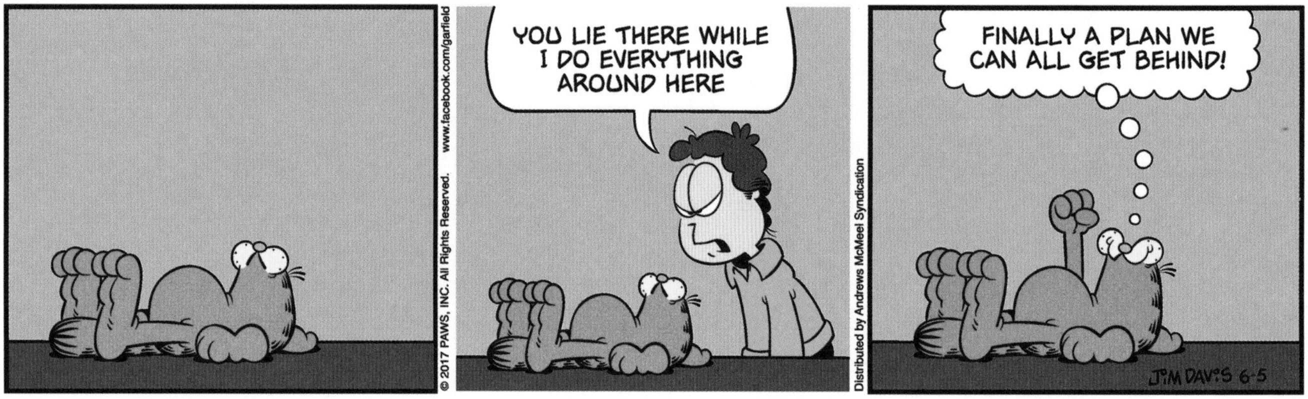
© 2017 PAWS, INC. All Rights Reserved. www.facebook.com/garfield
YOU LIE THERE WHILE I DO EVERYTHING AROUND HERE
Distributed by Andrews McMeel Syndication
FINALLY A PLAN WE CAN ALL GET BEHIND!
JIM DAVIS 6-5

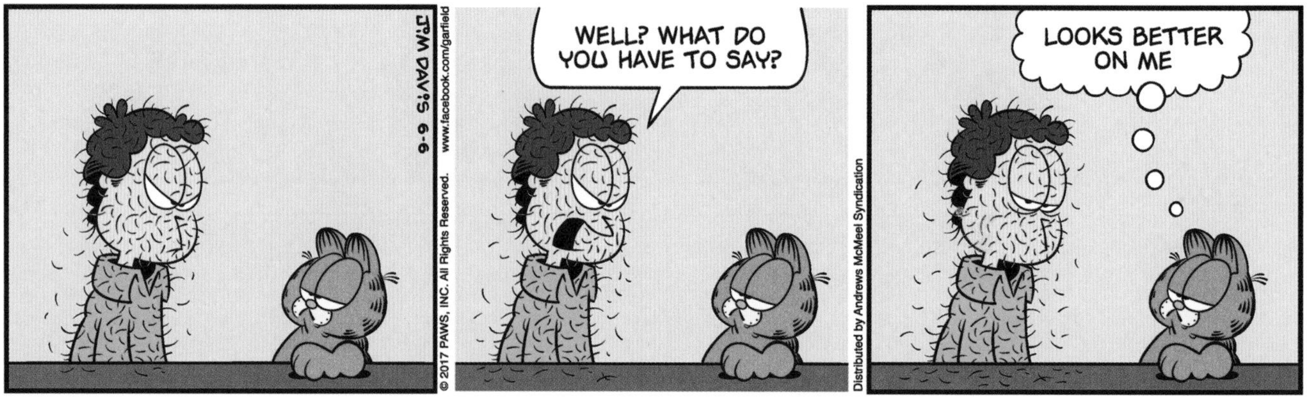
JIM DAVIS 6-6
© 2017 PAWS, INC. All Rights Reserved. www.facebook.com/garfield
WELL? WHAT DO YOU HAVE TO SAY?
Distributed by Andrews McMeel Syndication
LOOKS BETTER ON ME

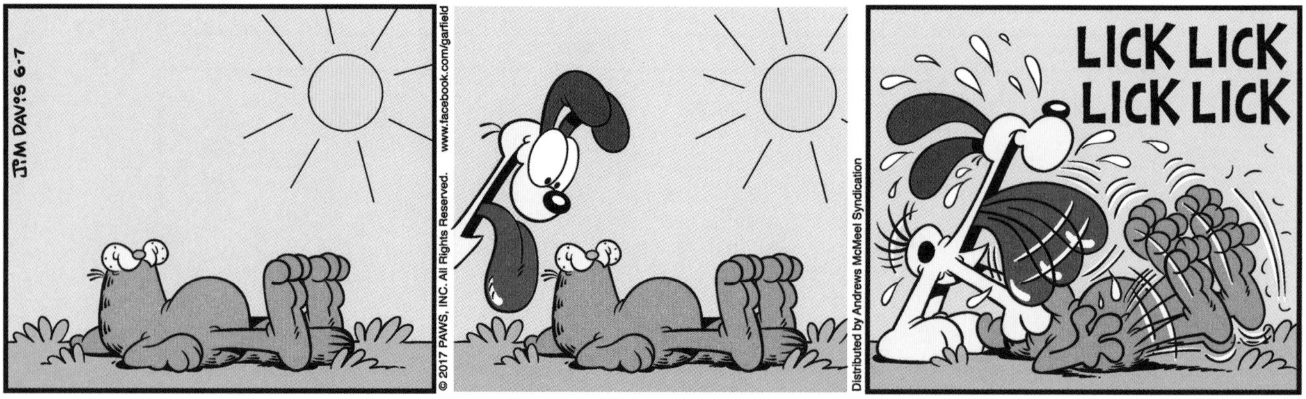
JIM DAVIS 6-7
© 2017 PAWS, INC. All Rights Reserved. www.facebook.com/garfield
Distributed by Andrews McMeel Syndication
LICK LICK
LICK LICK

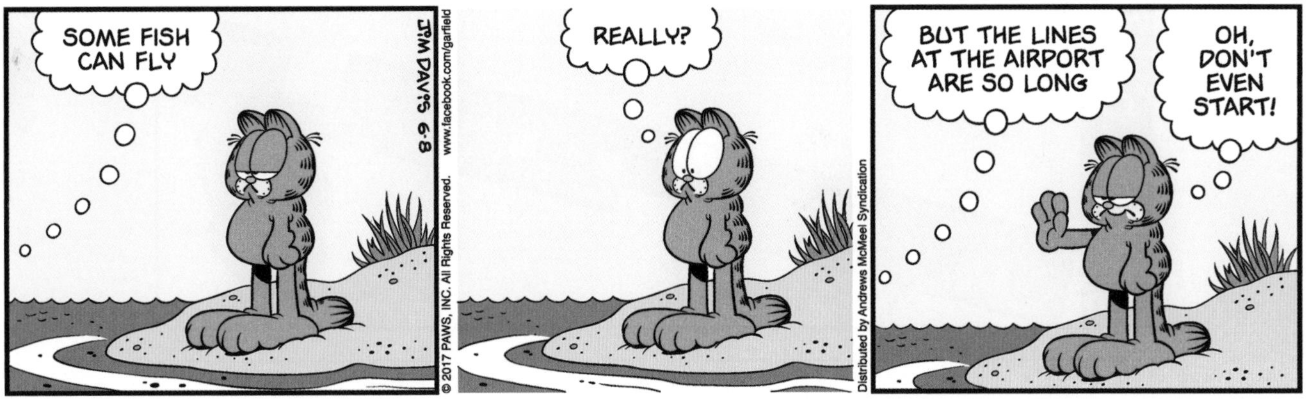
SOME FISH CAN FLY
JIM DAVIS 6-8
© 2017 PAWS, INC. All Rights Reserved. www.facebook.com/garfield
REALLY?
Distributed by Andrews McMeel Syndication
BUT THE LINES AT THE AIRPORT ARE SO LONG
OH, DON'T EVEN START!

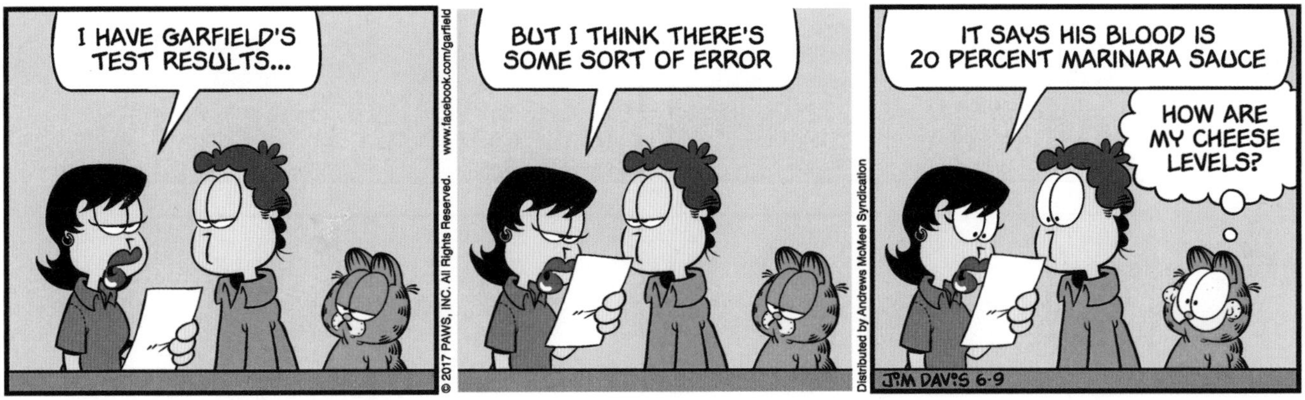
I HAVE GARFIELD'S TEST RESULTS...
© 2017 PAWS, INC. All Rights Reserved. www.facebook.com/garfield
BUT I THINK THERE'S SOME SORT OF ERROR
Distributed by Andrews McMeel Syndication
IT SAYS HIS BLOOD IS 20 PERCENT MARINARA SAUCE
HOW ARE MY CHEESE LEVELS?
JIM DAVIS 6-9

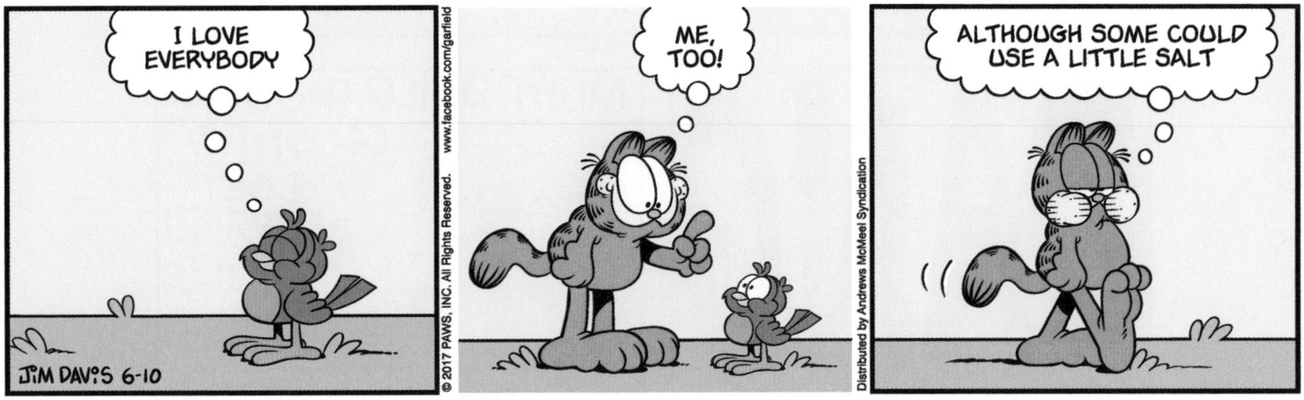
I LOVE EVERYBODY
JIM DAVIS 6-10
© 2017 PAWS, INC. All Rights Reserved. www.facebook.com/garfield
ME, TOO!
Distributed by Andrews McMeel Syndication
ALTHOUGH SOME COULD USE A LITTLE SALT

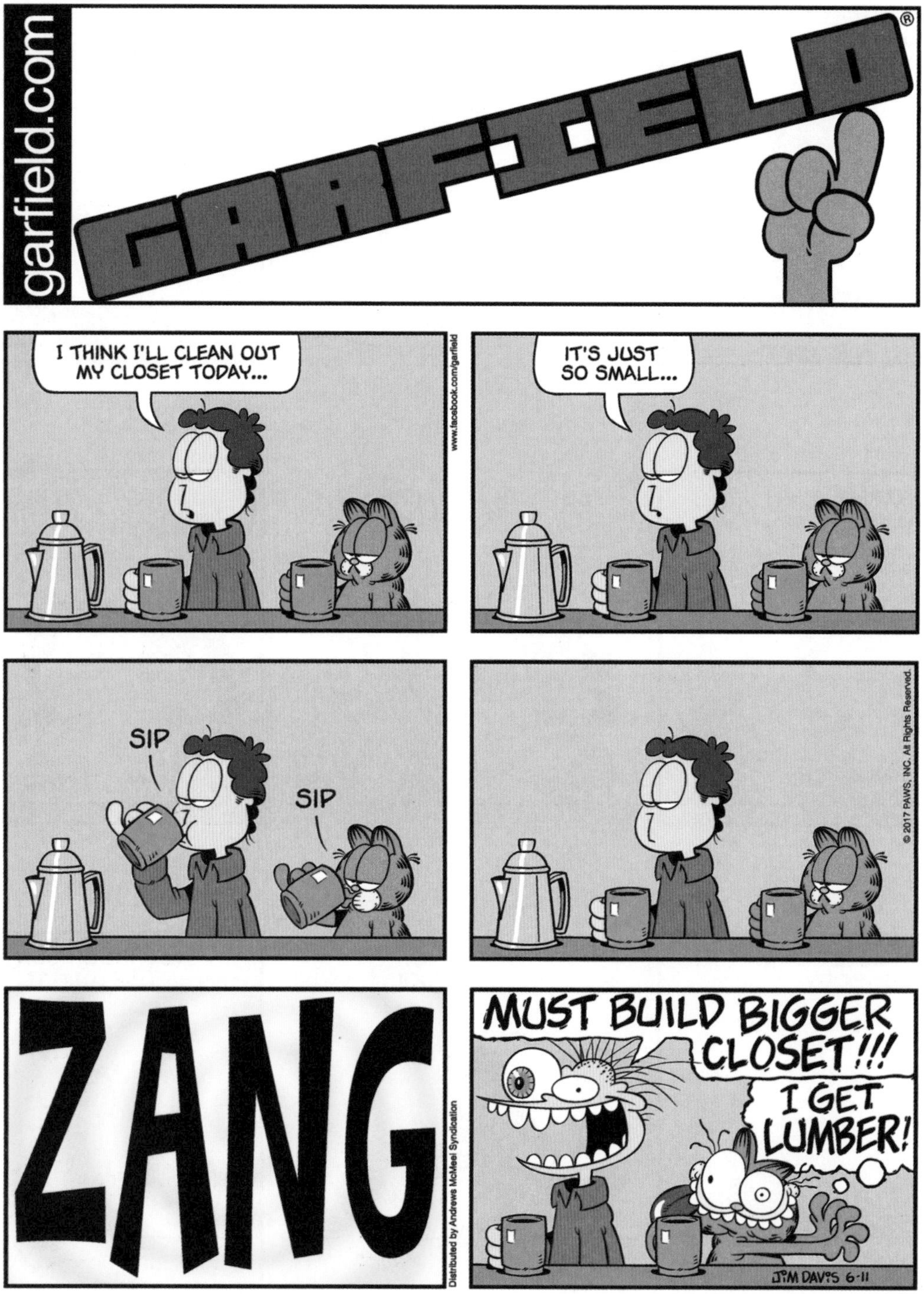
garfield.com
GARFIELD®
I THINK I'LL CLEAN OUT MY CLOSET TODAY...
www.facebook.com/garfield
IT'S JUST SO SMALL...
SIP
SIP
© 2017 PAWS, INC. All Rights Reserved.
ZANG
Distributed by Andrews McMeel Syndication
MUST BUILD BIGGER CLOSET!!!
I GET LUMBER!
JIM DAVIS 6-11

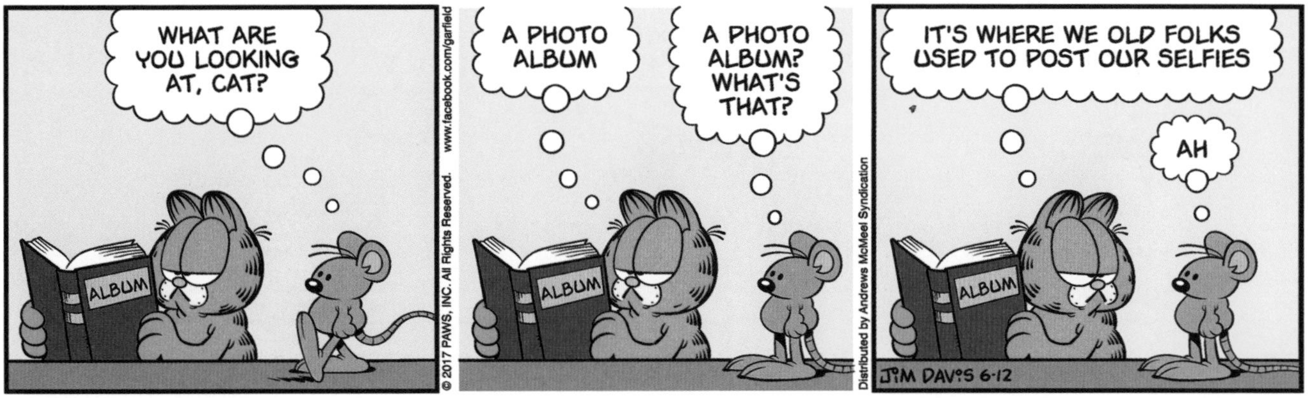
WHAT ARE YOU LOOKING AT, CAT?
A PHOTO ALBUM
A PHOTO ALBUM? WHAT'S THAT?
IT'S WHERE WE OLD FOLKS USED TO POST OUR SELFIES
AH
ALBUM
© 2017 PAWS, INC. All Rights Reserved. www.facebook.com/garfield
Distributed by Andrews McMeel Syndication
JIM DAVIS 6-12

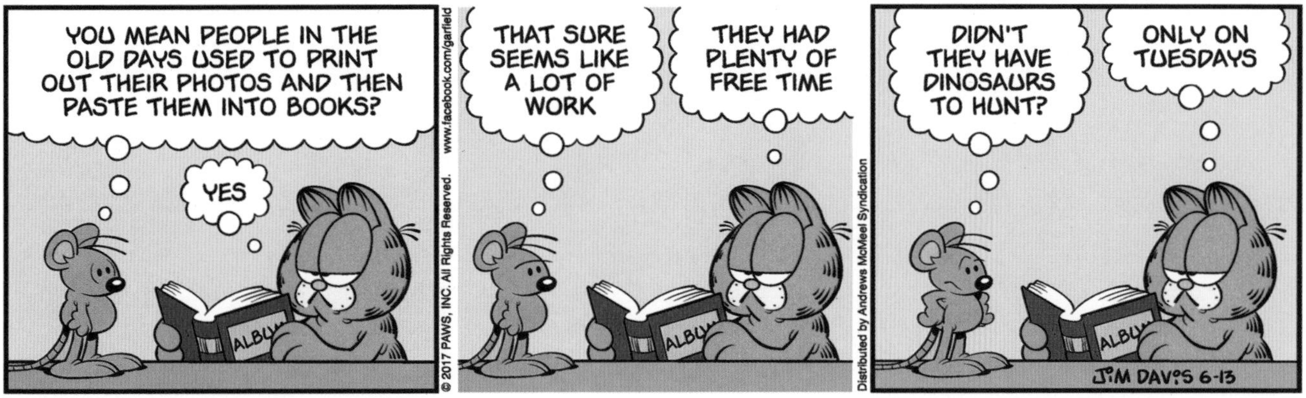
YOU MEAN PEOPLE IN THE OLD DAYS USED TO PRINT OUT THEIR PHOTOS AND THEN PASTE THEM INTO BOOKS?
YES
THAT SURE SEEMS LIKE A LOT OF WORK
THEY HAD PLENTY OF FREE TIME
DIDN'T THEY HAVE DINOSAURS TO HUNT?
ONLY ON TUESDAYS
© 2017 PAWS, INC. All Rights Reserved. www.facebook.com/garfield
Distributed by Andrews McMeel Syndication
JIM DAVIS 6-13

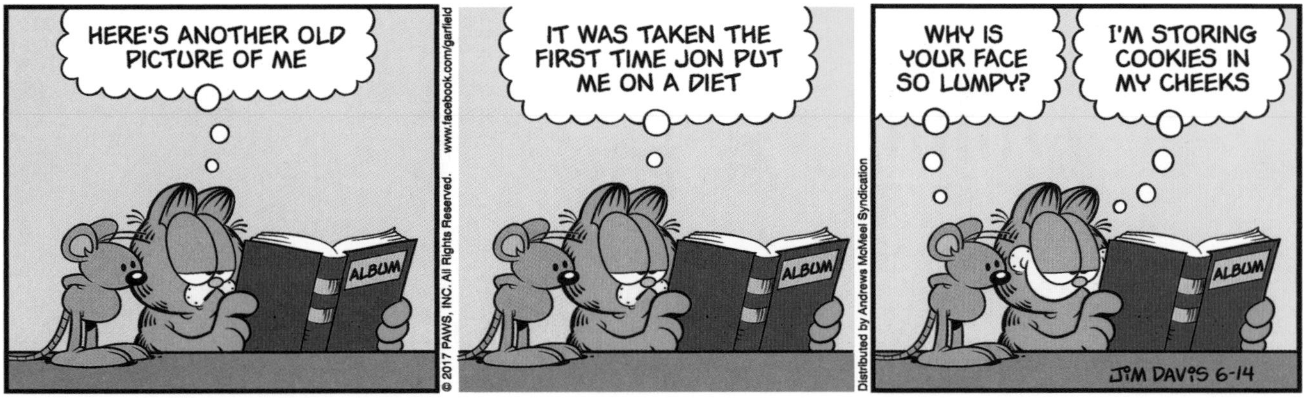
HERE'S ANOTHER OLD PICTURE OF ME
IT WAS TAKEN THE FIRST TIME JON PUT ME ON A DIET
WHY IS YOUR FACE SO LUMPY?
I'M STORING COOKIES IN MY CHEEKS
ALBUM
© 2017 PAWS, INC. All Rights Reserved. www.facebook.com/garfield
Distributed by Andrews McMeel Syndication
JIM DAVIS 6-14

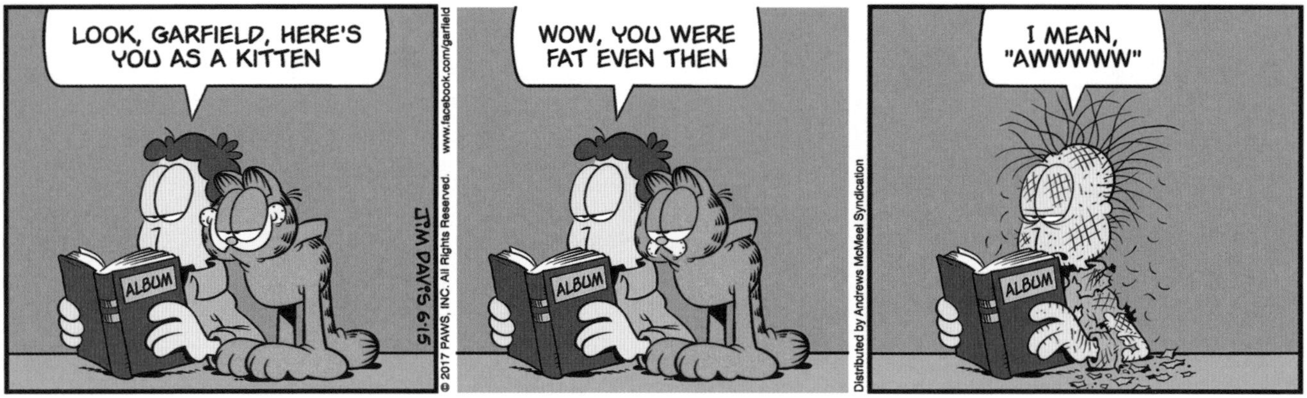
LOOK, GARFIELD, HERE'S YOU AS A KITTEN
ALBUM
JIM DAVIS 6-15
© 2017 PAWS, INC. All Rights Reserved. www.facebook.com/garfield
WOW, YOU WERE FAT EVEN THEN
ALBUM
Distributed by Andrews McMeel Syndication
I MEAN, "AWWWWW"
ALBUM

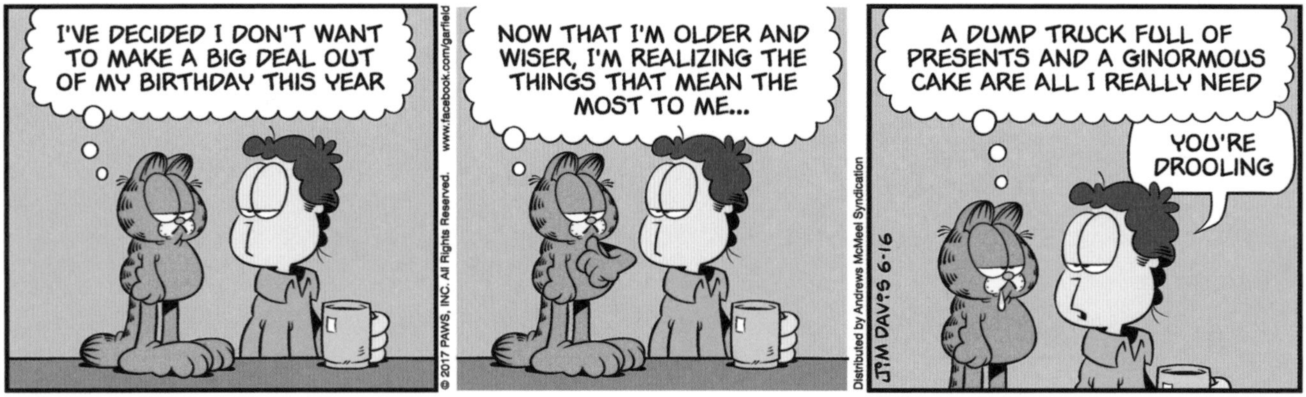
I'VE DECIDED I DON'T WANT TO MAKE A BIG DEAL OUT OF MY BIRTHDAY THIS YEAR
© 2017 PAWS, INC. All Rights Reserved. www.facebook.com/garfield
NOW THAT I'M OLDER AND WISER, I'M REALIZING THE THINGS THAT MEAN THE MOST TO ME...
Distributed by Andrews McMeel Syndication
JIM DAVIS 6-16
A DUMP TRUCK FULL OF PRESENTS AND A GINORMOUS CAKE ARE ALL I REALLY NEED
YOU'RE DROOLING

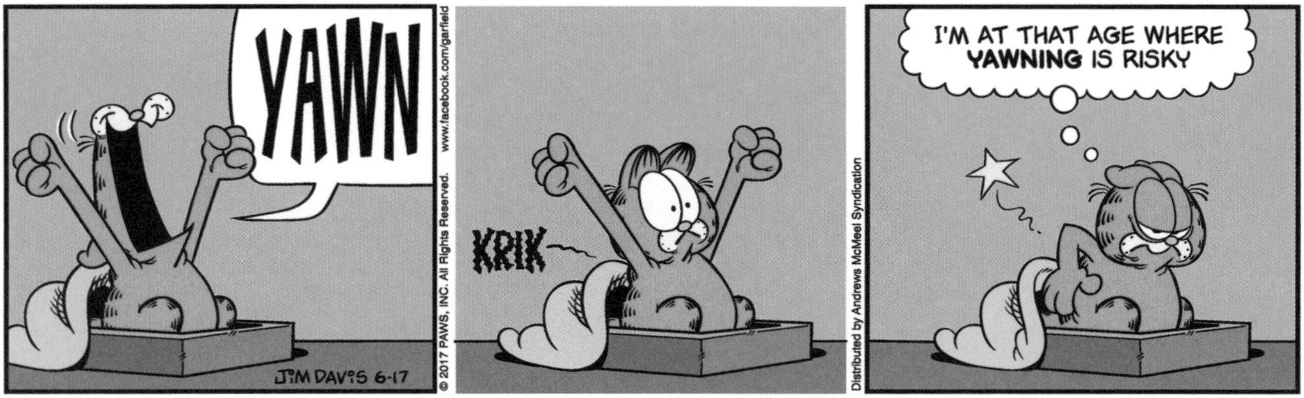
YAWN
JIM DAVIS 6-17
© 2017 PAWS, INC. All Rights Reserved. www.facebook.com/garfield
KRIK
Distributed by Andrews McMeel Syndication
I'M AT THAT AGE WHERE YAWNING IS RISKY

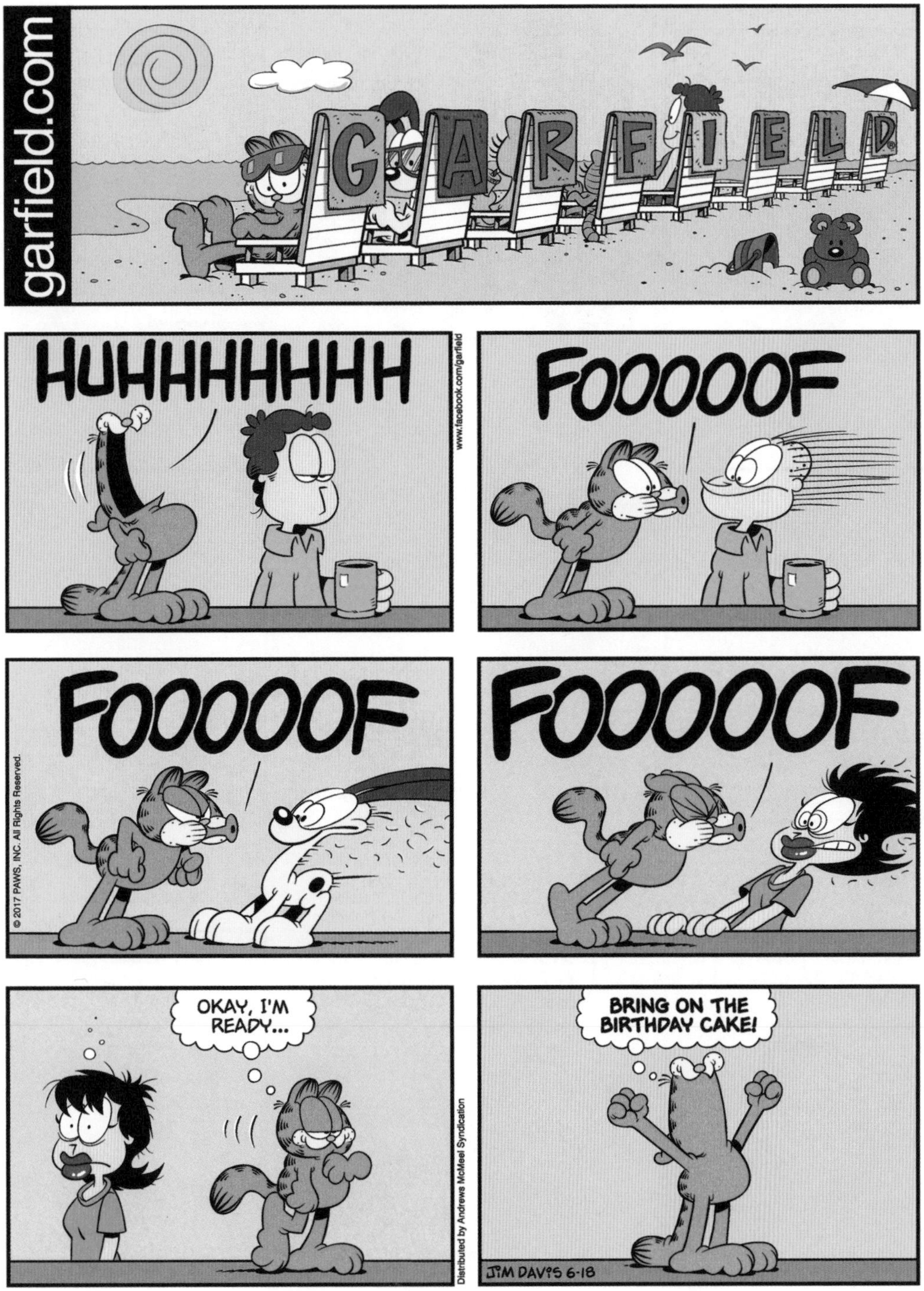
garfield.com
GARFIELD
www.facebook.com/garfield
HUHHHHHHH
FOOOOOF
© 2017 PAWS, INC. All Rights Reserved.
FOOOOOF
FOOOOOF
OKAY, I'M READY...
Distributed by Andrews McMeel Syndication
BRING ON THE BIRTHDAY CAKE!
JIM DAVIS 6-18

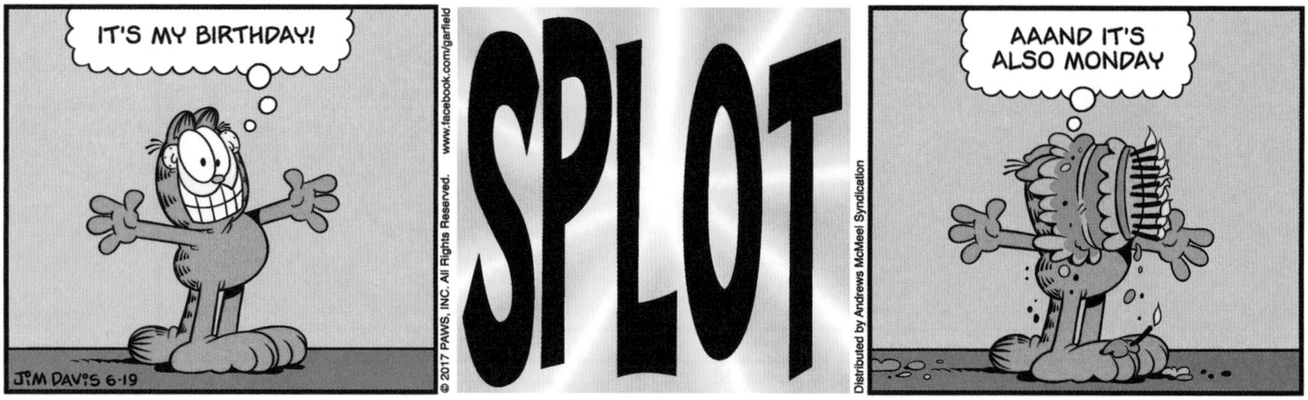
IT'S MY BIRTHDAY!
JIM DAVIS 6-19
© 2017 PAWS, INC. All Rights Reserved. www.facebook.com/garfield
SPLOT
Distributed by Andrews McMeel Syndication
AAAND IT'S ALSO MONDAY

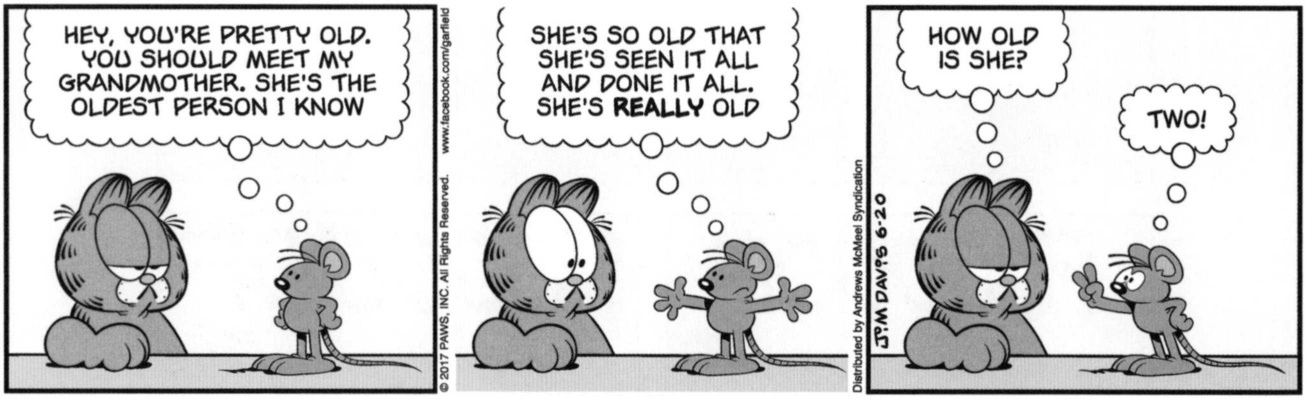
HEY, YOU'RE PRETTY OLD. YOU SHOULD MEET MY GRANDMOTHER. SHE'S THE OLDEST PERSON I KNOW
© 2017 PAWS, INC. All Rights Reserved. www.facebook.com/garfield
SHE'S SO OLD THAT SHE'S SEEN IT ALL AND DONE IT ALL. SHE'S **REALLY** OLD
Distributed by Andrews McMeel Syndication
JIM DAVIS 6-20
HOW OLD IS SHE?
TWO!

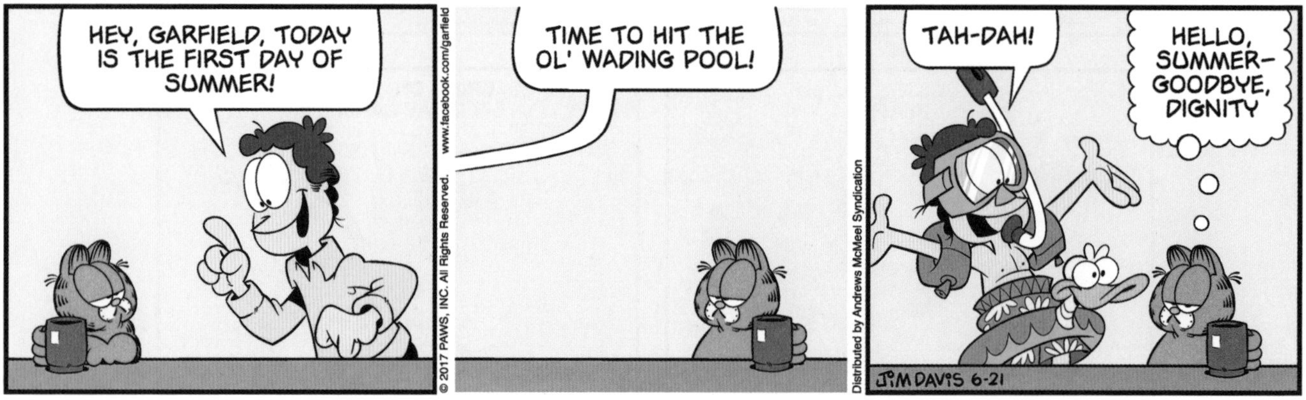
HEY, GARFIELD, TODAY IS THE FIRST DAY OF SUMMER!
© 2017 PAWS, INC. All Rights Reserved. www.facebook.com/garfield
TIME TO HIT THE OL' WADING POOL!
Distributed by Andrews McMeel Syndication
TAH-DAH!
HELLO, SUMMER– GOODBYE, DIGNITY
JIM DAVIS 6-21

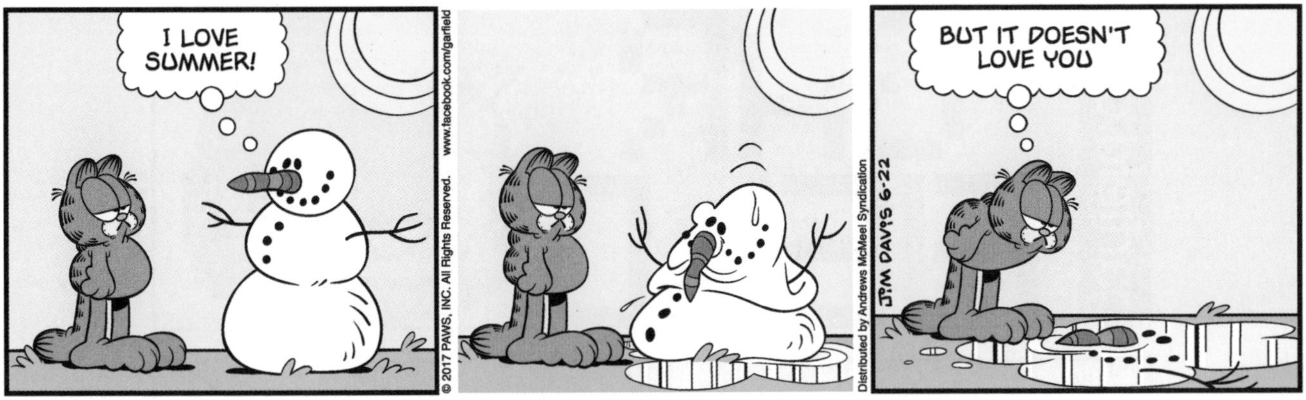
I LOVE SUMMER!
© 2017 PAWS, INC. All Rights Reserved. www.facebook.com/garfield
Distributed by Andrews McMeel Syndication
JIM DAVIS 6-22
BUT IT DOESN'T LOVE YOU

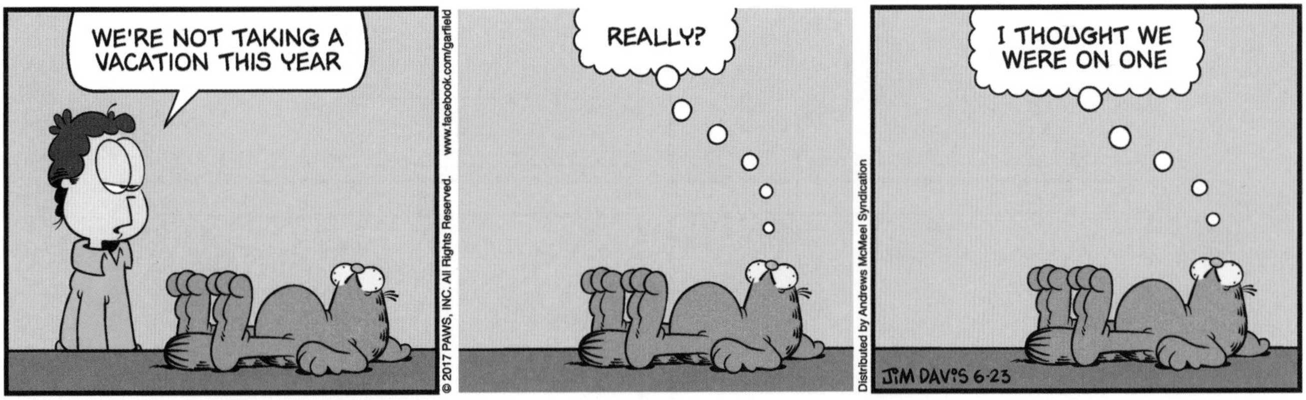
WE'RE NOT TAKING A VACATION THIS YEAR
© 2017 PAWS, INC. All Rights Reserved. www.facebook.com/garfield
REALLY?
Distributed by Andrews McMeel Syndication
I THOUGHT WE WERE ON ONE
JIM DAVIS 6-23

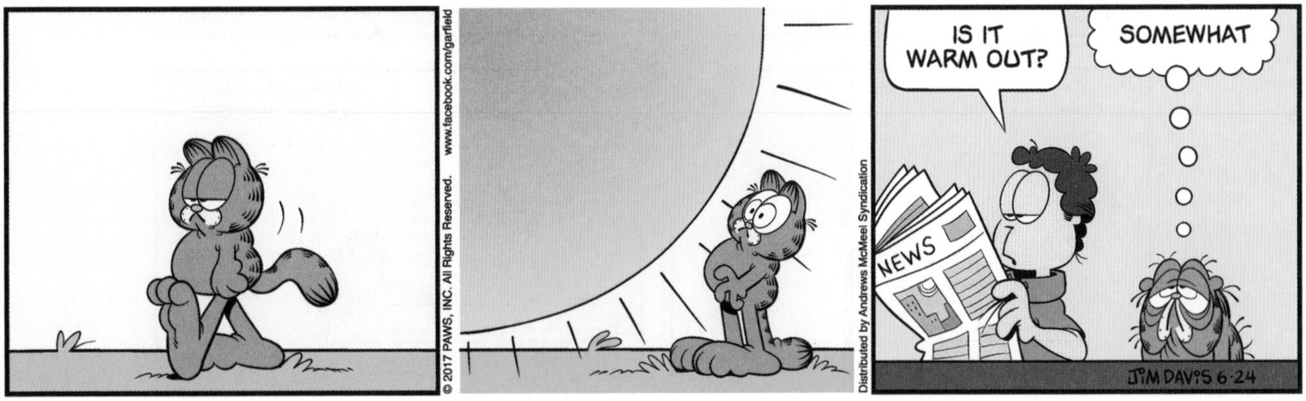
© 2017 PAWS, INC. All Rights Reserved. www.facebook.com/garfield
Distributed by Andrews McMeel Syndication
IS IT WARM OUT?
SOMEWHAT
NEWS
JIM DAVIS 6-24

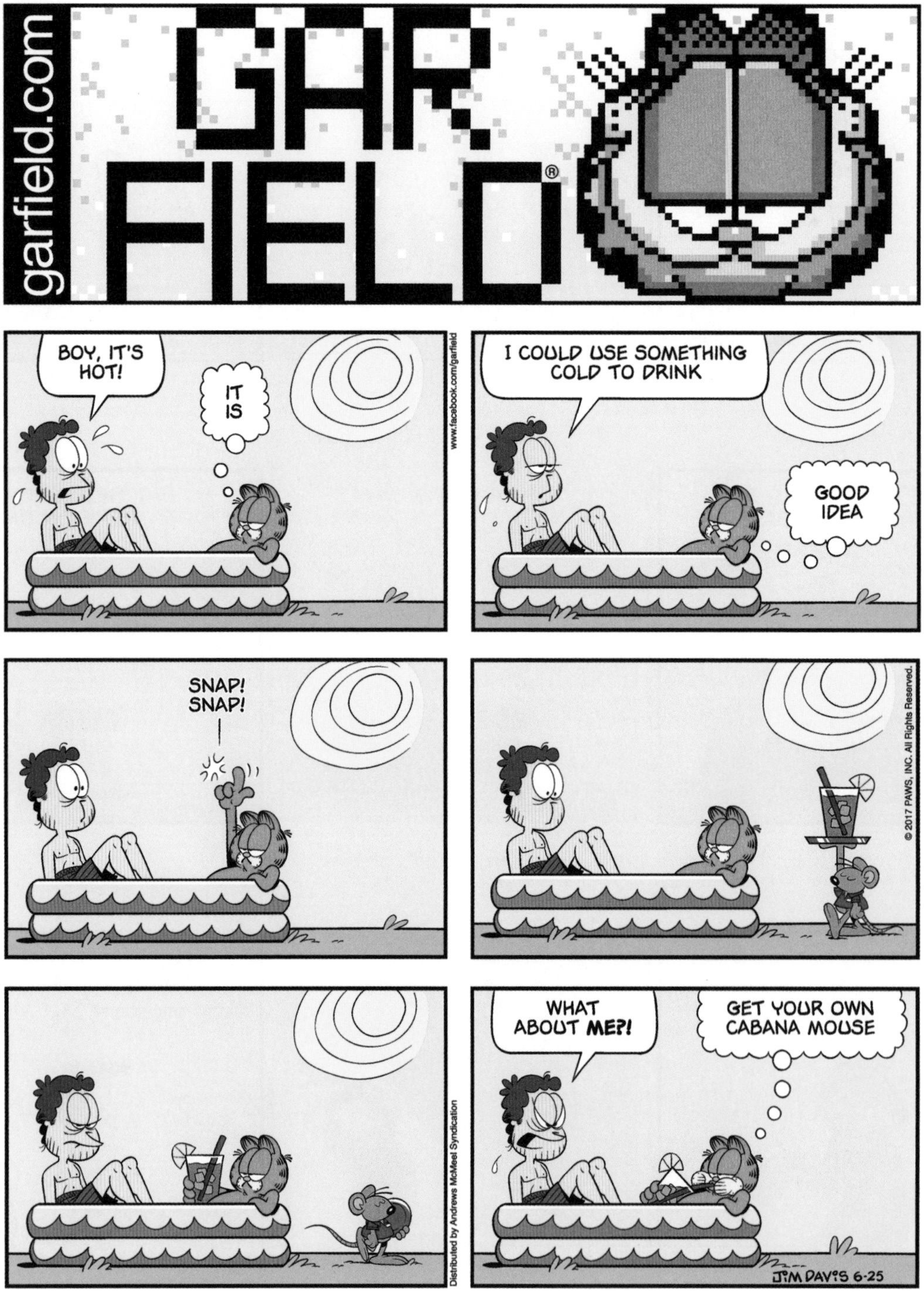
garfield.com
GARFIELD®
www.facebook.com/garfield
BOY, IT'S HOT!
IT IS
I COULD USE SOMETHING COLD TO DRINK
GOOD IDEA
SNAP! SNAP!
© 2017 PAWS, INC. All Rights Reserved.
Distributed by Andrews McMeel Syndication
WHAT ABOUT ME?!
GET YOUR OWN CABANA MOUSE
JIM DAVIS 6-25

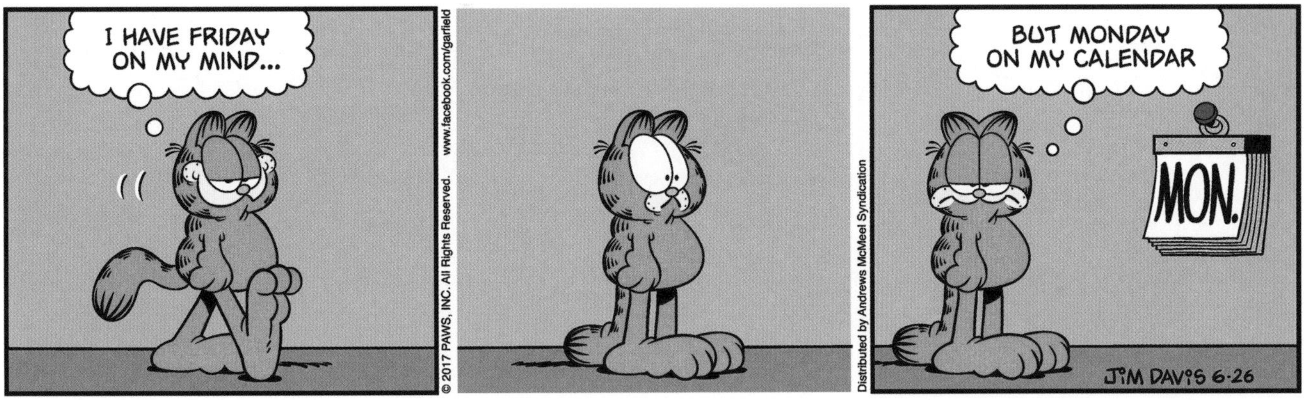
I HAVE FRIDAY ON MY MIND...
© 2017 PAWS, INC. All Rights Reserved. www.facebook.com/garfield
Distributed by Andrews McMeel Syndication
BUT MONDAY ON MY CALENDAR
MON.
JIM DAVIS 6-26

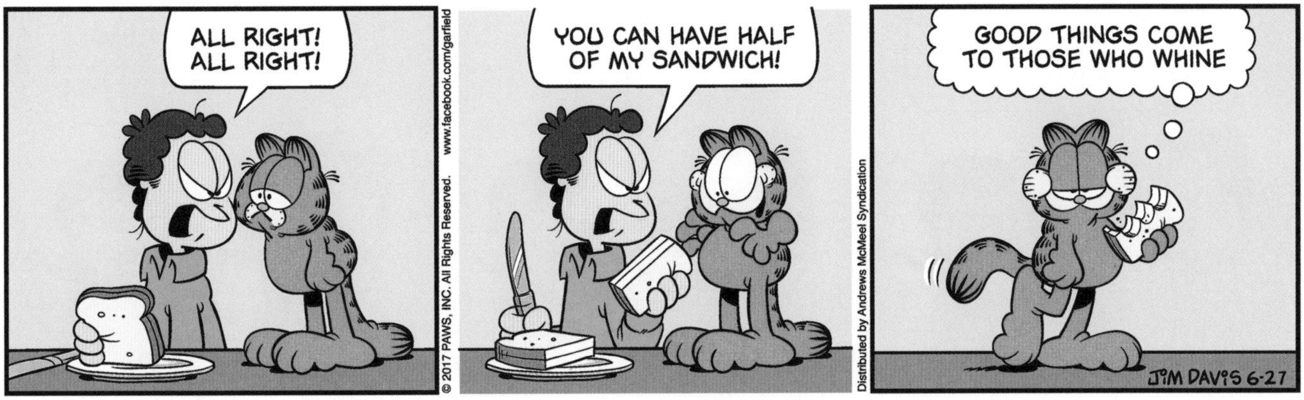
ALL RIGHT! ALL RIGHT!
© 2017 PAWS, INC. All Rights Reserved. www.facebook.com/garfield
YOU CAN HAVE HALF OF MY SANDWICH!
Distributed by Andrews McMeel Syndication
GOOD THINGS COME TO THOSE WHO WHINE
JIM DAVIS 6-27

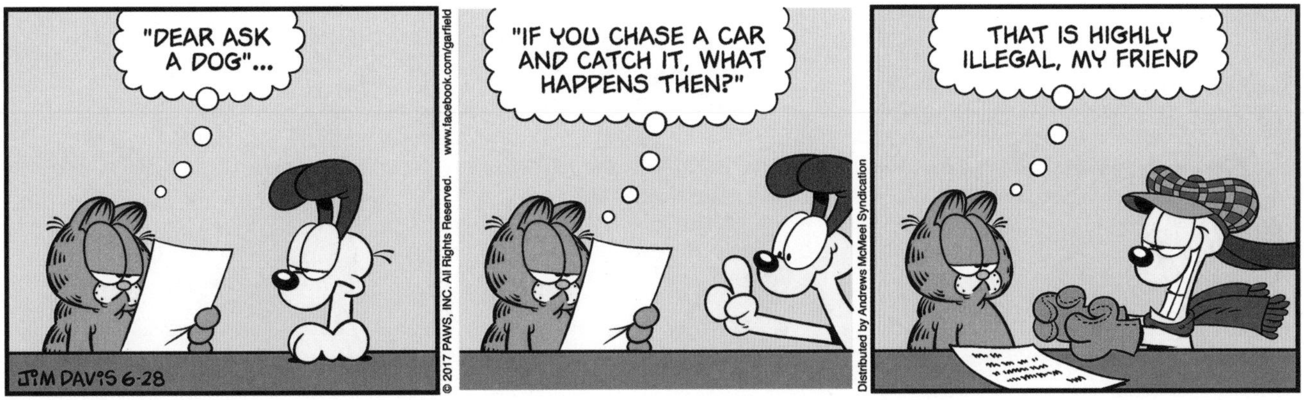
"DEAR ASK A DOG"...
JIM DAVIS 6-28
© 2017 PAWS, INC. All Rights Reserved. www.facebook.com/garfield
"IF YOU CHASE A CAR AND CATCH IT, WHAT HAPPENS THEN?"
Distributed by Andrews McMeel Syndication
THAT IS HIGHLY ILLEGAL, MY FRIEND

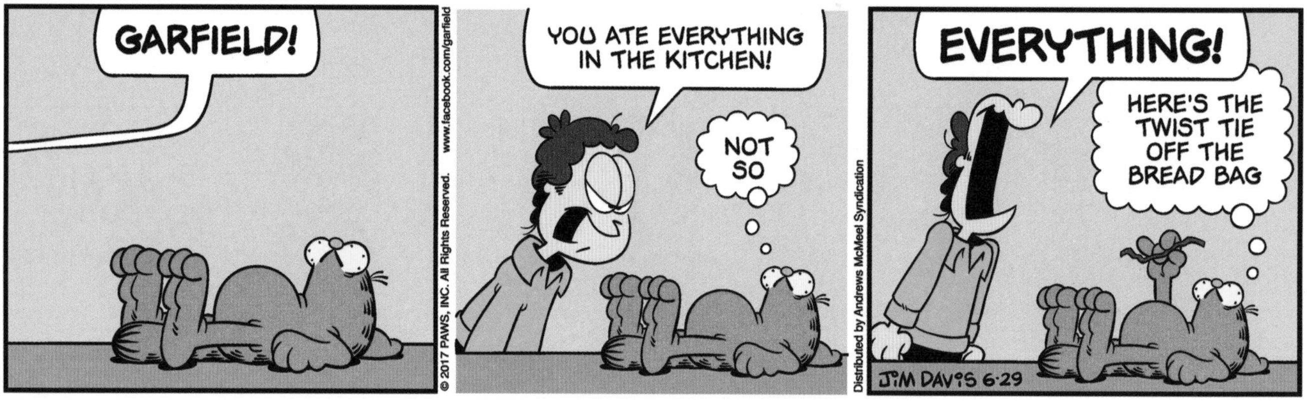
GARFIELD!
YOU ATE EVERYTHING IN THE KITCHEN!
NOT SO
EVERYTHING!
HERE'S THE TWIST TIE OFF THE BREAD BAG
JIM DAVIS 6-29
© 2017 PAWS, INC. All Rights Reserved. www.facebook.com/garfield
Distributed by Andrews McMeel Syndication

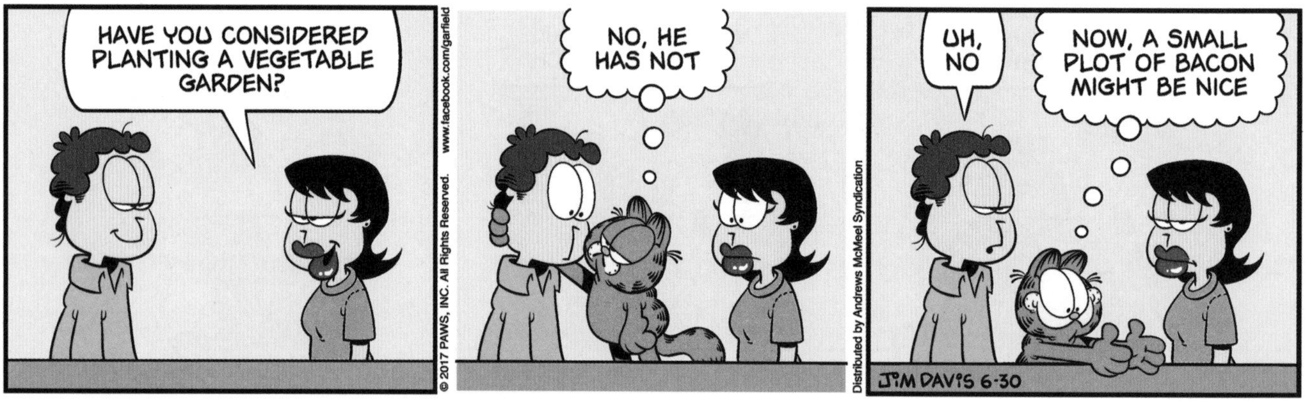
HAVE YOU CONSIDERED PLANTING A VEGETABLE GARDEN?
NO, HE HAS NOT
UH, NO
NOW, A SMALL PLOT OF BACON MIGHT BE NICE
JIM DAVIS 6-30
© 2017 PAWS, INC. All Rights Reserved. www.facebook.com/garfield
Distributed by Andrews McMeel Syndication

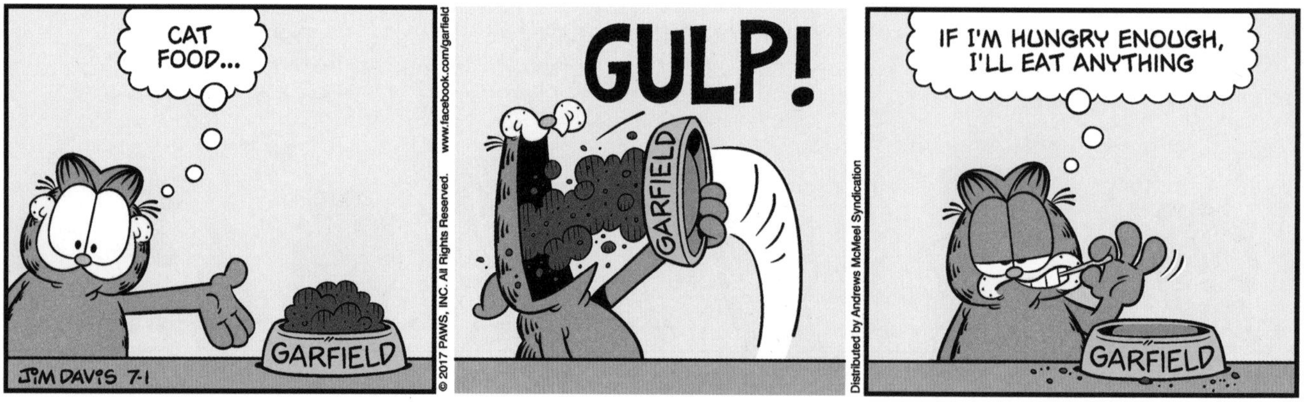
CAT FOOD...
GARFIELD
JIM DAVIS 7-1
GULP!
GARFIELD
IF I'M HUNGRY ENOUGH, I'LL EAT ANYTHING
GARFIELD
© 2017 PAWS, INC. All Rights Reserved. www.facebook.com/garfield
Distributed by Andrews McMeel Syndication

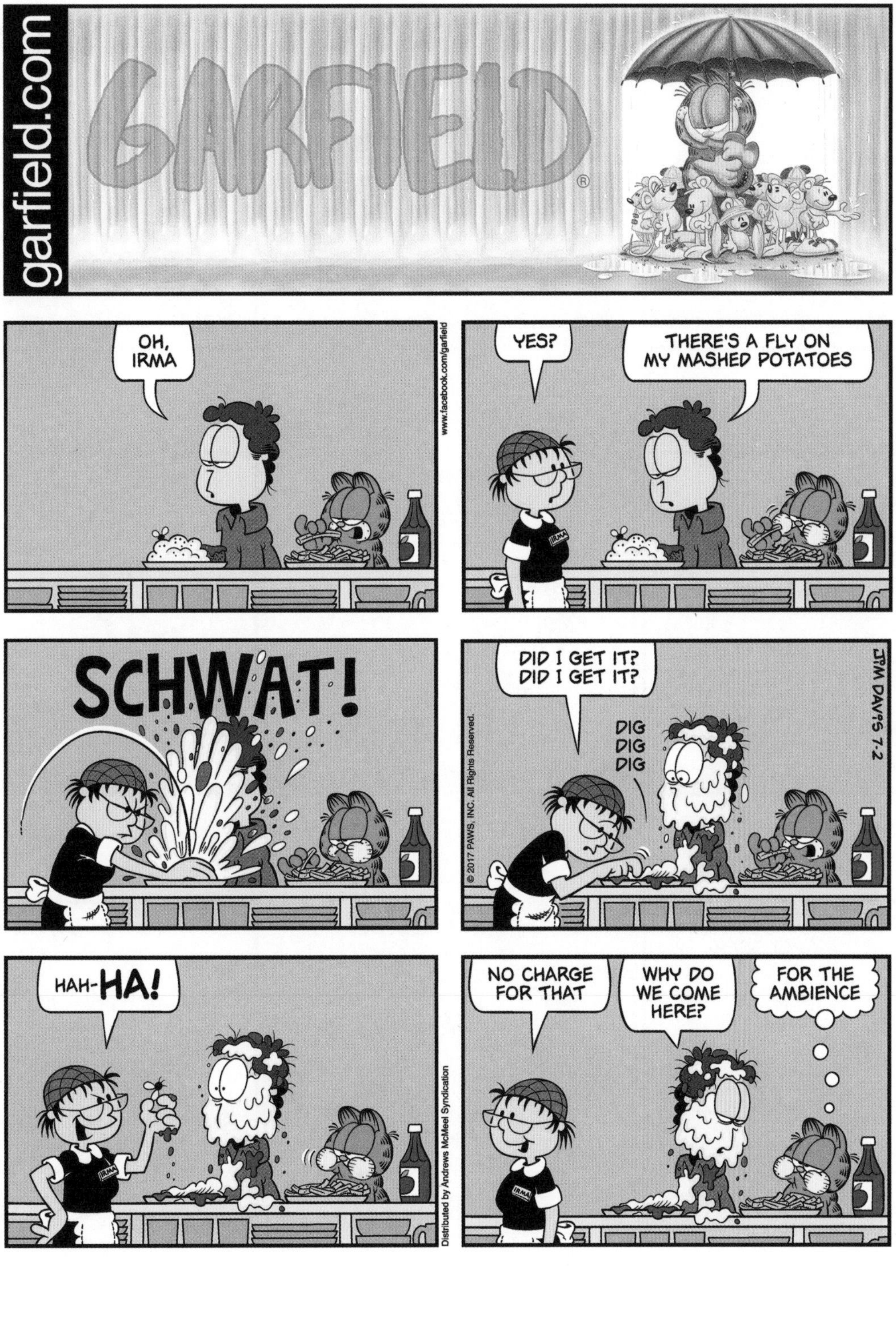
garfield.com
GARFIELD
OH, IRMA
www.facebook.com/garfield
YES?
THERE'S A FLY ON MY MASHED POTATOES
SCHWAT!
© 2017 PAWS, INC. All Rights Reserved.
DID I GET IT? DID I GET IT?
DIG DIG DIG
JIM DAVIS 7-2
HAH-HA!
Distributed by Andrews McMeel Syndication
NO CHARGE FOR THAT
WHY DO WE COME HERE?
FOR THE AMBIENCE

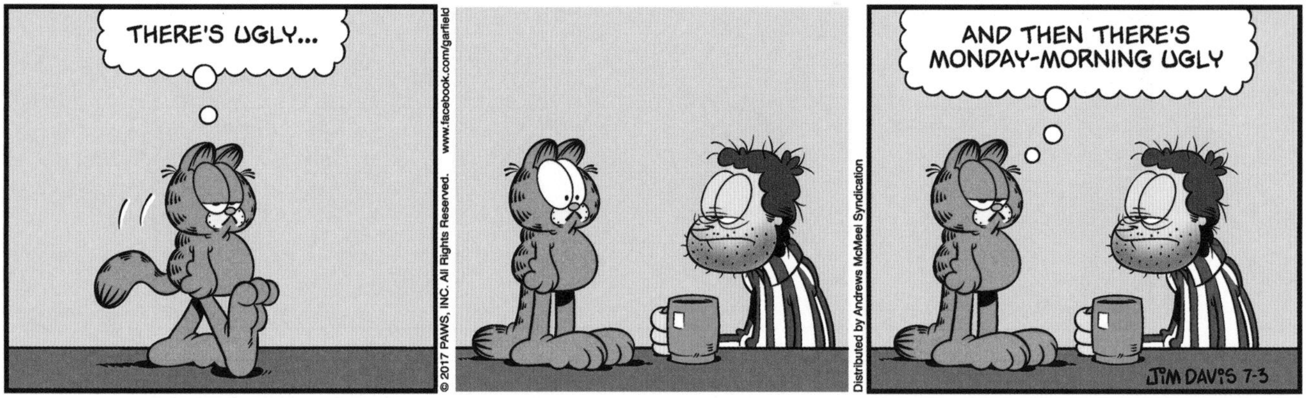
THERE'S UGLY...
© 2017 PAWS, INC. All Rights Reserved. www.facebook.com/garfield
AND THEN THERE'S MONDAY-MORNING UGLY
Distributed by Andrews McMeel Syndication
JIM DAVIS 7-3

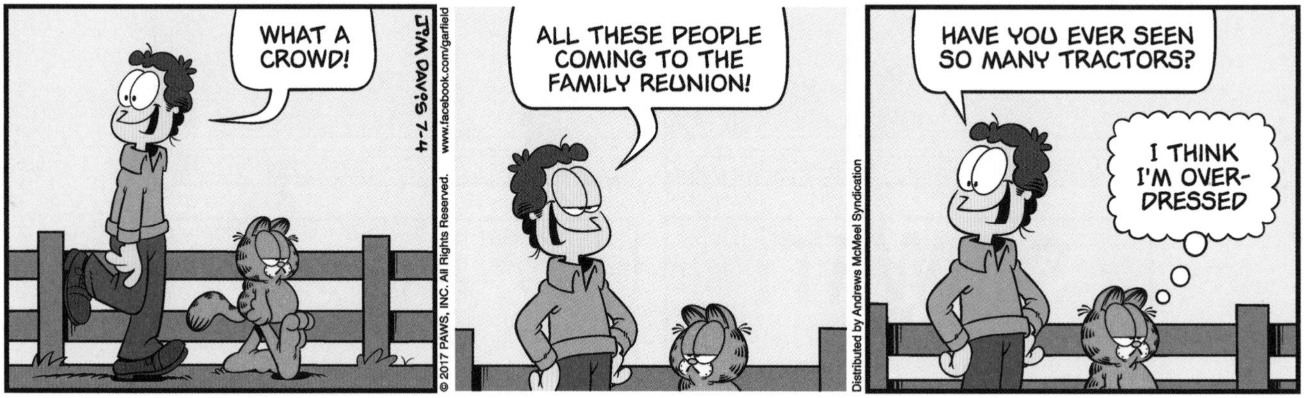
WHAT A CROWD!
JIM DAVIS 7-4
© 2017 PAWS, INC. All Rights Reserved. www.facebook.com/garfield
ALL THESE PEOPLE COMING TO THE FAMILY REUNION!
Distributed by Andrews McMeel Syndication
HAVE YOU EVER SEEN SO MANY TRACTORS?
I THINK I'M OVER-DRESSED

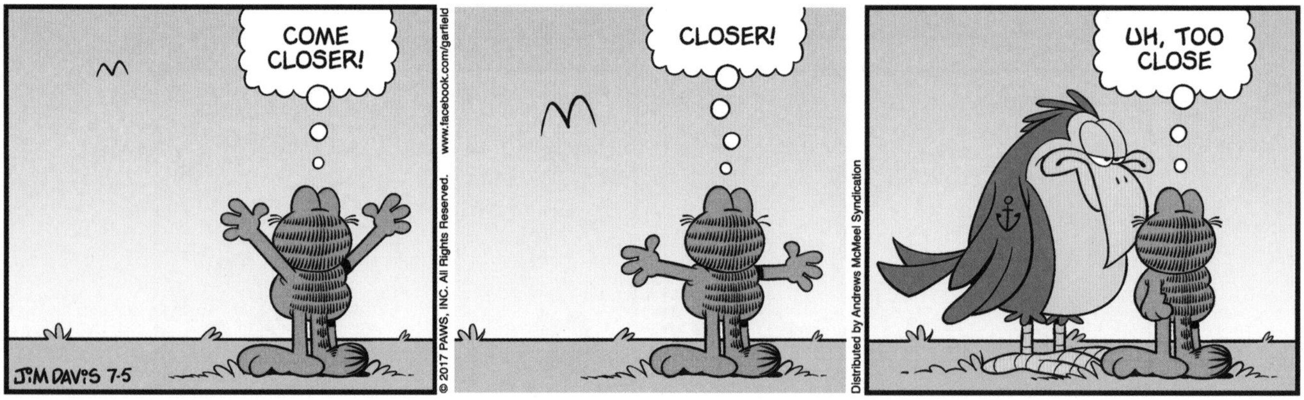
COME CLOSER!
JIM DAVIS 7-5
© 2017 PAWS, INC. All Rights Reserved. www.facebook.com/garfield
CLOSER!
Distributed by Andrews McMeel Syndication
UH, TOO CLOSE

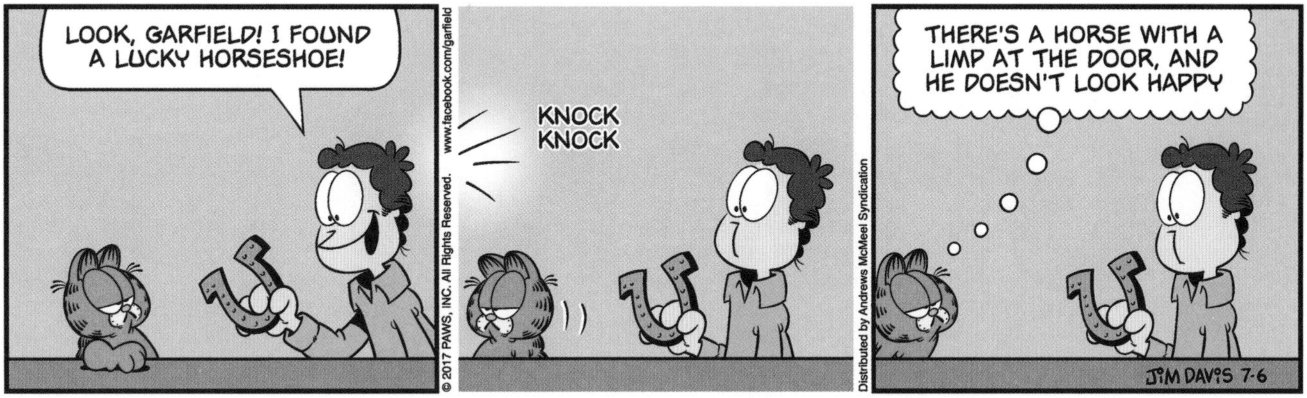
LOOK, GARFIELD! I FOUND A LUCKY HORSESHOE!
© 2017 PAWS, INC. All Rights Reserved. www.facebook.com/garfield
KNOCK KNOCK
Distributed by Andrews McMeel Syndication
THERE'S A HORSE WITH A LIMP AT THE DOOR, AND HE DOESN'T LOOK HAPPY
JIM DAVIS 7-6

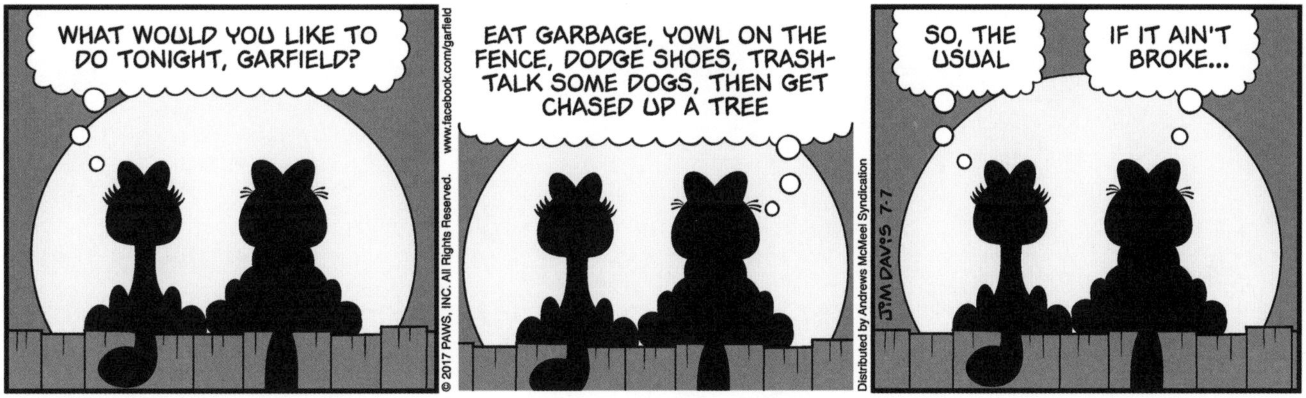
WHAT WOULD YOU LIKE TO DO TONIGHT, GARFIELD?
© 2017 PAWS, INC. All Rights Reserved. www.facebook.com/garfield
EAT GARBAGE, YOWL ON THE FENCE, DODGE SHOES, TRASH-TALK SOME DOGS, THEN GET CHASED UP A TREE
Distributed by Andrews McMeel Syndication
JIM DAVIS 7-7
SO, THE USUAL
IF IT AIN'T BROKE...

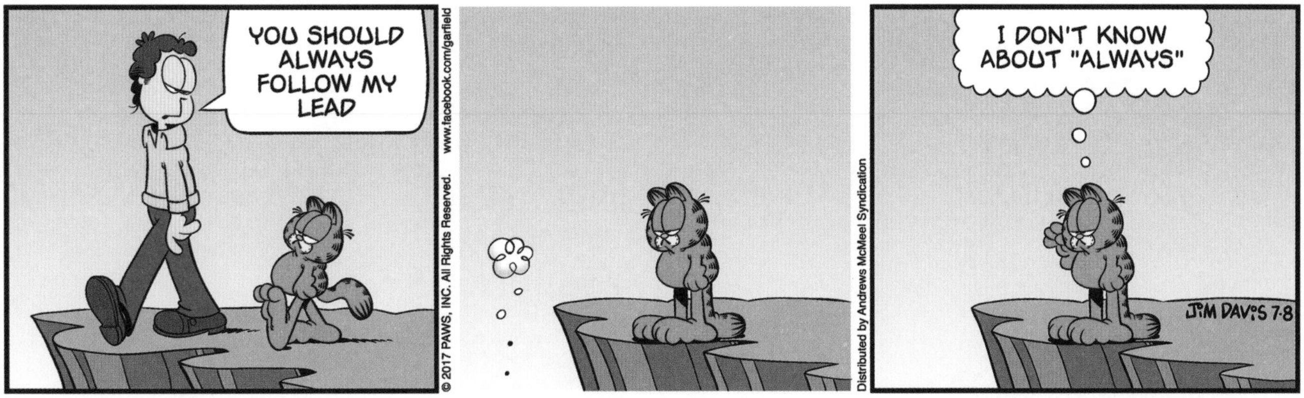
YOU SHOULD ALWAYS FOLLOW MY LEAD
© 2017 PAWS, INC. All Rights Reserved. www.facebook.com/garfield
Distributed by Andrews McMeel Syndication
I DON'T KNOW ABOUT "ALWAYS"
JIM DAVIS 7-8

Garfield's Green Tips

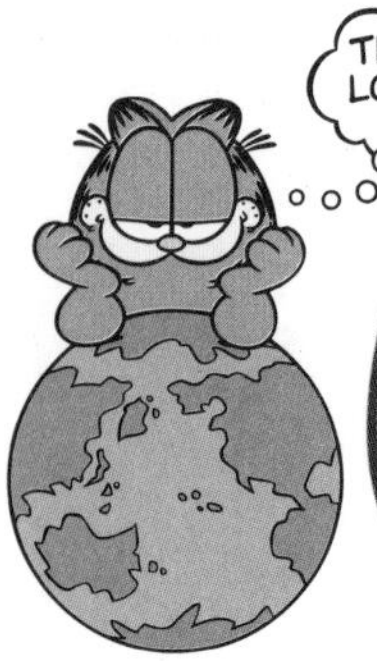
THIS PLANET LOOKS GOOD IN GREEN

Turn down your water heater

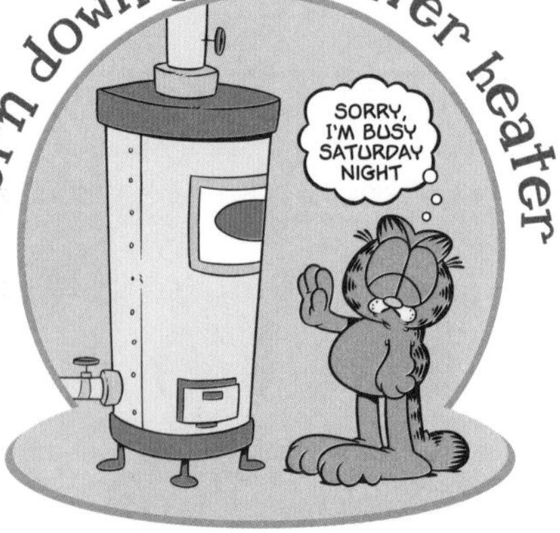
SORRY, I'M BUSY SATURDAY NIGHT

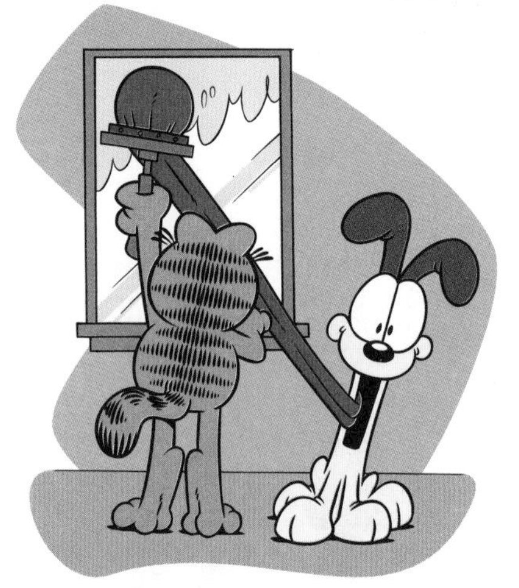

USE ORGANIC CLEANERS!

INSTEAD OF DISPOSABLE CUPS, USE A MUG

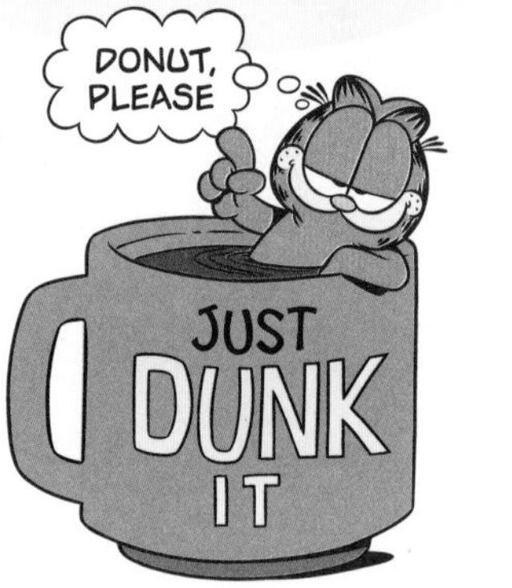
DONUT, PLEASE
JUST DUNK IT

Don't keep opening the refrigerator– empty it the first time

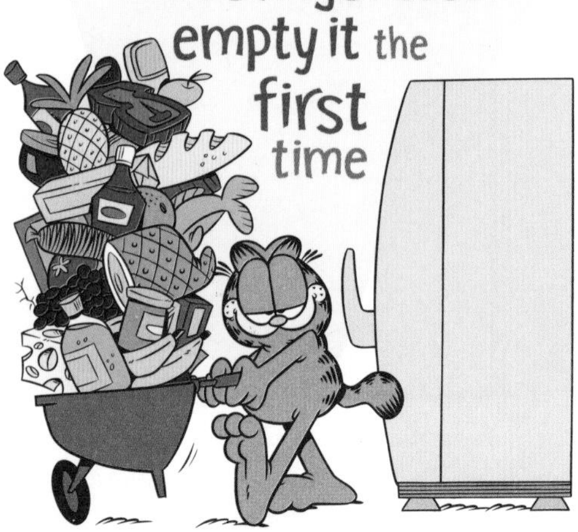

UNPLUG ALL UNNECESSARY APPLIANCES– LIKE THE ALARM CLOCK

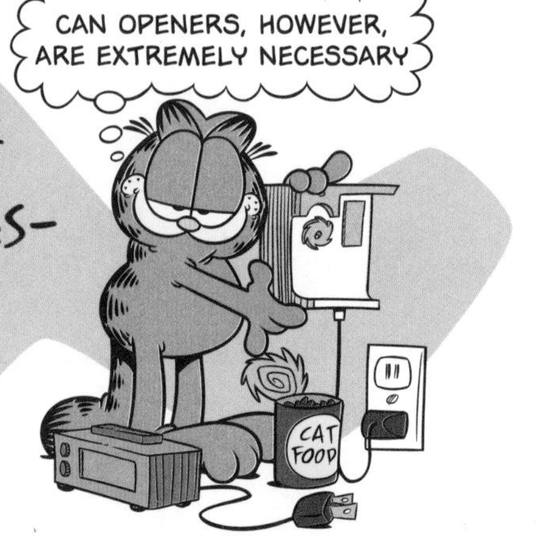
CAN OPENERS, HOWEVER, ARE EXTREMELY NECESSARY
CAT FOOD